COSMOPOLITAN

December 1976 • 30p

Elizabeth Taylor– As Never Before. See Page 92

Bodypower– The New Way to Rid Yourself of Stress And Tension

How to Say No to a Rapist And Survive

Did You Miss The Glittering Prizes? Read Frederic Raphael's Novel Based on the Compelling TV Series About The Bright Young Things of the Fifties

y Living
ether
Rotten

p Up
stmas-
Failsafe
Page Guide

ensational
-Look

£6.95

onia Fraser's
ourite
e Letters

New Sexual

ou Feel
if
Hold Back?

nantic Are
? (Quiz)

COSM

The Pill No One Can Decide For You But Here Are the Latest Findings

How To Be Thoroughly Efficient Without Turning Into An Iron Maiden. Special Get-Organised Section

Men's Greatest Fears And Why You Should Be Aware of Them

Would You Believe, The Spaghetti Diet!

Win a Volvo. See Page 90

How is Your Marriage? Recognise the Danger Signals Before It's Too Late

Luscious Embroidered Afghanistan Rig-Out At a Down to Earth Price

Monday Lunch In Fairyland From Angela Huth's Latest Collection of Sophisticated Stories

COSMOPOLITAN

September 1976 • 30p

How to be Truly Sexual– Rather Than Merely Sexy

Have You Got What it Takes to Work In Television?

How to Understand And Enjoy Men. A New Approach, By Irma Kurtz

A Quiet Life The Latest and Most Intriguing Story By Prize-winning Novelist Beryl Bainbridge

e-Your-Life
by
avid Reuben.
w This
olutionary
Eating Plan

at to do
out People
sbands,
ses, Lovers,
nds) Who
g You Down

Psychology
ossip

u're Not
y or
er You Need
zpah;
n Get You
thing
Want

COSMOPOLITAN

February 1976 • 30p

What to Do When You Go Off Sex

Gore Vidal: What It's Like to be Rich, Talented and Bisexual

How One Woman Cured Her Fear of Breast Cancer

Cardiff: Cosy or Constricting? Inter-City Report

The Softest Dress of Spring— Yours for £9.45

Happiness: What It Is and What It Isn't

How to Have a Dazzling Smile. Give Your Teeth The Treatment

Who is Your Favourite Fantasy Man? See Page 83

How to be a Self-Made Woman

Laurie Colwin's Poignant Novel About a Girl's Love for Two Brothers

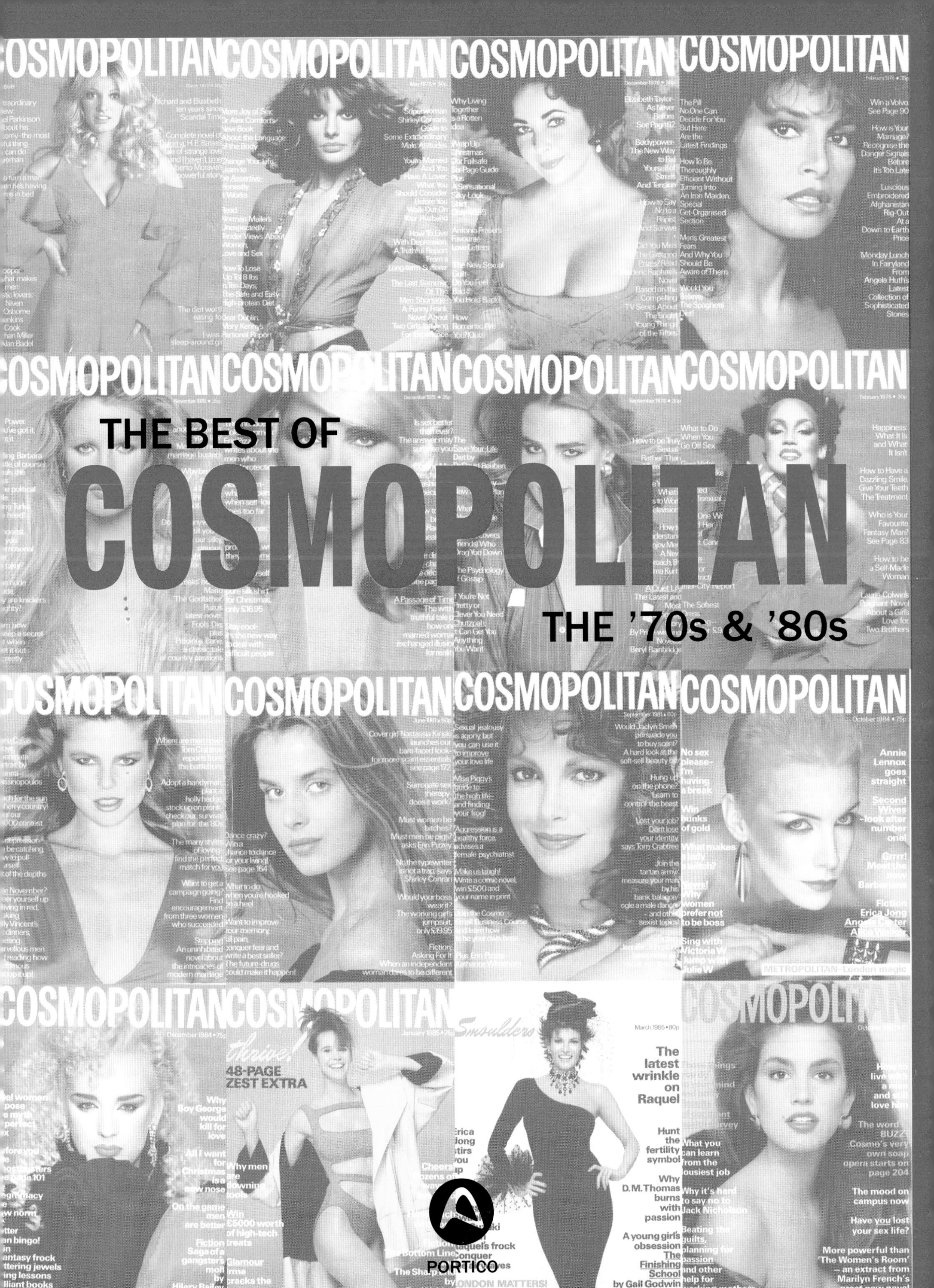
THE BEST OF
COSMOPOLITAN
THE '70s & '80s
PORTICO

First published in the United Kingdom in 2007 by
Portico
10 Southcombe Street
London
W14 0RA

An imprint of Anova Books Company Ltd

ISBN 10: 1 90603 215 7
ISBN 13: 9781906032159

A CIP catalogue record for this book is available from the British Library.

10 9 8 7 6 5 4 3 2 1

Compiled and edited by David Salmo
Designed by Nichola Smith

Reproduction by Mission Productions Ltd, Hong Kong
Printed and bound by Mondadori, Toledo, Spain

This book can be ordered direct from the publisher.
Contact the marketing department, but try your bookshop first.

www.anovabooks.com

CONTENTS

6 Office Exercising
8 The Most Beautiful Thing a Man Can Do for a Woman – and Michael Parkinson Has Done It
11 Cosmo Offer: Man Trap Scent & Sun Trap Bikini
13 What I Want in a Wife
16 Why the Abortion Law Doesn't Work
18 New Pairs: New Jeans
21 Things to Say in Bed
22 Vidal Sassoon – How to Succeed by Really Trying
25 Liberation Now
26 Quiz: How Sensual are You?
28 Dance Like Crazy – Shape up to a Great Figure with the Paris Showgirls
30 What Does the Difficult but Fascinating George Best Think about Women?
33 What Happens When Girls Make Passes/Men Do Need Women
34 The Tailor Maids … Wear Trousers Without Antagonising Men
38 Cosmo Pin-up: Ian McShane
40 Give Your Place the Designer's Touch
43 Should Men Do 'Women's Work'?
44 Join the Quick Set … for the Fastest Ever Party Style
46 Knit a Clingy Sweater
48 The Naked Lunch – Picnic Food
52 What Your Legs Say About You
54 Haven't Got a Thing to Wear…
57 Twenty Ways to Make him Come on Strong
60 Meet David Newton – He is that *Cosmopolitan* Man
63 Quiz: How Male Dominated are You?
66 Helen Mirren: 'I Dress to Look Sexy and to Raise a Laugh'
70 Irma Kurtz's Agony Column
72 Day for Night Fashion
74 He's Stingy If…
79 Who are the Flirts?/The 'Ladies' of London
80 Who Looks OK? Who Looks KO?/The Cosmo Girl's Guide to Fashionable Television Viewing
81 How I Learned to Stop Worrying About Being Fat and Got Thin
82 The Packaging of Farrah Fawcett-Majors
85 *Cosmopolitan*'s Young Journalist Contest
87 How to Cut Your Own Hair
89 Gentlemen Prefer Blondie
90 Christmas Day in the Morning
92 The Liberation Questionnaire – into the 'Eighties with Men at Our Side
95 Cut-price Chic
96 The Things That Make Life Worth Living
97 'Why are Women Such Sluts?'
98 Catch the Spotlight with Fantasy Fashion
100 Dynamic and Demanding – the Shape of Jobs to Come
104 Cosmo Offer: Stretch a Leg
106 Bold Brushwork – Cut-price Living
108 Who's Sexy Now?
110 Rollermania
115 Sexist Chat to Avoid…
116 Glamour at A. Price!
119 Cut-price Chic: Street Sheets!
120 In the Royal Pink – Paula Yates Investigates Britain's Most Glamorous Step-Granny…
122 'Women Will be Free the Moment they Stop Caring What Men Think About Them' by Quentin Crisp
123 Dear *Cosmopolitan*
124 'The '80s Man is More Inclined to Grab a Box of Tissues Than a Wooden Club'
125 Poetry: 'Cosmopoliten' by Marcelle D'argy Smith
126 Quiz: How Well Do You Know Cosmo?
128 Shocking the French – Paula Yates, Martin Kemp and Steve Strange in Paris
130 Heavy Petting
134 Futureworks – When Office and Home Merge and There'll Really be Time to Live
138 Miss Piggy – Work out with Moi!
139 Sexual Manners – When to Wait … When to Pounce…
141 'This Could be the End of Something Small' – The Morning After the Night Before
142 So You Think You're Independent?
144 Stab in the Back – What's in and What's out in 1985!
146 Male Orgasm – It's Good News
148 Irma Kurtz's Agony Column
150 Sex on the Job
153 'New Men are Worth Waiting For' – On the Couch with Tom Crabtree
154 Cheers for the Capitalist Feminist!
156 Vivat Vagina!
159 'Fatness is not a Problem – Other People's Attitudes Are'
160 Smart Girls Carry Condoms
162 Are You What the Lads are Looking For?
164 'A Jerk is a Jerk, no matter What Continent' by Ruby Wax
166 New Age Relationships
168 The Bimbo and the Post Feminist
170 What we Really are, What Men Really Want
174 Goodbye to all That!

FOREWORD

Thirty-five years ago the first ever issue of British *Cosmopolitan* went on sale. It cost 20p – and by lunchtime all 350,000 copies had sold out. It was a publishing sensation.

By the time the second issue went to press the print run was upped by 100,000 copies. Britain's women still couldn't get enough and it was impossible to buy a copy after only two days. An added attraction was Cosmo's introduction of the naked centrefold – which would later feature Ian McShane, who chose a strategically placed dachshund to hide his modesty.

As *The Times* put it: 'A mighty orgasmic roar was heard throughout the land. *Cosmopolitan* magazine was born.'

The philosophy behind this ground-breaking magazine was simple ... but in those days radical. American Cosmo legend Helen Gurley Brown wanted her readers to: 'Live big, go for it and be the best you can be in every area of your life.'

Britain's launch editor Joyce Hopkirk wrote to her readers: 'You're very interested in men, naturally, but you think too much of yourself to live your life entirely through them.'

This book shows just how far we have all come. It is a brilliant social commentary that makes you realise how different life was for a woman in the 1970s. There is a knitting pattern for a clingy sweater and adverts entitled, *Why three clever girls chose electronic typewriters* and *Who's afraid of word processing?* Others begged the reader to get the '80s look with beads and headbands like Bo Derek or a body like Victoria Principal's. And Michael Parkinson revealed that 'The most beautiful thing a man can do for a woman' was to have a vasectomy, apparently.

The cover girls are icons of their time, from Elizabeth Taylor to Paula Yates, Joan Collins, Jerry Hall and Farrah Fawcett-Majors.

Cosmo is as famous today for its sex coverage as it was then, and I am thrilled to say we still have the brilliant Irma Kurtz writing for the magazine. But it isn't just about sex and relationships. Cosmo still celebrates a fun, glamorous, optimistic passion for life, inspiring women to get everything they want out of it ... and not just in the bedroom, but in the bathroom or anywhere else the Cosmo woman fancies having it.

To quote *The Times* again: 'Cosmo is bigger than a magazine, it is a brand, an empire, a state of mind. Its greatest compliment has been not only that it has shaped all women's magazines in its image, but also that it has transformed a whole genre of men's magazines. They owe their attitude to the indefatigable Amazon that is *Cosmopolitan*. She could still teach them a few tricks.'

Read on and enjoy.

Louise Court – Editor, *Cosmopolitan*

OUR COSMO WORLD

Apart from being first to the moon, or *really* falling in love, there can't be anything more exciting than starting a new magazine. Especially when you know that there are thousands of girls out there who will love it and find it exactly what they need. Why so cocky? For the answer you just have to think about yourself. You are that *Cosmopolitan* girl, aren't you? You're very interested in men, naturally, but you think too much of yourself to live your life entirely through *him*. That means you're going to make the most of yourself—your body, your face, your clothes, your hair, your job and your mind. How can you fail to be more interesting after that?

Since news of Cosmo first leaked out everybody's been asking if it's going to be a female *Playboy*. Although I think *Playboy* is very entertaining it's got a completely different slant on life from us. *Playboy* preaches a doctrine in which all their men are fantastic looking, rich, exciting and successful. I don't think *you* are so sure of yourself. Certainly with a divorce behind me and who-knows-what in front, I've got my share of emotional hang-ups. Do you know anybody without any hang-ups at all? And that's why we are producing *Cosmopolitan*—to give help and advice on those aggravations like jealously, envy, and a feeling of just not being up to it that hits us all too often.

When we were looking around for an advertising agency to get Cosmo noticed, we talked to eight top London firms and met nearly 100 bright boys—and only one woman. There's scope for Cosmo girls. Beats me why agencies don't accept that women really do understand each other. *Cosmopolitan* magazine in America rocketed ahead when a woman took over. That's the clever editor, Helen Gurley Brown—remember she wrote *Sex and the Single Girl?*—in the picture (right) with me.

Cosmo writers do have fun. When Romany Bain flew to Rome to interview her old friends the Burtons, Richard was moved to write a poem specially for her. (You can read it on page 85.) "I may not be a beauty like Elizabeth but he certainly made me feel special," a delighted Romany said afterwards.

I haven't done so badly either. From sitting faceless behind an executive desk at *The Sun*—I had two glorious years there as woman's editor—I've had to get out and meet people. No hardship when they're as fascinating as Laurence Harvey—that's one of his houses you see embellishing the background of our fashion pictures. Then there was Michael Parkinson. Yes, he's even more attractive than on the TV screen.

So what kind of other lovely goodies have we got for your first issue? A great story on the said Mr Parkinson (p. 68) written by the lovely Stephanie Bennett, who is publisher W. H. Allen's publicity director. A top Cosmo girl. The irresistibly funny Jilly Cooper is married—to another publisher Leo Cooper. But it doesn't stop her speculating on what makes a good lover (p. 86). How to turn a man on when he has problems in bed (p. 114). You couldn't resist that one. A famous doctor who has helped hundreds of patients gives specific advice.

Our fiction is a bit tough. But, then, isn't life? Alberto Moravia's *I Haven't Time* describes too many girls I know. Although they'd never recognise it. Our complete novel is by that old master H. E. Bates. *Dulcima* has been made into an EMI-MGM film starring Carol White and John Mills. You won't be able to put it down.

Remember this is just the beginning . . .

JOYCE HOPKIRK

Office Exercising

What? Do exercises at the office? Why not, as long as no one's around? You have perfect props (desk, chair, filing cabinet). You'll save time and money and counteract the dreaded sit-down spread. Here are five clever and effective routines to do in your spare moments . . . we suggest you confine them to lunch-breaks, otherwise you risk frightening everyone else!

1

Push your chair away from desk until fingers can barely reach typewriter keys. This stretches your torso mightily so do wear a stretchable bra—or take it off.

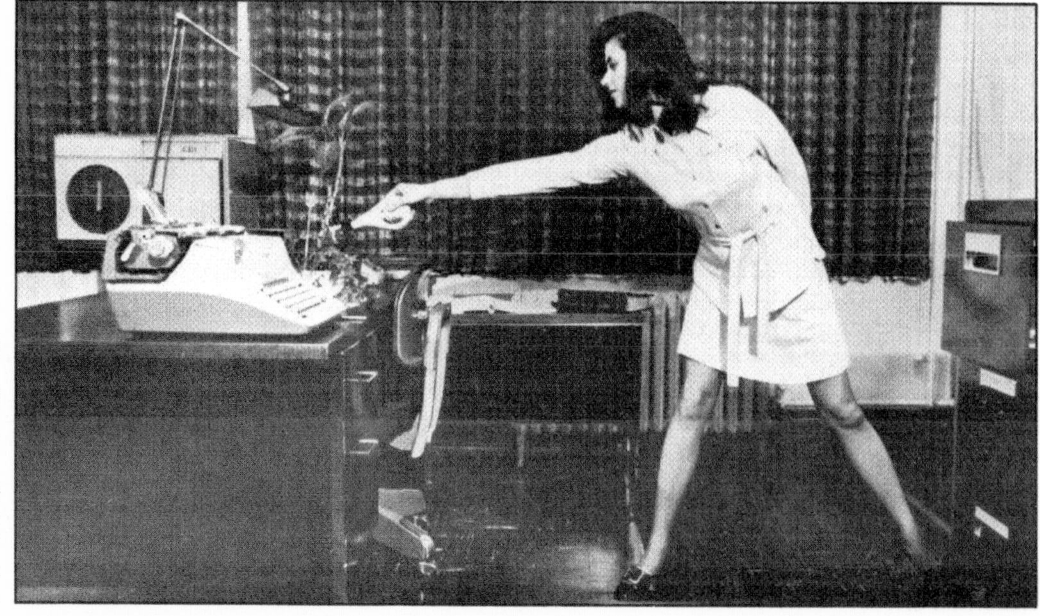

2

Angle your legs as far as skirt hem will allow. Lean over to left or right as if watering the office plant. No plants around? Stretch out and pick up paper clips.

Office Exercising
CONTINUED

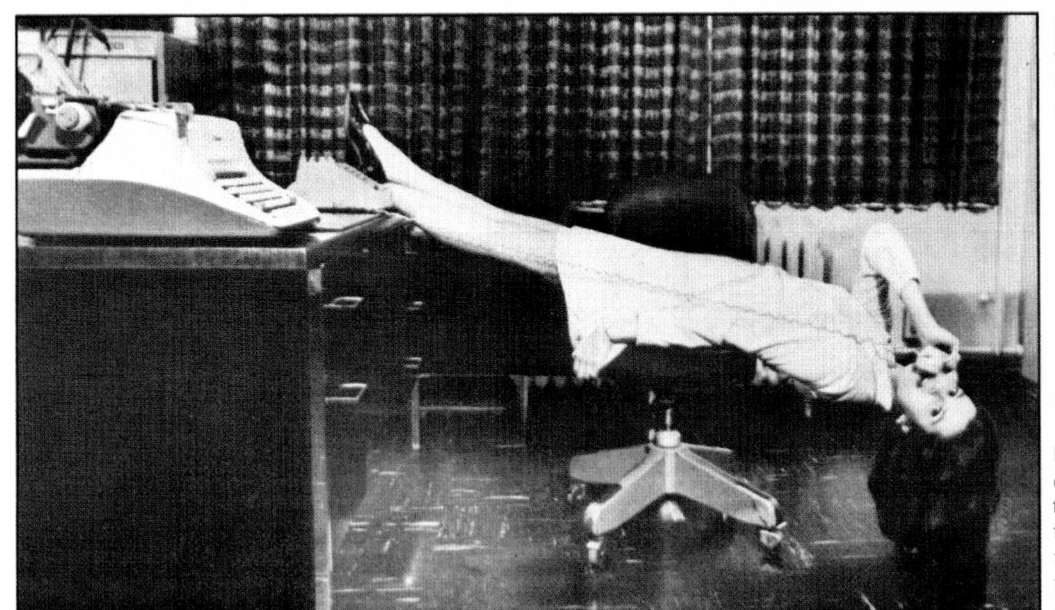

3

Lock the door before you do this one. Lie across the office chair balancing feet on desk, head towards floor. This firms the bottom and also revs up your circulation.

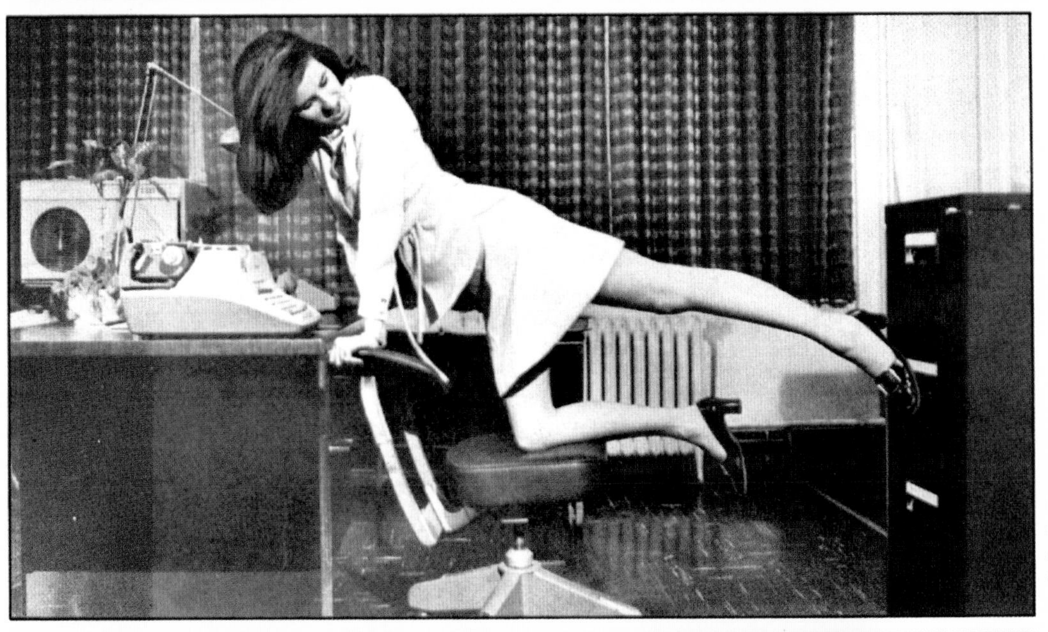

4

Ride your desk chair on castors like a child's scooter. This firms waist, trims thighs and strengthens legs.

5

Stand with back to open file drawer; bend body down from waist quickly, banging your bottom against the drawer. The drawer closes and you get a good firming thump on the bottom. You can achieve the same effect by bashing your bottom against a hard wall.

The most beautiful thing a man can do for a woman

and Michael Parkinson has done it

What would be the most beautiful thing a man could do for you? Take you on a second honeymoon, buy you a king-sized diamond, write you a poem? All these can be very romantic but in our opinion they don't measure up to the supreme compliment that Michael Parkinson has paid his wife. Read on and see if you agree with us . . . and him. BY STEPHANIE BENNETT

Parkinson keeps his halo well hidden. He doesn't come across as a man who's just made a Brave and Momentous decision. Away from the box his signature tune is unchanged—a blend of suavity and ingenuousness, offhand humour and down-to-earth comment. He can hardly be accused of taking himself over-seriously, so when he talks about "getting myself cut the other day" you could easily assume he was describing an after-programme binge.

But the flippancy is only a cover-up. A few weeks before we met, Michael had a vasectomy—and that's not something you do for a laugh. It may be the most effective method of birth control but, being virtually irreversible, it's also the most drastic. So when the television's king of chat not only goes through with the operation but is also prepared to talk about it, it has to be a subject he feels strongly about.

His example should also go a long way towards neutralising some of the prejudice. For although vasectomy is becoming ever more popular, there's no doubt it's an emotionally charged subject. Pick a random selection of men—happily married who have completed their families—and ask them what they think of the idea. Chances are they will hesitate, shuffle guiltily, agree that in principle, and for other people, it makes sense, but that, no, they can't really explain why, it's not something they'd like for themselves.

The reason for this reluctance is extremely complicated. Anyone who's investigated the subject of vasectomy knows that sterilisation has no effect whatsoever on sexual performance. But the aura remains. Perhaps men are afraid for their image, afraid of women's reactions, afraid of being thought less than a whole man. Parkinson answers that one every time he appears on television—flirting with Shirley MacLaine, crinkling his eyes suggestively at Joanne Woodward, gazing sensually at Sarah Miles's see-through neckline and generally making out with an endless succession of sought-after ladies. He's happily married—*they* may be happily married—nevertheless the sexual *frisson* is unmistakable and none of the people who watch Parkinson can doubt that they are indeed looking at a red-blooded, hundred per cent male.

Michael's reason for "getting cut" is beautifully straightforward and straightforwardly beautiful. "I did it for Mary," he said. "She's tried half a dozen kinds of Pill but each one affected her either physically or psychologically. In any case, she's only thirty-three and I just didn't like the idea of her being on the Pill for another ten years at least. There's a hell of a lot of risk involved for a women.

"As for other forms of birth control—they're either off-putting, messy, or ineffective. The diaphragm is a real passion killer—it turns sex into a mechanical performance. Most methods take away all the spontaneity and in the end you decide the easiest way is, don't. Well that's no fun is it, so I felt it was up to me to do something. I first got the idea when I read a funny article in *The Guardian*. The man made it sound so easy and civilised."

Michael says the decision was entirely his. "I've always felt that the man should share the responsibility for birth control—it shouldn't be left to the woman. Naturally I discussed it with Mary and she had to give her written approval. But if she had been the one to suggest it, I'm sure I would have felt castrated. I think a man must decide for himself, otherwise he would always feel resentful if he had any regrets afterwards.

"Of course I had some doubts about it, who wouldn't? In fact, just before the operation I was very nervous indeed. A lot of people I talked to who had had a vasectomy say that for a few months afterwards they did feel regretful."

Michael himself has no regrets. At thirty-six he is very happily married, he has three schoolboy sons and he proclaims proudly that since the operation his sex life is better than ever. "I'm much randier than before. You ask Mary."

The biggest problem was getting someone to agree to do the operation. "The real opposition came from my doctor. I saw him three times before he was satisfied that we understood the implications. Then we met the surgeon who turned out to be a sort of devil's advocate. He kept telling me that there was no way of going back, and he raised the inevitable point—what happens if your children are in a car crash and, bingo, they're gone? I'd thought about that of course, although it's impossible to envisage, but finally I said no, we wouldn't start again although we'd possibly adopt. In the end it turned out that the surgeon himself had had a vasectomy done, which was very comforting."

The operation itself is a very simple one. It's usually done with a local anaesthetic so that a busy man can take an hour off in the morning and be back at work in the office in the afternoon. Michael did. And was.

"Fortunately it was very early in the morning and I'm never properly conscious until midday. Which was just as well. In fact the nursing home is only 50 yards from where I live, so I just fell out of bed and into the operating theatre.

"I was told to take off all my clothes expect for my underpants, which struck me as very strange. But it transpired that the pants are whipped up immediately after the operation to cover the dressing, because they don't bother to put on a bandage. So there I was in my underpants lying on this table which was so small it must have been designed for a dwarf. Then I was given the

local. That was the part that hurt most—after that I didn't feel a thing."

Nothing at all? When the man is waving a shining scalpel over his genitals? Any psychiatrist would confirm this as one of the most persistent of male horror fantasies. Michael agreed.

"My first reaction was, Jesus Christ, what have I done? You know they say a man's brain is linked straight to his balls and there's this man carving away at my anatomy. The only reassuring thing was that I knew the surgeon himself had been through it—and *he* still looked all right. It's rather like buying a car from a salesman who owns the same model. Though I must say I wished he'd keep his mind on the job instead of chatting away about football.

"After it was over I got dressed and we shook hands, like English gentlemen who suddenly find themselves quite unexpectedly on equal terms."

Had Michael been a more nervous type he could have had a general anaesthetic, but that would have meant spending a day or two in hospital recovering. As it was he could carry on as if he'd just had a tooth out.

"When the anaesthetic wore off it began to hurt like hell. I'll never forget the television interview I had to do the day after. It was absolute agony sitting down but as I couldn't very well start pacing around, I just had to put up with it. There I was distracted with pain, chatting away and trying to laugh at the other chap's jokes, and thinking if only he knew what I was going through. It was about two weeks before I could even think about it without flinching. And then quite distinctly, I felt more randy than before."

This reaction is quite common, according to Professor Blandy, head of the Vasectomy Unit at the Margaret Pyke Clinic in London. He finds that the vast majority of his patients are much happier afterwards. "Some even say it's like a second honeymoon," says Professor Blandy. "A lot of people don't realise that, far from causing impotence, vasectomy was originally introduced in order to rejuvenate the waning powers of elderly men."

In fact, any lingering doubts about potency can be safely ignored because vasectomy in no way tampers with masculine hormones. What it does, in the simplest terms, is to prevent the sperm manufactured in the testicles from being ejaculated through the penis. This is achieved by making a small incision on each side of the scrotum (which holds the testicles) so that the tubes can be located and part of them snipped out. The scars that remain are so microscopic that they could only be located by the keen eye of a surgeon.

Some people are puzzled about what happens to the sperm after the operation. Professor Blandy explained that only part of the ejaculatory liquid is actually composed of sperm. The rest of it is a fluid created to carry the sperm and this is ejaculated in the normal way, while the sperm, whose passage has been blocked by the operation, is simply absorbed.

Disappointingly for those who think their sacrifice deserves instant results, vasectomy isn't immediately effective. The patient has to return to the hospital with specimens of his semen over a period of three months, and until the emission is clear of all sperm other precautions must be taken. This is because sperm is still stored in the tubes and the length of time they take to empty varies from man to man. But once over this hurdle, the chances of a woman getting pregnant by a man who's been sterilised are practically zero.

Although Michael is delighted with the results of his operation, he maintains it's not something any man should rush into "I don't think, obviously, that vasectomy is the great answer to everybody's birth control problems. After all, you've both got to be very sure you don't want any more children."

In any case there's little danger of anyone getting a rush job done. Although, in theory, the operation is sometimes reversible, doctors insist that all candidates consider it as permanent and subject them to a very thorough screening. So if you're a Casanova type who imagines being sterile would add to your chances, forget it. And an unmarried man, even if he was sincerely determined not to have children, would find it almost impossible to find a doctor to agree to the operation. After all, what if he should fall in love with a girl and *she* wanted children. Even ideal candidates, like Michael and Mary, are made to examine their motives in depth. Michael said, "It did actually occur to me that Mary might run off and leave me one day. But then I'd chase her to the ends of the earth."

You cannot have a vasectomy on the National Health unless there are strong medical grounds, for example, if you can prove that other methods of contraception are a hazard to either the husband's or the wife's health. But a Private Member's Bill, which was recently given a second reading, is aiming to make voluntary vasectomy available on the same basis as other contraceptives.

The Family Planning Clinics charge £15 for the operation (far cheaper than the Pill in the long-term) or it can be done privately as Michael chose, when the cost is usually between £20 and £25. Unfortunately, however, not enough facilities are available, and there are long waiting lists at most of the clinics.

The queues are likely to get longer for, despite the hang-ups, more and more men are turning towards vasectomy. There are no records of how many operations are arranged privately but between 1966 and 1970, the Family Planning Clinics alone performed 9,000 vasectomies and dealt with 60,000 enquiries. In Windsor, where Michael Parkinson lives, twenty operations a week are being done. "Two men in my own street have had vasectomies and those are just the ones I know about. There are more people around who have had it done than you would ever suspect."

Perhaps men are realising at last that contraception is not exclusively a female responsibility. And the equivalent operation for a woman is far more drastic. Michael was adamant when I asked for his views on female sterilisation. "No, I absolutely object, because there is an alternative. Sterilisation for a woman means a lot more pain and maybe two weeks in hospital. It's a much more serious undertaking."

Vasectomy may be simple, but what about the psychological effects? Although the capacity for orgasm is unimpaired, many men confuse virility with propagation. In other words, the fact that they *can* have children is a tangible proof of their potency. Often they worry about the effect of sterility on their marriage, and wonder if their wives will react with the same passion, feeling cheated of that element of risk.

It seems to me that most women would feel more passionate once the fear of unwanted pregnancy was finally removed. And Dr Edey, a psychiatrist at the Sanger Clinic in America confirms this view. "My impression is that most of the couples who come here have a pretty good marriage. I like the way they talk to each other. If you ask them how their sex life is, they grin."

Michael Parkinson's own grin should be enough to dispel any lingering doubts. For a television idol, particularly one with a frankly sexy image, it takes a good deal of courage to talk about such a controversial subject. But, speaking for the female sex, I don't think he has a thing to worry about. Certainly we'll admire him for his unselfishness, and we'll envy his wife for having a husband who cares so much about her. But when Parkinson appears on the box, we'll forget about all these high ideals and just wish we were the girl he happens to be chatting up that night.

COSMO'S FIRST GREAT OFFERS -FOR YOU

MAN TRAP SCENT

For only 50p

What is as personal as your pulse beat, as pervasive and warm as a new love affair? The answer is *Intimate*, one of the world's most successful fragrances. For Cosmo girls alone Revlon is offering one full ounce of *Intimate* toilet water at the unbeatable price of 50p, a great saving on what you'd have to pay in the shops. A guaranteed man trap, *Intimate* is one of the frankly female scents that, having warmed on your pulse area, lasts and lasts and lasts. And like all great beauties, you do want your presence to linger on long after you've left the party. Beautifully packaged, this exclusive Cosmo offer (actual size shown above) is simple to order. Send a cheque or money order for 50p to the address on the coupon on page 144. No lovely Cosmo girl can afford to miss these so-special offers, so order NOW.

SUN TRAP BIKINI

JOHN KELLY

For only £2·90

What is tiny, clingy, light as a powder puff—and packs more punch than a ton of Miss World one-piece swimsuits? The answer is the Cosmo bikini that traps all the sun you need while making the most of your vital statistics. This is the sexy swimsuit of summer 1972 that you know will look right on every beach from Biarritz to the Bahamas. Exclusive to Cosmo readers, it is yours for the unbeatable price of £2·90. Available in bust sizes 32 to 40 in. Both bra and pants are fastened with gilt rings and the bra has string straps that knot to fit your measurements. The stretch towelling fabric is flower printed in a choice of three colours—red, green or brown—and has a built-in sparkle that glints in sunlight. Send a cheque or money order for £2·90 to the address on the coupon on page 144 and your size and second colour choice.

COSMO TELLS ALL

Produced by Margaret Goodman

COSMO PIN-UP: USA STYLE

Unless you've a will of iron you'll already have flipped over to page 76 to have a good gawp at Paul du Feu. And here, for your extra entertainment is American actor Burt Reynolds who this month is revealing all on the pages of American *Cosmopolitan*. Burt, who used to be married to *Laugh In* lady Judy Carne, has his first major film role in *Deliverance* which will be around later this year. Posing in the nude, he says, struck him as a very funny idea. One thing that fascinates us is the contrast between Paul's smooth skin and Burt's all-over furriness. In Cosmo's office, voting is six to one in favour of our British smoothie, but we'd love to have an opinion from you.

TIPTOE THROUGH THE TULIPS

You could scarcely tiptoe through the tulips in THESE clogs. Propped up on nearly four inches of cork a girl has to stride out—if she does not want to tip over. Love That Daisy shoe in suède and cork by Elliotts, £7·95; Carmen Miranda clog in yellow with red and green straps by Sacha, and bright yellow leather sandals also by Sacha—both £5·99.

DRAWINGS JANET SEAWARD

AND AFTER THE ORGY . . . ?

If you think sexy films and royal romances don't mix, Christina Lindberg, 21, is here to prove you wrong. She recently starred in *What are you doing after the orgy?* and if you asked Christina that question, she might tell you she was having dinner with a Prince. Christina is the new girl in the life of Sweden's Crown Prince Carl Gustav, but she keeps the rumours under control by insisting she doesn't believe in marriage.

MEET THE OYSTER CHAIR

So-called because it clamps up tightly enough to keep all the weather out. Designed for outdoor living-it-up, it would also be a great asset to any short-of-space Cosmo pad. It comes in vivid red, yellow or white and costs, alas, £40. Available at Heal's, Tottenham Court Road, London WC1.

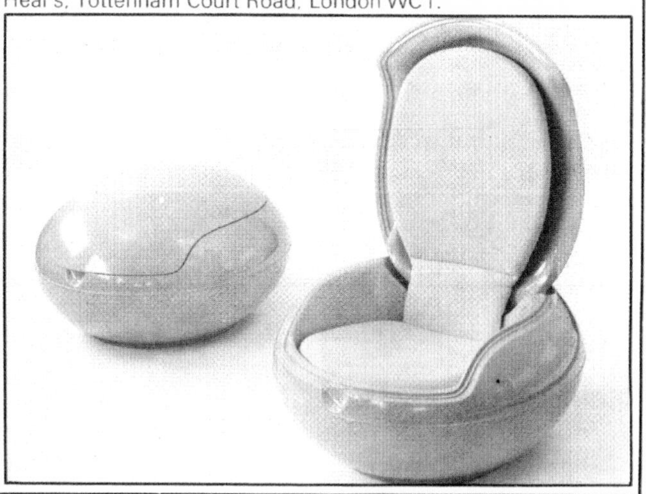

FREDERICK'S NEW LOOK

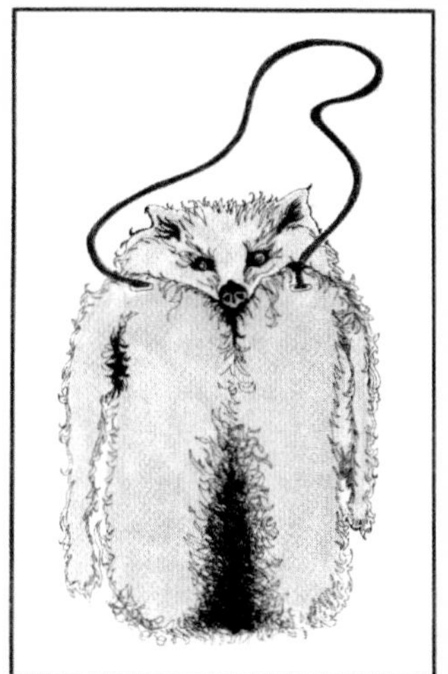

KEITH MATHIAS

Frederick the Fox turned up at Cosmo the other day disguised as a handbag and found himself the centre of attraction. If you want to copy, hunt around the junkshops for one of those fox stoles that Auntie Minnie used to snap on around her shoulders—this one cost £3·10 in the Paris flea market. Cut off the tail, front legs and snap fastening at the jaw and neaten off the lining. Fold the tail end round to meet the head just behind the ears and sew in two pieces of suède to make side gussets. Thread cord through each gusset for handle.

WHAT I WANT IN A WIFE

What do Britain's most eligible bachelors look for in a wife? Are they switched on by physical perfection, do they look for a definite personality type or is it simply a question of chemistry? We've tracked down forty very desirable men—single when we talked to them—and while we can't give you their telephone numbers, we can tell you what would turn them on to marriage, although we couldn't possibly agree with some of their views. Could it be you they've been waiting to meet?

compiled by Shirley Percival

GYLES BRANDRETH (writer and panellist):

"Someone who's kind, jokey and talks even more than me. She'd have to do an interesting job and earn as much or more than me. To marry a housewife would be terrible. I'd want her quite demanding and passionate, but even so I wouldn't marry her if she smoked."

DAVID BROOME (show jumper):

"I like a girl with a lot of character and a will of her own. Good looks would get me started and character would hold me."

MARK CAINE (male model):

"A good cook and good-looking. Faithful, too. A reasonable amount of self-confidence but not too much. I'd prefer a homely type to an out and out career girl. And I've always had a soft spot for Scandinavian birds."

ROBERT CARRIER (gourmet):

"Surely marriage is outdated what with the permissive society and the Pill. Most people I know live together. If I did marry it would have to be someone paper thin—they say opposites attract—who's able to eat and eat and still look sensational."

MAX CLENDENNING (designer):

"She would have to be very natural and interested in people rather than objects or money. The attraction comes from a human quality of aliveness, understanding and interest. A beautiful girl whose one idea is to grab a millionaire would become very dull and boring. It would show in her eyes."

TOM COURTENAY (actor):

"My favourite woman at the moment is Charley's Aunt. In my thirty-four years I have learnt a good deal about women . . . which is why I'm still single."

ROGER COLLINS (hairdresser from French of London):

"Someone who constantly looks glamorous, is always groomed and immaculate. She should have an abundance of personality, be liked by everyone but superior to other girls. Having a profession might help. So far there's always been something not quite right."

BRIAN STRANGE (champion weight-lifter):

"She'd have to put up with me training six times a week. She must be a first-class cook and not moan about the housekeeping money she wouldn't get. I prefer small girls, otherwise I take them as they come."

MICHAEL FISH (fashion designer):

"I think of an old-fashioned wife who knows her duties. I was once told you choose a wife like you choose a cow—so that there's regular times when she comes in for milking. I wouldn't want her trendy."

BENNY HILL (comedian):

"Dear heart, I haven't the faintest idea. I've lots of charming girl-friends. One I take to the theatre, one to boxing and one I leave at home as it's more fun. Let's say I like girls to surprise me which they frequently do. A woman who's an enigma and takes me off guard."

JOHN HURT (actor):

"She'd have to be up-beat, punctual and independent, and never jealous. And positively, but positively, anti-Women's Lib. Well, we can't all be perfect."

SIMON JENKINS (journalist):

"I'd want a working wife, someone who considers herself liberated and able to look after herself if I wasn't around. Most of my friends are journalists but I'd rather not marry one. I couldn't envisage marrying anybody who wasn't attractive."

EDDIE KULUKUNDIS (wealthy impressario):

"A woman who's attractive, intelligent and capable of entertaining people at short notice. Well-informed and able to fend for herself. Tactfully dressed so as not to embarrass me. Faithful? That depends. I imagine it comes afterwards."

Charlotte Rampling, who has made the headlines by living with two men and "loving them equally"—Randall Lawrence here is one—has recently married the other, Brian Southcombe. But there's no breakup in wha she calls "her family". Here Charlotte cuddles up to he Best Man, a champagne girl in a pop outfit. Pepsi top £9·45 trousers £7·20, by Harriet

Fabergé for the love of life.

The world famous delay spray helps the considerate man to prolong the act of love. Available at leading Chemists from £1.75. Or send direct to Stud Holdings Ltd, Dept. 78, 45 Brompton Road, London SW3 IDE.

WHY THE ABORTION LAW DOESN'T WORK

Abortion became legal in this country in 1968, but anyone who expected that termination would become as easy as tonsillectomy has been sadly disillusioned. True, the Act has averted numbers of tragedies and prevented thousands of unwanted children being born, but for many women, and for all sorts of reasons, it simply doesn't work. It doesn't work because:

- Unsympathetic doctors often make girls feel embarrassed, ashamed or even as if they have committed a crime.
- A girl who decides quite rationally that she wants a termination frequently has to put on a great show of hysteria to convince a gynaecologist or psychiatrist.
- Lack of facilities and co-ordination often result in decisions being delayed until termination is very dangerous or no longer possible.
- Difficulties in obtaining NHS abortions mean that those with the knowhow and the cash to have private treatment have preference over less fortunate women who may well be in greater need.

These problems can only be solved by a vast increase in facilities for abortion and by the acceptance that every woman who wants an abortion should be allowed to have one. Abortion on demand is a very sensitive subject. The anti-lobby will talk about religious implications, will argue that the life of the foetus is sacred, that abortion is psychologically damaging and that the girl who is refused an abortion will afterwards be grateful. These are such powerful arguments that surely every woman has the right to work them out for herself and decide what she wants to do with *her own body* and *her own life*. This is our opinion, and many well-known women agree with us and feel strongly enough to allow their views to appear in print (see overleaf). We admire their courage.

THESE WOMEN HAVE HAD ABORTIONS

Buzz Goodbody

Maxine Audley

Shirley Ann Field

Joan Heal

Lelia Goldoni

Georgia Brown

Ann Lynn

Melissa Stribling

Ann Firbank

Patricia Cutts

BUZZ GOODBODY
Associate Director of the Royal Shakespeare Company

"To have a child for the wrong emotional reasons is disastrous, and it's hard to separate the subject of abortions from why people get pregnant. When young, I had an affair with a married man, and the one hope of getting him away from his wife was to have a child. He wanted me to. Then he left. I had an abortion. Anyone with a job in her own right must be able to decide whether she wants it or not. What a tragic future for an unwanted child from an affair that had gone wrong."

SHIRLEY ANN FIELD
actress

"The psychiatrists, supposed to deal in the milk of human kindness (particularly in view of their work), are experts at mental torture. They almost gloat. They take the payment as quickly as possible and still try to inflict misery. They ask ridiculous personal questions, and reduced me, and everyone else I have spoken to, to tears. They seem to humiliate deliberately. I believe abortion should be available to everyone, and cost no more than dilatation and curretage [a simple operation of dilating the cervix and gently scraping away the lining of the womb]—that is £30. Otherwise it encourages private doctors (obviously of a certain temperament) to become racketeers making thousands of pounds a week."

JOAN HEAL
actress

"It is diabolical that there are brilliant, eminent surgeons who never accept a cheque, but who remove £200 in tax free cash from beneath the clinic pillow, and run a filthy racket. When I've wanted a child I've had it. When I didn't, I've had an abortion, because I believe it is a hundred per cent a woman's responsibility to see she doesn't give birth unless she wants to. To me, abortion is no more murderous than contraception. You are preventing a birth."

MAXINE AUDLEY
actress

"No doctor should refuse a woman an abortion if she wants one, whatever the reason . . . if she has missed the Pill, forgotten the cap or been raped. The point is, it must be done quickly; delay is the danger. I had three abortions, when I was in my early twenties (of course, all illegal), each because of my own carelessness. And I wasn't yet ready for the responsibility of a child. Happily, and luckily, I now have a beautiful seventeen-year-old daughter, who was conceived and born because she *was wanted*."

LELIA GOLDONI
actress

"What incenses me is the masculine attitude that women are second-class citizens and if they get into trouble, they must pay for it. How dare they put us in the position of having to beg some National Health doctor for something which should be our personal right. There should be no stigma and no shame. My abortion was a drag. It went wrong and cost a fortune to be fixed. This was ten years ago and in America—I think it's an international problem. I felt no guilt then. But now I have a child, I think I would feel guilty."

MELISSA STRIBLING
actress

"People go on about the foetus as a separate being. You might as well say a boil is. Abortion should be as easy as having your appendix out. I chose to have this operation twice. I'm sorry for people who can't conceive, but I'm certainly not prepared to be a breeding factory for other people to adopt. A woman should be able to say 'I'm pregnant, I don't want it. I'll pay a reasonable sum to have it removed.'"

GEORGIA BROWN
singer

"Abortion will always be a traumatic experience, but it's not as dirty a word as when I had one at twenty-two. Women need every sympathy and every facility so they are not tempted back to the old gin and needle panic. So few people are educated to understand that the sexual act is a freedom and a joy, not just something you do to produce children. Contraceptive advice should be more freely available. But I feel very strongly that unwanted children are a tragedy."

PATRICIA CUTTS
actress

"Why should the doctor be God? It's right that 5,000 doctors should fly to Bangladesh to abort 20,000 women raped by West Pakistani soldiers. But outrageous that a doctor here should refuse one girl who has suffered the same fate. Nurses often dislike doing abortions because they have been trained to save lives. God knows, it's always traumatic. Mine was. But a woman should be able to choose freely."

ANN LYNN
actress

"Once the decision is made, the process should be simple, easy and safe, with sympathy all round, no stigma and no moral indignation. Years ago, I was humiliated, neglected and practically treated like a criminal, whereas a friend of mine had one through the National Health this spring and the nurses couldn't have been kinder. There's no simple answer to the problem."

ANN FIRBANK
actress

"I had the most humiliating, under-the-counter experience, ages ago. I was unmarried and not sufficiently involved with the father to want his child. Having children is a very serious business. Some women are capable of bringing them up on their own. But I believe children should be the result of a loving relationship. I feel very strongly about overpopulation, and to have a child, unless you desperately want it, is a selfish act. Abortion is common sense in this day and age, and should be made easily available to any woman who feels she needs it."

These Women have Strong Views on Abortion

ADRIENNE CORRI
actress

"I don't care what people think. I chose to have my two children, but I could easily have chosen abortion. To shove people into general hospitals is ghastly. The system is ham-fisted, masculine and Victorian. There should be properly administered centres run by sympathetic people."

GLENDA JACKSON
actress

"The present, wider grounds for legal abortion are a great step forward, but the scheme is unfair because of the individuals who run it. It is monstrous that in certain parts of the country it is almost impossible to get one because of the beliefs of the doctors and the prejudices of the nursing staff."

JILL BENNETT
actress

"People don't always love babies. If the Pill doesn't work it's not your fault. But it's still the same school credo, 'you've been found out'. If you've got to have an abortion—and I never have—do it fast and enlist a sympathetic doctor and boyfriend. Money and influence are a great help. I'd need a good reason. It's terrible to have one because you are just going to start in a good play."

ANNIE ROSS
singer

"It should be abortion on demand with no stress or strain. No woman should suffer the indignity of being put through an emotional hoop by a psychiatrist. She should be able to say 'I want one,' or 'I don't want one'."

SARAH LAWSON
actress

"At forty-three, it would be ludicrous to start a family again. I'd have it out like a tooth."

ADRIENNE POSTA
actress

"Why should a man have such power over a woman's body? Look at the Pope. I feel abortion is murder, and wouldn't want one. But if you conceive the first time you have sex, it's tragic."

NANETTE NEWMAN
actress

"People get so hysterical, forgetting the end product is an unwanted child. If it's done soon enough, I would compare it to a minor operation. Surely that's more sensible than ruining a woman's life?"

NEW PAIRS: NEW JEANS

Fashion by Deirdre McSharry. Photographs by Norman Eales

Blue jeans never die, they simply fade away. As most people prefer them that way—old and faded—the bottom *ought* to have dropped out of the market ages ago. A market that boomed in Europe when Brigitte Bardot and Audrey Hepburn swapped their respective ginghams and Givenchys for imported cowboy denims. You might think that saturation point had arrived when everyone from Princess Anne to Liz Taylor turn up in their nice, old jeans. But the likely lads at Levis (who have been selling jeans since 1848) and elsewhere are keeping the sales soaring this summer with an extra ingredient—sex. Noting that one of the essential differences between the sexes is the gap at the back of the waist caused by the pear shaped female bottom, jeans manufacturers are plugging that gap with specially shaped and seamed jeans that cling round the bottom and flare at the hem. Style extras for '72 include brighter colours and stud and badge decorations. When a pretty girl turns her back this summer the well-rounded sight ought to do wonders for the £40 million jeans market. Those saddle-weary ole blue denims have come a long way . . .

When not appearing in a well-cut bra and knickers in the current Brian Rix farce *Don't Just Lie There Say Something,* actress Joanna Lumley (this page) lives in jeans. "Jeans are the acid test, if I'm one ounce overweight I can see and feel it." For summer she's giving up her rolled-hem blue jeans for dazzling white flares. "A girl in white jeans turns men on," she says. Her chum, actor Richard Warwick of TV's *Please Sir* fame, agrees. Jeans, £5·50 and jacket, £5·35 by Levis. His star-spangled jeans from The Jean Machine £5·95. The Triang Pedigree bike is £30·95. Pins from Lord John. Joanna's hair by Paulene at Michaeljohn.

Proving that the best fitting jeans don't *have* to come from America, British designer Alistair Cowin teams up with American cover girl Ann Turkel (inset) to show off his all-English jeans: "I sold 45,000 pairs last year, not bad for fashion jeans." Ann bought ten pairs on the spot. Alistair Cowin jeans £3·95, shirts £6·95 and £5·90 from Way In, Harrods.

"If you are not wearing jeans you *must* be over thirty," says Renate Zatsch (opposite page) twenty-five-year-old German cover girl in her Dietrich accent. "Jeans are a way of life, who doesn't wear them?" says her boyfriend Michael Calderon. Renate likes jeans that fit. These white cotton pop jeans are seamed over the bottom to fit like flypaper, and the off the shoulder blouse is bursting out all over. "It's a gas," says Renate. Jeans and blouse £7 each by Anthony Price. His jeans £7·50, sweater £18 at Browns. Renate's hair by Ricci Burns.

PHOTOGRAPH PATRICK HUNT

THINGS TO SAY IN BED

Do you sometimes feel that your performance in bed is great but your dialogue could be more effective? Here are a few *bon mots* that should encourage a repeat performance and a few more that are calculated to banish him forever—if that's your intention.

- Whoever said sex was an overrated pastime?
- On a scale of one to ten that was *twelve*.
- You're one of the few people who look better out of clothes than in them.
- Seconds? I know *I'd* like some.
- You could put the electric blanket industry out of business.
- Don't go to work today!
- Did you write *The Sensuous Man*?
- How can something so good be non-fattening?
- I don't want to know about your past, but it certainly taught you a thing or two.
- Sleeping with you is like spending a week in Marrakesh.
- I reckon you could cope with six girls but don't let me catch you near one of them.
- Where do I send the cheque?
- Let's stay here all day.
- You know you're beautiful without your glasses/executive frown/hippie headband.
- Who needs champagne?
- I'm so glad we kept the light on.
- You must have been reading my *Cosmopolitan*.
- Mmmmmmmmmmmmm!
- And to think I once thought I was frigid!
- Let's not waste time talking.

REMARKS UTTERED TO MEN WHO DIDN'T RETURN

- How much did you say you weigh?
- I'll bet you can run a *mile* in three minutes, too.
- Listen, you know that Masters and Johnson study . . . ?
- There's a man with binoculars across the street!
- There, if that doesn't hold you, nothing will!
- That hurts!
- Is that the doorbell?
- Let's see . . . did I take my Pill this morning?
- For God's sake, it's only 7 am.
- Maybe we should get a vibrator?
- Did you read about the girl who got pregnant in a swimming pool?
- Could we get rid of some of these covers? I get a terrible rash when I'm overheated.
- Oh it's just a small infection but the doctors don't seem able to get rid of it.
- Did you put the rubbish out?
- Hey. You know, you're improving.
- Would you mind moving to the sofa? I can't bear anyone in bed with me when I'm sleeping.
- Do you always get hiccoughs?
- You only want me for one thing.
- But I *always* wear pyjamas.
- I can't breathe.

VIDAL SASSOON

This is a picture of a man who has made it. Vidal Sassoon is the tycoon of the crimping trade and he's got all the perks—a film-star wife, a jet-setting life, a penthouse in New York and a permanent seat at Chelsea football ground. All this and muscles too. Not bad for an East End boy who cheerfully admits to being forty-four. Years old, that is. If you are interested, his measurements are: 40 in. chest, 29 in. waist, 37 in. hips.

When Terry O'Neill finally angled Vidal in front of his camera at the David Morgan gym at 8.15 am, it was the end of a typical Sassoon schedule. In the previous month he had opened his first men's hair place in London, cut the hair of Chelsea football team, been to Manchester to check the salon there, crossed the Atlantic twice, taken a week off for sunning—nightclubbing too—in Miami with his wife Beverley, been to Paris to see hairdresser Alexandre, been filmed cycling in New York, and survived a fifteen-hour session in the TV studios for a series of hair-product commercials. He loved every minute, and, unlike that other jet setter David Frost, does *not* have bags under his eyes.

A ham at heart, Vidal—who in private life is a nice, rather shy guy—loves to be "on stage" publicly. When he hosts a TV show, he says they have to drag him away from the cameras. Lunching with him in London is like having Frank Sinatra by your side. Vidal knows everyone and everyone wants to say hello.

Mary Quant's husband, Alexander Plunkett-Greene, said to him on Vidal's last London visit: "Isn't it about time you stopped working your guts out?" Typical Sassoon retort: "If I had to live in the country, I would die. I'm forty-four, but I feel like a kid. I'm having a ball. I keep my body in shape by going to the gym three times every week. Beverley and I cycle in New York's Central Park, and we are health nuts. I'm not ashamed of my body—the body is the greatest machine ever invented. I love to watch the athletics at Madison Square and I hate to miss a Chelsea match. The appeal is mind over matter, like the four-minute mile. As in hairdressing, a great haircut is fine but what are you doing to your *hair*? You are what you eat.

"I had bags under my eyes but I got them taken away. Why not? Beverley is twenty-six and incredibly beautiful. My kids are three and two and it's up to me to stay young as long as possible. And no one needs an old chairman in *my* company. I say to the kids in the salon, 'I'm just starting, how about you?'

"I wouldn't give it away for a million dollars, the way I feel now. My son has black eyes—and handsome, wow! I think, where does he come from? Sure, I have a few grey hairs, but there's no way I'd have them dyed."

As with Liz Taylor, when you look at Vidal's sterling silver threads among the rich black, you understand why their spouses like them that way. Beverley Sassoon, whose own dark hair is shorter by about three inches than Vidal's—"Howard in London cut it that way. I think it's all part of a plot, so Vidal's looks longer," she laughs—says Vidal looks better than ever. "Like a French film star, don't you think? I used to feel like a gym-widow when he went off. Now I really appreciate what he does because he looks so good. The generation gap? I feel *older* than him sometimes, he's so active. But his health routine *does* work, at 8 st. 3 lb., I'm lighter than I've ever been. We never have a tin in the house, only fresh food. As I do almost as many TV commercials in America as he does, now we joke about sharing screen space!"

Could TV star be Our Hero's next role? He could certainly beat some of our telly stars at the cheesecake stakes hollow. Or should I say rounded?

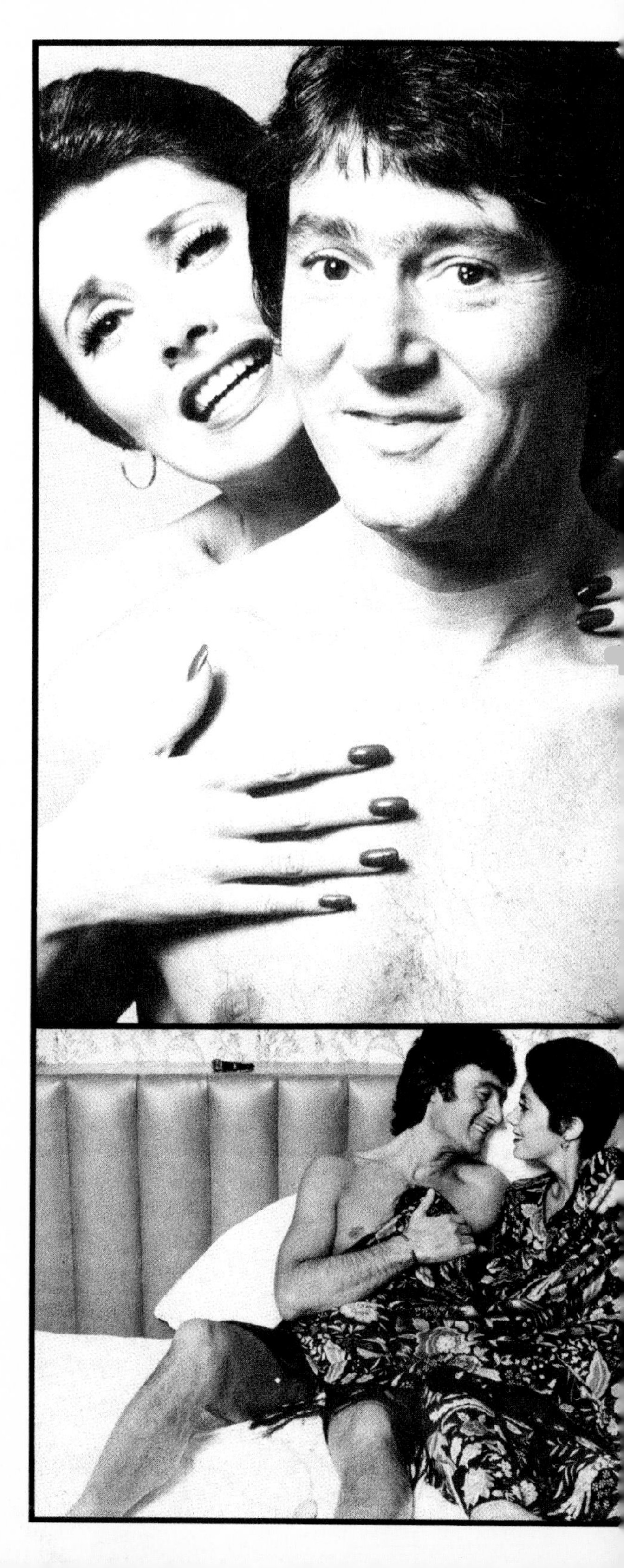

Muscle Man Vidal Sassoon swops the cutting shears for something tougher—the body-building equipment at London's David Morgan gym. This page, with his wife Beverley.

How to succeed by really trying

by Deirdre McSharry
photographs by Terry O'Neill

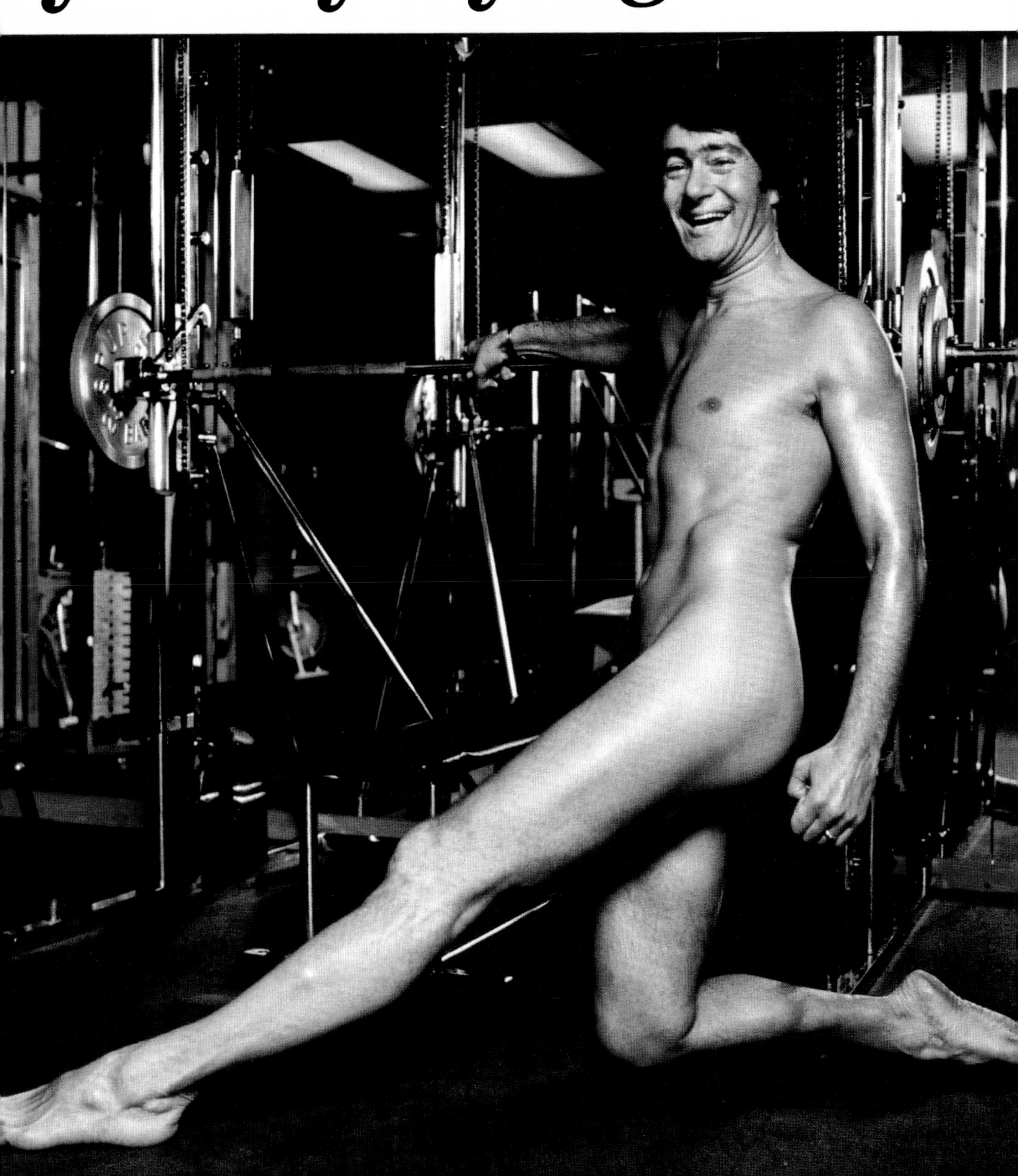

LIBERATION NOW

We all know we live with a double standard. The question is what are you doing to change it to a single? Had you thought of these possibilities?

- Ask him to hunt for a birthday present for your sister.
- Turn the television over to your favourite channel while he's engrossed in Match of the Day.
- Ask him if he's seen the missing button from your shirt just as he's rushing off to work.
- Arrive on time and look pointedly at your watch when he turns up.
- Next time he takes you to dinner, you select the wine.
- When you're walking together, look the attractive men you see on the street up and down. Let your eyes glitter a little.
- Invite some colleagues to dinner and let him prepare the meal so that you can talk office politics.
- Send him flowers on his birthday or after a special night out.
- Tell him your new assistant is extremely sexy—and he's *single*!
- Ask him to wash out your tights.
- Pick up the bill after a night on the town.
- Sleep on the outside of the bed.
- Phone at six o'clock and say you have to work late . . . *again*.
- Explain Value Added Tax to him.
- Let him pack and unpack your things for trips.
- Hire a lover and install him in a nice cosy little flat round the corner from your office.
- Let him feed the dog, the cat, the parakeet and the goldfish.
- Insist on carrying his suitcase.
- Offer to work out his income tax returns.
- When he goes to the men's room, give him 5p to tip the attendant.
- Tell him, "You're very clever—you think like a woman!"
- Stop faking orgasms.
- If your husband or the man you live with won't do his share of the housework, insist he hires a cleaner to do it for him.
- Walk into your place tonight after work and say, "What's for dinner?"
- Offer to *help* him with dinner.
- At the airport, ask him to wait over by that post while you check both of you in.
- Let him pick up your discarded clothes from the floor, and fold or hang them up.
- Bury your nose in work when you get home tonight . . . make numerous business phone calls.
- Insist on reading to him out loud just as he has got absorbed in a good book.
- Get out of bed only after he's got the coffee on and brought you orange juice in bed.
- Ask him to let you help open that bottle.
- When he hits a hole-in-one or drives a ball into your court say, "Not bad . . . for a man."
- Teach him how to work the washing machine.
- Invite him to the cinema . . . march right up to the box office and *pay*. Buy him a packet of crisps, too.
- Wash exactly half the kitchen floor.
- Stop wearing your wedding ring but insist that he wears his.
- Ask him to let you take out the rubbish once in a while.
- Throw a fit next time he asks "Where do you keep the sugar . . . towels . . . frying pan . . . soap . . ." etc.
- Tell him you'll need your grey silk trouser suit back from the cleaners by Wednesday.
- Don't take him on your next trip, but bring him the miniature bottles of booze from the aeroplane.
- Bellow like a wounded bear next time you're ill.
- Teach him to play chess.
- Give him a bigger allowance from your next salary increase. ◘

HOW SENSUAL ARE YOU?

by Carole Hay

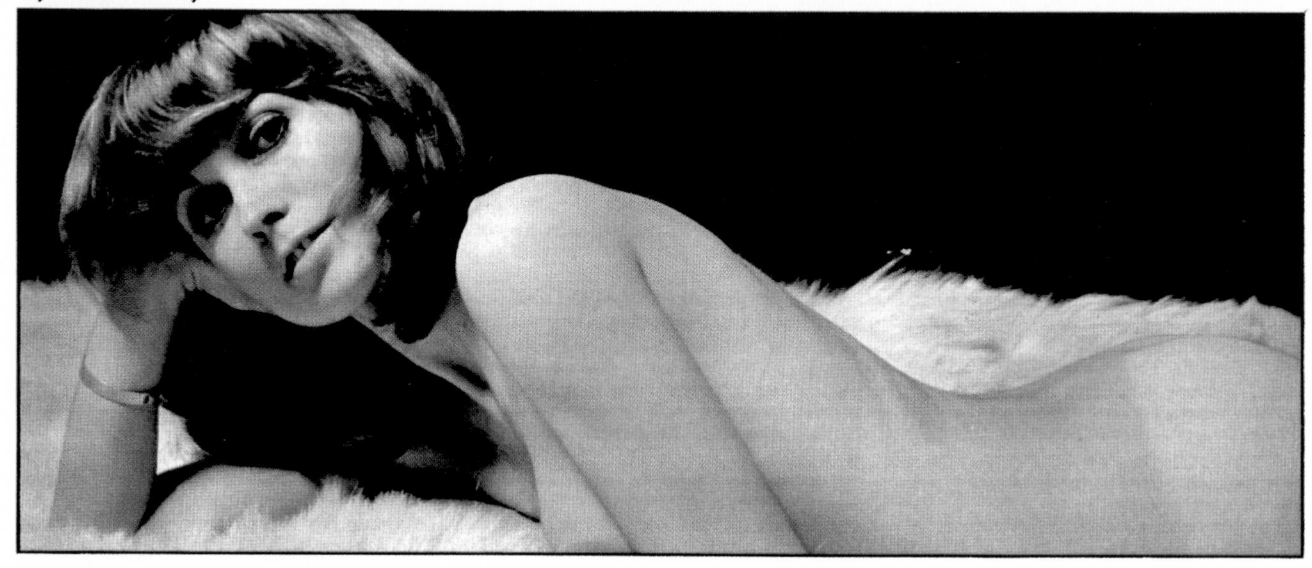

We all have the same five senses, but what we do with them—what we respond or vibrate to (or shun or shudder at)—varies widely according to our individuality. What type of sensuous person are *you*? Take this test and find out. Be sure to answer every question (pick answer a, b, c or d) and if none of the responses seems exactly right for you, then pick the one that's least unlikely. Be honest: there are no right or wrong answers, and besides, the questions don't always measure what they seem to be measuring.

1 You would most like to slip off to sleep in
a glamorous, silky, incredibly expensive sheets, à la Jackie Onassis.
b the same old . . . even rather sweaty . . . sheets that last night he made glorious love to you on.
c nice, white, clean-smelling, sunshine-dried sheets, like Grandma used to give you.
d a sleeping bag under the stars.

2 During the night a fire breaks out. When the firemen rescue you, you are found
a wearing nothing but *his* old sweater.
b in a sinuous lavender negligée that shows off your cleavage, and trailing clouds of scent.
c totally naked.
d in trim, elegant Dior pyjamas.

3 What you like best about your dog is
a stroking that marvellous fur and scratching those floppy ears.
b the fact that he loves and depends on you.
c taking him for long, exhilarating runs.
d his gorgeous looks and good manners.

4 You are shipwrecked on strange shores clinging to the one personal item you cannot live without. This is
a suntan lotion—if you're going to be stuck outdoors you might as well get a tan rather than burn to a cinder.
b that burnouse you brought back from Morocco—it will protect you from the weather and keep you looking attractive besides.
c your make-up kit—to keep you beautiful and your skin protected.
d the farewell fruit basket you never got a chance to dip into.

5 You have been skiing the slopes of Gstaad all day and are *very* cold. You drink
a a smooth, fulfilling hot chocolate with whipped cream atop.
b a fiery, intoxicating hot buttered rum.
c an opalescent green Chartreuse—just what the St Bernards used to carry to snow-stranded travellers.
d a simple but fragrant tea with lemon.

6 You're off to buy a new sofa. Price is of little object. You select
a deep-toned velvet, with squashy, sink-into down-stuffed pillows.
b Mies van der Rohe *moderne*—chic, spare, and glossy.
c something both beautiful and *sturdy*—you want the man to *enjoy* being there.
d the one piece in the showroom that makes you want to *snuggle*.

7 While lolling on your new sofa you listen to
a Bach, Vivaldi, or Scarlatti.
b Creedence Clearwater or the Rolling Stones.
c Janis Joplin or Marlene Dietrich.
d Frank Sinatra or Barbra Streisand.

8 When was the last time you squished your bare toes in the mud?
a sometime last summer, while sitting by a lake or stream.
b not for years . . . sandals are sexier than mud.
c last week, when you were caught in a rainstorm and saw a puddle.
d Yukk, you *hate* mud!

9 Your plane is hijacked to a Middle Eastern country. You are unharmed, but, due to political exigencies, are not allowed to leave. You
a find somebody rich and haunt the bazaars from his limousine, allowing him to buy you trinkets and baubles.
b move into the Hilton and sun-bathe by the pool.
c fall in love with a shepherd . . . sleep with him on his dirt floor.
d find an obscure native inn with a gorgeous view of the hills.

10 Of these scents, you prefer
a Patchouli or essence of musk.
b new-mown hay.
c the barest hint of jasmine.
d Chanel No. 5.

11 You are walking with your love in a lonely but beautiful wood when a cloudburst descends. You
a huddle under a leafy tree and hold each other close.
b run joyously through the rain, holding hands.
c pull him down on the ground to make love.
d walk quietly on, letting the rain caress you.

12 You are about to develop an allergy, making it impossible for you to wear certain fabrics or materials. Which would you least like ruled out of your life?
a mink, fox, and sable.
b lamb's wool and cashmere.
c cotton and drip-dry fabrics.
d silk, satin, and Irish linen.

13 You win a free trip to Italy in a contest. Immediately on arrival you find yourself
a in bed with an Italian.
b sipping Cinzano on your terrace overlooking the Bay of Naples.
c whisking through town, glorying in the sights—and the appreciative stares of Italian men.
d shopping at Gucci, Pucci, and Valentino.

14 You meet a film director who wants you in his next picture, but you're so skinny you must gain ten pounds. You eat
a caviar, champagne, and *babas au rhum*.

b steak, baked potatoes, and milk shakes.
c lobster, asparagus, and *crème brûlée*.
d all the famous specialities in all the best restaurants.

15 The picture finished, you wish to be skinny again. You do it by
a running, dancing, and swimming.
b going to a weight-reduction spa.
c dieting on smoked salmon and dry white wine.
d quietly fasting for six days.

16 You are planning to redecorate your bedroom. For the predominant colour scheme you would choose
a yellow and black.
b varying shades of red and pink.
c purple, maroon, and gold.
d forest green.

17 Your current man, frankly, is a bit of a drag, but you can't resist him because
a he surprises you by wanting to make love at unexpected times and in daring (even semi-public) places.
b he is passionate and loving, with a need for you that never abates.
c he's incredibly sensuous, inventive, and versatile in bed.
d he has a magnificent body.

18 Of the following books, which, as a child, did you like best (or dislike least)?
a *Little Women*.
b *Black Beauty*.
c *The Wizard of Oz*.
d *Alice in Wonderland*.

19 Of these sensual experiences, your favourite would be
a swimming naked by moonlight.
b wearing a fur coat with *nothing* underneath.
c slipping naked into cool sheets.
d a soothing, sensuous bath at day's end.

20 If he wants to make you feel terrifically sexy, all he has to do is
a tell you he wants to go to bed with you *right now*.
b whisper outrageously naughty suggestions in your ear.
c undress you (but very subtly) with his eyes.
d hug you and tell you how mad he is about you.

SCORING

1	a 4	**6**	a 4	**11**	a 2	**16**	a 1
	b 2		b 1		b 4		b 2
	c 1		c 3		c 3		c 4
	d 3		d 2		d 1		d 3
2	a 2	**7**	a 1	**12**	a 4	**17**	a 3
	b 4		b 3		b 2		b 2
	c 3		c 4		c 3		c 4
	d 1		d 2		d 1		d 1
3	a 4	**8**	a 2	**13**	a 2	**18**	a 2
	b 2		b 1		b 1		b 3
	c 3		c 3		c 3		c 4
	d 1		d 4		d 4		d 1
4	a 3	**9**	a 4	**14**	a 4	**19**	a 3
	b 1		b 2		b 3		b 4
	c 4		c 3		c 1		c 1
	d 2		d 1		d 2		d 2
5	a 2	**10**	a 4	**15**	a 3	**20**	a 3
	b 3		b 3		b 2		b 4
	c 4		c 1		c 4		c 1
	d 1		d 2		d 1		d 2

80 to 66: You are extravagantly sensuous—flamboyantly so at times. You love things that make a strong or vivid impression on the senses—clouds of exotic perfume, deeply saturated colours, opulent jewellery, lush bubble baths, rare foods and wines, soft, suggestive lighting, luxurious, sybaritic surroundings. Sexually you are ingenious and fanciful, with a knack for bringing out the beast in even the most lamb-like man. In dress you tend to be theatrical—nobody's ever going to accuse *you* of being classic! At times people accuse you of being phony, or a show-off but in truth you *do* need more sensual stimulation than the average person.

65 to 50: A nature girl, you are deeply in tune with the earth, the tides, the moon, the seasons. You enjoy just being *you*. The feel of the ground beneath your feet, the sight of sunlight slanting through the trees, the smell of new-mown grass, hearing the roar of a distant thunderstorm—these are what help make life a joy for you. You're a very *physical* person, and may take great delight in activities in which you use your body—sports, for instance, or driving very fast in a car or surfing. By no means a gourmet, you nevertheless have an intense enjoyment of food: a barbecued steak or an ear of corn, when you're hungry, can be as satisfying as the fanciest meal. If you drink at all, it's because you enjoy the effects of alcohol—you're not the wine-snob type or an *aficionada* of fancy beverages. Sex to you is as natural as breathing, and you enjoy it without hesitation.

49 to 35: You are the *true* sensualist . . . *satisfaction* is what you seek and crave. Of your home, you demand that it be above all comfortable and filled with objects that make *you* feel good, even if an interior decorator might not approve. You adore everything about eating, especially the glow that comes from having had a marvellous meal (even at the cost of filling yourself a little *too* full and having to worry about your weight). You could easily be a gourmet, or be renowned for your excellent cooking. Another important area of sensuality for you is *sexuality*—your keen enjoyment of almost everything in bed makes it easy for you to find and hold a man. You may or may not have a flair for aesthetics and the finer points of the sensuous life—what *really* matters to you is not appearances but deep, pleasurable fulfilment.

34 to 20: You have an elegant austerity in your approach to the life of the senses. A discriminating person, you insist on clean, spare lines, sensitive, just-right colour combinations and an uncluttered, serene atmosphere in your surroundings. You never over-indulge in food or drink, preferring small portions impeccably prepared and attractively served. There is something of the spiritual in your sensual life, and you are apt to have strong artistic leanings. You can be quite demanding sexually, however, and are apt to be *very* choosy in selecting a partner—a task made somewhat easier because men tend to flock to you. Even if you don't possess great beauty, you attract because of your sense of style. Of the senses, the *visual* is most important to you.

Shape up to a great figure with the Paris Showgirls

by Deirdre McSharry

The Eiffel Tower is said to be a bit rocky on its pins, the gourmets say the French cuisine is not what it was, but one Paris attraction is as solidly glittering as ever—and that's the Crazy Horse Saloon.

When you look at the pictures you can see this famous landmark is built on a flawless base—the nubile charms of the fifteen Crazy Horse girls. Don't call them strip teasers, these girls are *dancers* who are beautiful enough to take off their clothes in public. They are the couture mannequins of show biz. That's the firm opinion of owner Mr Alain Bernadin, who runs his club and guards his girls as if the Crazy Horse was a finishing school.

"What we do here is a kind of art form. I love women—everything about them—and my show celebrates this fact. No wonder we have such appreciative audiences. Onassis brings Jackie *and* his daughter. It's my rule that the show should be for the family. If my best friend's sixteen year old daughter thinks I'm a dirty old man I'll close the place down.

"I know *everything* about my girls. I am—do you say—their father figure? I watch over their boys, their marriages, what they eat. Fifty per cent of the girls were born under the sign of Gemini (I'm Capricorn), the sign of the exhibitionist. But off-stage the girls look like any girl on her way to work. No make-up, blue jeans.

"The fact that they are more graceful is their only trademark. That and their beautiful figures. They must be under twenty when they begin. Have small hips—it makes the bosom look bigger. I look for girls all over Europe, a mixture of English and German is best. Never Scandinavians, they are all alike—like fish.

"The way they move is what I watch for. In a natural way. Not contrived like some classical dancers. And they should look uninhibited. If she has the basic qualities I feel I can train almost any girl to be a Crazy Horse star."

The working star-maker is Victor Upshaw, a black American who walks around like the movie bad guy in stetsons and high-heel boots. Star of his own weekly French TV show, he's put more dancers through his hands than most men have had hot dinners. He too thinks he can shape up any girl—if she's willing to work. For your own personal private Upshaw lesson read on:

"You must make the whole body WORK. Once you start to move, it's easy. It starts in the head. Think about movement. Start with walking—the hardest thing to do well. The back is the centre of your existence. Hold your back up and not your breath. Think to the music—there's a beginning and a climax. Think of yourself as if you are being photographed. The image you make in someone's mind. No blurry gestures.

"Once you start dancing it is easy. Stretch the head—keep the neck working so the double chin is out. Work the arms as much as you can—that lifts the breasts. Dance is better than gym; it gives tension, which you need. It's better than relaxing, there's too much relaxing. Everything must stretch, you must have the intent—that makes for pretty movement. Jazz dancing is best. Stretching does make legs longer and thinner. Stretch and stretch. Watch yourself in the mirror. You can spot a wrong movement. My girls train at least two hours a day. Start with ten minutes and work up. The dance works all the muscles, weight is lost in certain areas. Yes, especially around the hips. Watch dancers on TV, in the movies. Make a movement style of your own, it should be part of you, like your clothes. Smile a lot, that's a good exercise. It moves all the facial muscles. With a pretty girl it's like turning on the light."

PHOTOGRAPHS BY ALICE SPRINGS. JEANS BY LEVI'S

DANCE LIKE CRAZY

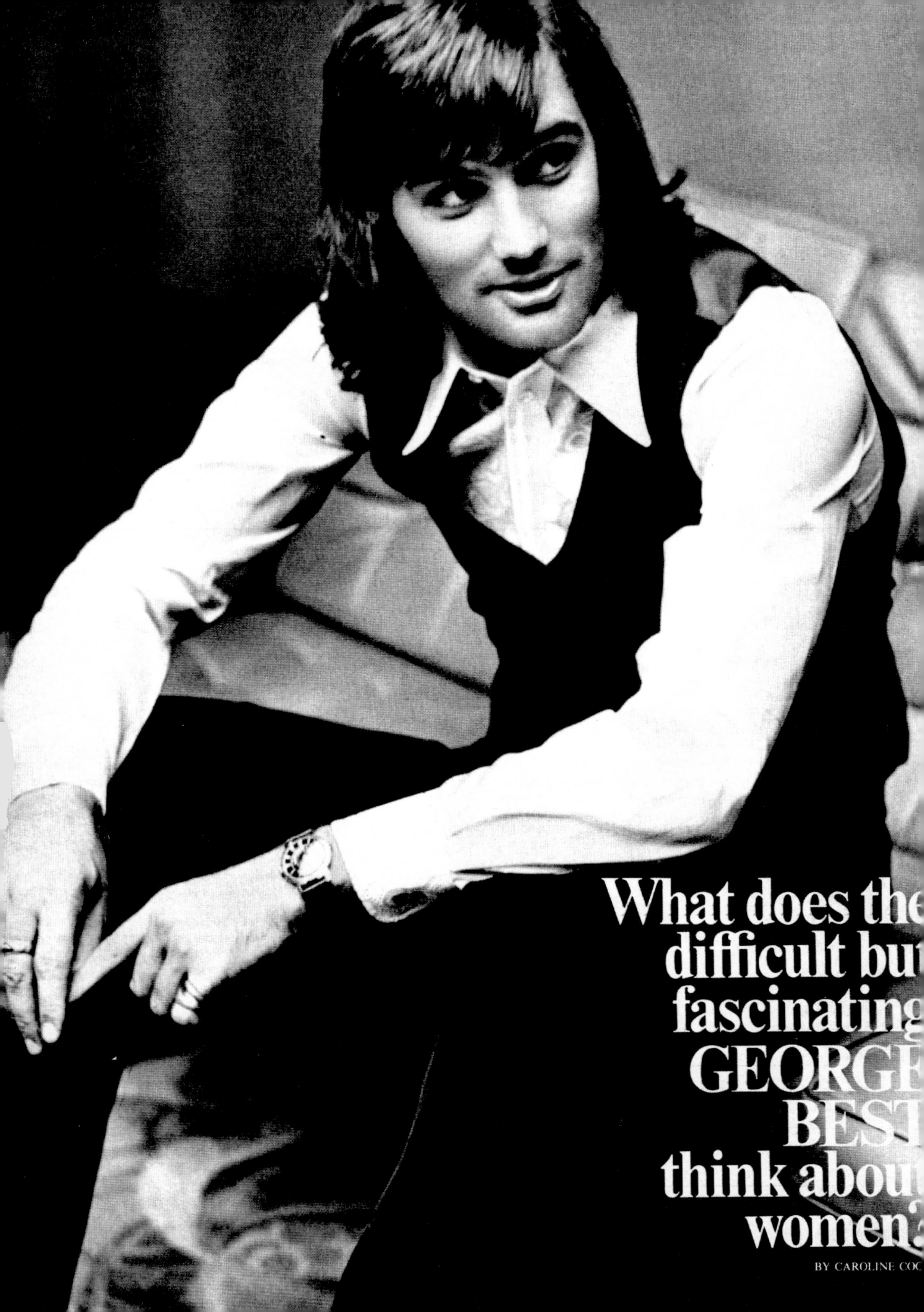

What does the difficult but fascinating GEORGE BEST think about women?

BY CAROLINE COC

It's anyone's guess where George will be today, tomorrow or this time next year . . . but wherever it is, he's sure to have a stunning girl in tow. Spoiled he may be, arrogant he certainly is, but no one can deny the magnetic attraction that draws the crowds, hits the headlines and makes women queue up for his attentions. What's the real secret of this erratic Irish genius? What does George Best really want from his women? And what do they get from him?

Even if you don't know what is meant by "off-side", or who "linesmen" are, even if you don't know the first thing about football, you'll know George Best plays the game. He plays it better, in fact, than almost anyone in the world, and certainly better than any footballer in the living memory of his fans in Manchester, where he played for Manchester United, or in Northern Ireland, where he has been the star of their International team.

At about 2.15 pm every Saturday afternoon from August to May, 600,000 men all over the country gulp down their lunch or a last pint at the pub. By 2.45 pm, complete with brightly coloured club scarves they are thronging their way, shoulder to shoulder, to the local football stadium for kick-off at 3 pm. Along the last hundred yards or so, they are escorted by the policemen, often mounted on huge horses, who are there to keep things cool. At this tense time, nothing will arouse a man's passion more than the sight of someone rooting for the opposing team—so there are ambulances in the vicinity too. Hot dogs pass hands at a furious rate, the boards of the rosette sellers flutter high above the heads of the crowd and, over the noise of general hilarity there are the shouts of lads with bundles of official programmes. The huge industry of football is having its weekly carnival.

George Best will be sitting with ten team mates, in his clean shorts, waiting for the team manager to open the dressing room door and let him out on to the pitch. When the crowd see him they roar. Forty thousand voices open out in full cry as the two teams, in single file, jog into view. After a few minutes warm-up and the toss-up to see which team will play into which goal first, the referee blows his whistle and the fun starts. All ninety minutes of it! Twenty-two fabulously fit men, after a night of abstention (so their managers hope) try, with a battery of hard learnt techniques and skills, to smash a small white ball past the opposing defenders, past the goalkeeper and into the goal. When this happens the crowd goes berserk—and the player who scored the goal will get hugged and kissed by his jubilant team mates.

When George Best puts the ball, with one of his master shots, into the back of the net, his fans chant "Geor-Gee! Geor-Gee! Geor-Gee!" Most of them have kicked an identical ball round a back yard, a side street, the school sports ground and plenty have dreamed of becoming a Professional. To the list of fighter pilot, cowboy and train-driver, add footballer—and then think how many small boys get the chance to watch real fighter pilots or cowboys, compared to those who for fifty pence can see a real footballer do his stuff! When a Hero can be seen for real, rather than gawped over in comics or at the movies, he is the instantly available object feeding the thwarted dreams of his worshippers. They expect and want to see him behave how they, for one reason or another, are unable to behave themselves. Each cheer and accolade they give their Hero is to some extent an act recognising the Hero in themselves who never got out. That Hero is incarnate in men like George Best.

When he was fifteen a talent scout spotted him playing for a youth club in Belfast. He was sent to England to train as an amateur for Manchester United. He couldn't sign a contract as an apprentice professional, training during the day and drawing a wage from the club, because the Irish and Welsh football associations were accusing England of "taking all the young talent out." The first morning he arrived in England he was taken to see United's football factory at work. The sight of so many athletes pounding about their morning training session, muscles rippling and sweat pouring, put the fear of Garth into George's yet undeveloped hamstrings. He saw what he had to do to put his body into footballing shape. To a "skinny little kid from Belfast" it was a daunting proposition and he was on the next ferry home to Ireland. Two weeks later his father had given him the confidence to return, and from that day on he has devoted himself to the game.

A year after signing professionally with Manchester United he was at London airport with a victorious team, being fêted after a triumphant match with Benfica in Portugal. It was an astonishing win, quite unpredicted by the critics who believed that Benfica and their wizard Eusebio would make mincemeat of the young team that Matt Busby was building up after the Munich air disaster. George at nineteen had played only four games with the first team, and yet he had scored two of the goals against Benfica! The next morning his picture was splashed over the front of the nationals, beaming from beneath the brim of a huge sombrero, his hair curling down the back of his neck. He had secured himself a permanent place in the most glamorous of the English football teams.

George's football is unique. He can play anywhere on the pitch, but his usual place is nearest the opposing team's goal. He's a striker! He's there to get the goals! He skims over the turf, his masterful sense of balance and control masking the exertion so obvious in less skilful players. When he wins the ball from an opponent everybody holds their breath. They know he can pick and dodge and skip his way through the most formidable defence, creating a goal in a situation which looked impossible.

His fans love him when he's scoring goals and they probably love him when he's not. The sporting pundits take a more bilious view of his off moments. Full of sanctimonious moralising, they give him advice in their columns about the way he should conduct himself off the pitch, so that when he is on it he is able to play his best. Heroes must expect some aggravation along with the adulation, but George Best rouses in his critics a hysteria which transcends concern for football. Well, he is more than a footballer. He holds his own, along with Alain Delon, Mick Jagger and Rudolf Nureyev as one of the world's most beautiful and unconventional men. He's twenty-seven, unmarried and a self-made millionaire. He loves fast cars, hip clothes, beautiful girls, and he has plenty of them. And they have all been blamed for his lack of form when he has not been scoring goals. If only he would settle down and get married cry his critics, often using him as an excuse to attack the permissive society. But it is his disregard for convention which makes him a brilliant player on and off the pitch. He experiments with football style as well as social behaviour. And this makes the fuddy-duddies in the football industry hopping mad.

He smiles after every other word as if to say, "you don't think I'm being serious, do you? He watches your dilemma and then bursts out laughing. He's very beautiful, but not at all sure of himself. The tall talk and bravado at the bar is a smoke screen behind which he hides his shy, sensitive self. Recently his friends asked a bartender mate of theirs to do an impersonation of George Best. To their surprise, all he did was to stand in a corner with a glass of lager. He stood there doing nothing, for five minutes.

George finds it difficult sometimes to believe he is a star. "It doesn't sink in—I mean, when I read about myself, it's like reading about someone else. And the other night after a game—we were in the players' lounge having a drink—a chap came over and said 'I hope you don't think I'm being a nuisance, but someone has asked if he can come over and say hello to you, if you don't mind.' And it was Gene Barry—and *he's* coming to ask *me* if I mind him saying hello. It seems so strange! The press often call me a big head. But I like to think I'm as much on the ground as possible. I know I'm different from other people, but I don't think I'm better. I know I'm a better footballer! That's the only thing I've got confidence in. Put a ball at my feet and I'll take on anybody. But in other things I'm nothing in comparison, so why should I think I'm better than anybody?"

The smile and the laugh, the skin and the hair must make it very difficult for a lot of girls to refuse an invitation from George Best, even if they realise that the intimate details of the event will provide the fodder for bar room jokes. His charm will also help them forget how often he shows up hours late for dinner, but is quite likely to pop round at one o'clock in the morning. Anybody who loves football will want to see George shoot into the back of the net for a long time yet. But it looks as if he's getting bored with it all. Surely the star who Michael Parkinson asked Matt Busby to evaluate, only to be asked in return "how deep is the ocean?" will somehow stay in the game. Surely there are enough girls who, in the interest of sport, will keep him amused? And while they are about it, couldn't just one of them find the time to tell him something about women?

In September 1928, Monsieur Francois Coty introduced his new fragrance, l'Aimant.
That October, Madame la Comtesse de l'Arbour St. Aubin, was the first woman in Paris to wear it.
Today, you can exhibit the same chic.
Coty

WHAT HAPPENS WHEN GIRLS MAKE PASSES

BY CAROLE IRBY HAY

My friend Sandie is a charming, pretty girl . . . all skinny curves, wide grey eyes, smiles and elegance. Clever, too . . . she earns more than enough to dress like a dream and pay the exorbitant rent on her luxury studio flat. Recently, Sandie, who'd just broken up with her lover of two years and had determined not to plunge into a blue period, started going to a lot of parties. At one of these, she sighted a tall, worldly-seeming facsimile of Michael Caine, a visiting out-of-towner . . . smart, successful, sexy! Now, Sandie is optimistic and always has an eye open for the possibility of true love; she is also a sensualist and her Michael-Caine-of-the-moment struck a definite chord. Love might come later but, right now, bed was her object.

Elbows brushed, eyes met, conversation began. He appeared to be definitely attracted to her, she reported to me later, and a girl like Sandie is not apt to misread a man's signals. When he asked for her number, though, she smiled and said why didn't they adjourn for a drink right now? Later at the hotel bar, when he seemed to be fumbling around for an excuse to ask her up to his room (so shabby!), she hospitably suggested that they go on to *her* place. There, Sandie struck a languorous pose and waited. When nothing happened, she ambled across the room, perched on his knee, and put a hand caressingly through his hair.

At which point, he coughed, disengaged her hand, edged her from his lap, and asked rather stagily if she knew anything about *love*.

"Er . . . about as much as most people, I suppose," replied Sandie. "Why do you ask?"

"You don't behave as if you do," said the man in a shocked, somewhat paternal tone. "I mean, you invite me up here without a second's hesitation, and, well, it appears that you're prepared to go to bed with me . . . just like that!"

"Oh, I am," said Sandie, smiling cheerily. Then she paused; she must have misread this man, after all—evidently she wasn't his type. "Look," she said, "I'm sorry. I thought we were mutually attracted."

"It's not that," he said, scornfully, "but you're acting as if you've no respect for yourself . . ." his eyes turned sombrely downwards ". . . or for me either!"

My God, thought Sandie, galvanised by sudden insight, he doesn't want to go to bed with me because *I've* taken the initiative. By this time, Sandie no longer wanted this man, but she did want to determine whether or not her insight was correct; therefore she dropped her cheery, sexy, impudent air, retired discreetly to a dim corner, gazed at him diffidently, and began to talk in a shy and stumbling way. Sure enough, half an hour of this and she had to pry a prone, gasping, fully aroused man off her settee.

Unfortunately, Sandie's experience is hardly unique. A canvass of my (sexiest, most-liberated) friends indicates that for a woman to show more than a hint of sexual aggressiveness is apt to turn many men off faster than the news that you've got infectious hepatitis. Men are so accustomed to doing the seducing that they promptly lose identity—not to mention potency—when a woman indicates there's no need to prevail against her moral scruple or "feminine" timorousness . . . that, in fact, she's ready to be a willing, even aggressive, partner in the act.

How sad if men (or some men, anyway) want us only when sex is a kind of rape, when they have to inveigle and cajole, bully and threaten us into bed. Sandie's would-be lover was something of a sissie . . . and also a hypocrite. He ceased worrying about love the second that she demonstrated a "properly" fetching and demure manner. Like a woman of the Fifties, the man was muddling up sex and love, doing the old cop-out routine girls used to do simply because he was afraid to meet a female in bed as an equal!

And when a man can't *bed* as an equal, then the likelihood is he doesn't regard a woman as an equal in any other way either . . . not when he's employing her or marrying her or simply sitting across a conference room from her. You can't separate the sexual tyranny men are accustomed to exercising over women from any other kind . . . and you can't really have liberation until girls are free to actively select bed partners and men are willing to accept that our urges are just as irrepressible as theirs! ☒

MEN DO NEED WOMEN

BY JANE WALTERS

Now that Women's Lib has begun to demythologise the relations between the sexes, here's one more floating fallacy that needs to be anchored and then sunk—the myth that while a woman may pine and long to have a man of her own, men have no correspondingly intense need for females. Oh, they may put up with women for the sake of some good cooking or superior sex, but only a very weak-minded chap would be eager to trade his freedom for such cheap comforts. Then again, a man may be temporarily crazed by a passion for one particular female, but the frenzy of love fades quickly, and the "normal" male returns to the ordinary masculine condition—as soaringly independent as a sparrow hawk!

Well, this myth, fortunately for us man-loving females, does not reflect true emotional realities. Men *do* need women . . . and badly! Perhaps what prevents them from admitting this is merely some shrewd sexist logic. The myth that men can painlessly dissolve a sexual bond whenever they choose keeps us women rooted timorously in our "place," quaking with the fear of being left. Think how uppity a girl might become if she believed her man couldn't get along without her.

Dispassionately considered, though, the notion of men's splendid independence doesn't hold up at all. Most of the evidence scraped together by psychologists, anthropologists, and ethologists (they study the animal origins of human behaviour) supports the conclusion that the impulse to mate—to find a single life comrade of the opposite sex—is shared more or less equally by men and women. True, men have traditionally been given greater freedom than women to "sow wild oats"; until the recent sexual revolution, a man's life was expected to be far more liberally dosed with premarital adventure than a girl's. But even in those dark, pre-Sixties days, men would carouse for a while, and then yield to the almost universal impulse to settle down and build a family and career with the loving co-operation of a woman.

And what of the supposedly strictly female insecurities that prompt girls to seek anxiously for husbands—the "what good am I if I don't have a man" syndrome? Some of these fears may indeed be neurotically based, but on the whole these "insecurities" are merely our psyche's way of urging us towards maturity—and that generally means forming a permanent, adult bond with a member of the other sex. Are you really surprised to learn that men, too, share these "insecurities", that they feel their masculinity is diminished if they are not able to win and keep the devotion of a desirable female? If men didn't share these psychic promptings with women, no marriage would ever have been successfully made or maintained.

OK, men do need women, or, more specifically, *one* woman to love and help them through their lives. But here's another less palatable truth—males in our culture have been traditionally discouraged from acknowledging this need. A stern, self-sufficiency is part of the masculine mystique, and many men would perish by lingering torture rather than admit that inside they are basically "dependent clingers" —just like us.

Now and then, a rare, liberated man will indicate that he'd be lost without his woman, but more often men answer the charge that they actually require a girl's love with a loud, insistently "masculine" guffaw.

Pay attention, though, to what men do rather than what they say. Just about every normal man does eventually find a girl of his own, live with—and finally (if sometimes grudgingly) marry her. When made bereft by divorce, desertion or death, these same men go out and find another woman. Why? Because they don't need us? No, because, despite a pseudo-masculine reluctance to admit such needs, a man without a woman is quite as lost as a woman without a man. ☒

CHELSEA BROWN, ex-star of TV's *Laugh* is the perfect clothes horse for a pants "In New York they call it tuckus—your derr I mean," says the singer who has a nota one. "When you wear pants—and I alw do—that's where they've got to fit. My says 'do you ever wear a dress?' I thou they'd stopped making them. I'm built li boy, except for my bozoom, but no one mistake me for a man in pants. I wear th with high heels and hats. I'm a mo dresser and like most women I dress for man. What do I go for? The disastrous ty You know, jeans, suède and a Merced Chelsea here wears a cream suit by Wa £17·95, with Chelsea Cobbler shoes, £14

CILLA BLACK (right) who has been star in her own TV series, celebrates by buyin suit from the tailor who started the n gent's suiting craze—Tommy Nutte couldn't afford one before," says C "Tommy is a friend from Beatle days. I jealous when I saw Bianca and Joan Col in a Nutter job so I had my hair cut, a mage streak put in, and had my outside measured. I *do* look a bit like a blok these checks, but *he*—my husband Bo —likes me in trousers. I try to hav new look for every series. I can you I have to suffer to look thin, I my arms to look like snakes. I prefer pa for telly. Ringo Starr says he lo Tommy's suits—the crotch is cu high you walk out like th Cilla mimes an uptight walk, to stu applause. In the picture, howe Cilla looks relaxed in Prince Wales tweed suit and her c diamonds. Hair by Le at Smile. Suit £170 order at Nutt (01-437 685

The Tailor Maids...

ive you a lesson in how to wear the rousers—without antagonising the men

ashion by Deirdre McSharry
'hotographs by Norman Eales

'here's a story that Coco Chanel created the ashion when she arrived in Venice in the Twenties, vith the inevitable Duke in tow, and decided that ants were the only thing to wear while being anded in and out of a gondola. So trousers for emales were adapted from the side-buttoning arb of the gondoliers. There were no flies on :hanel. . . . Since then Garbo, Dietrich, Jackie)nassis and Bianca Jagger have worn the rousers. And no one ever mistook any of them or a man. The secret, the tailored ladies say, is o walk tall in high heels, move in a cloud of cent and make sure your pants fit where it hows—when you beat a retreat . . .

JOAN COLLINS stars in the thriller *Dark Places*, and in TV's *The Man Who Came To Dinner* she plays opposite Orson Welles in a grey flannel trouser suit. "What else?" says Joan. "I'm quite secure in my femininity and I've never felt butch in trousers. People used to turn round in the street, but now you can go anywhere in pants—even the Connaught. I've always thought that men look better than women and it's got to be their suits. In films, pants don't date the way skirt lengths do and I've learned how to sit down, cross my legs like a man—but sexier. Men pay me compliments when I'm in trousers. A girl in fella's clothes is appealing, don't you think?" Joan wears cream gaberdine suit, £20·90, and print blouse, £6·95, by Lee Bender at Bus Stop. Bangles from Butler and Wilson. Hair arranged by Michael at Michaeljohn.

ELIZABETH HARRISON has had two men in her life, Richard Harris and Rex Harrison. "Both my husbands love women and I'm a womanly woman. I know my place," she laughs. "The most important thing a woman can do is make a man want to protect her. I have never wanted to be a man. But if you are 'his' lady a man doesn't want you to look too odd. Rex is never sloppy (unlike me). He is a formal person and likes formal clothes. Rex has views—and how. But since I've put my clothes life into Gordon Luke Clarke's hands (he owns *Luke* in Chelsea) he is pleased with the way I look in trousers. I feel freer and not so responsible. No, I don't wear much underwear underneath. I hate that constricted feeling. Undies aren't necessary, are they?" Beautifully put-together outfit in navy jersey and green silk by Gordon Luke Clarke. Jacket £40, trousers £18·45, shirt £25. Jewellery and scarf also at Luke. Hair arranged by Clifford at Leonard. Make-up by Pierre LaRoche.
FOR STOCKISTS SEE PAGE 131

CHELSEA BROWN wears a Donegal tweed suit by Stirling Cooper, £22·95, silk shirt by Deborah & Clare, £12·95. Beads from a selection at Paul Stephens. Hair specially arranged by Christine at Mane Line.

For Ian McShane, there's nothing remarkable in being photographed sprawling across a bed. He's spent much of his career doing just that, but instead of a dachshund, his bedmates have included lovely ladies like Ava Gardner, Raquel Welch, Dyan Cannon and Gayle Hunnicut. And if you take a leisurely tour round that muscular torso and inspect those what-are-you-waiting-for eyes, you'll understand why he's picked for all those torrid love parts.

Despite those Latin features, thirty-one year old Ian was born in Blackburn. His father, Harry McShane, played for Manchester United and Ian grew up expecting to be a footballer until somewhere his ambitions changed direction and he went to RADA. Immediately afterwards he was given the lead in a film called *The Wild and the Willing* and since then his career has advanced steadily if not spectacularly. He's appeared several times in the West End theatre, acted in, on average, one television play a year and taken major parts in about eight films including *Sitting Target, If it's Tuesday it Must be Belgium* and *The Last of Sheila*, co-starring Raquel Welch and Dyan Cannon, which should be released in the late summer.

His performances have been consistently praised and there's little doubt that, if he chose, Ian could turn out twice as many films. He admits, however, that he doesn't like working too much. "The good thing about making a bit of bread is that you can do what you want to. I hate the thought of work for work's sake."

Instead, Ian likes to play the dilettante . . . commuting between pub and home, reading, listening to music, playing squash and football. He lives in an elegant Edwardian house in Roehampton, South London, with his wife Ruth, an ex-model from Manchester, their three year old daughter Katie and Nicky, seven, Ruth's son by a previous marriage. Their two dogs, Morrie, a neurotic dachshund (that's him preserving discretion in our photograph) and Wolfie, an extrovert, over-sexed mongrel, are regarded as third and fourth children.

Perhaps because his first wife, Susan Farmer, was an actress, Ian displays an almost total disenchantment with the breed. "I don't like them very much, I don't know why they do it. An actor I can understand . . . but an actress is quite a different species. They're too aware of what they are . . . always discussing how they should do the part, actresses are very full of that."

He's still recovering from tussles on location for *The Last of Sheila* where, according to Ian, the leading ladies were continually jockeying for first place. "It was all right when they were in front of the camera. The problems were about extraneous things like who took the longest to get their lip gloss on. He describes his first encounter with Dyan Cannon. She, chewing gum, sizing him up quizzically: "What's your name?" "Ian McShane." Chew. Chew. "You married?" "Yes." Chew. Chew. "Got any kids?" "Yes." Chew. Chew. "See ya."

His black list includes Elsa Martinelli ("an Italian spaghetti"), Senta Berger and Virna Lisi who all came in as guest artistes on one of his films and "were terribly blasé about their roles. I suppose they had a right to be. But you feel that terrible anger, you think 'how dare you come on this set for two days messing about'." Yet, if you accuse Ian of being too hard on women, his wife immediately defends him. "He's the most easy-going, tolerant man, not even grouchy when he's out of work."

He admits he has enjoyed working with some actresses, notably Ava Gardner, "A knockout, totally larger than life", and Gayle Hunnicutt, "A lovely lady and a very good actress". As for those passionate love clinches: "They're very clinical because it's all worked out beforehand. My most pleasurable ones were with Ava Gardner on *Tam Lin*—that was a big laugh. But these scenes are always enjoyable. After all it's just acting."

Many actors would shudder at that word "just". But Ian, although he takes his acting seriously enough, has kept a rare sense of proportion. His real life—driving his 1957 blue Rolls, taking his wife to gambling clubs ("She plays roulette, I stick to the fruit machines"), or doing nothing in particular at home—takes a high priority.

He's delighted, though, about his next film. He plays Bramwell in *Bramwell Bronte*, a part he has wanted for several years. "I have a lot of naive confidence. I always hope that the next one will be the best film, the best people, the nicest wine. It's very important that you should have a lovely time when you're working."

Having a lovely time seems to be a pretty good ambition and it's nice to talk to an actor who isn't all tortured anguish. On screen, Ian McShane can be brutal, arrogant or passionate to order, but look again at that impudent half-smile and you'll find the humour and animal warmth that make him such a huggable Libran.

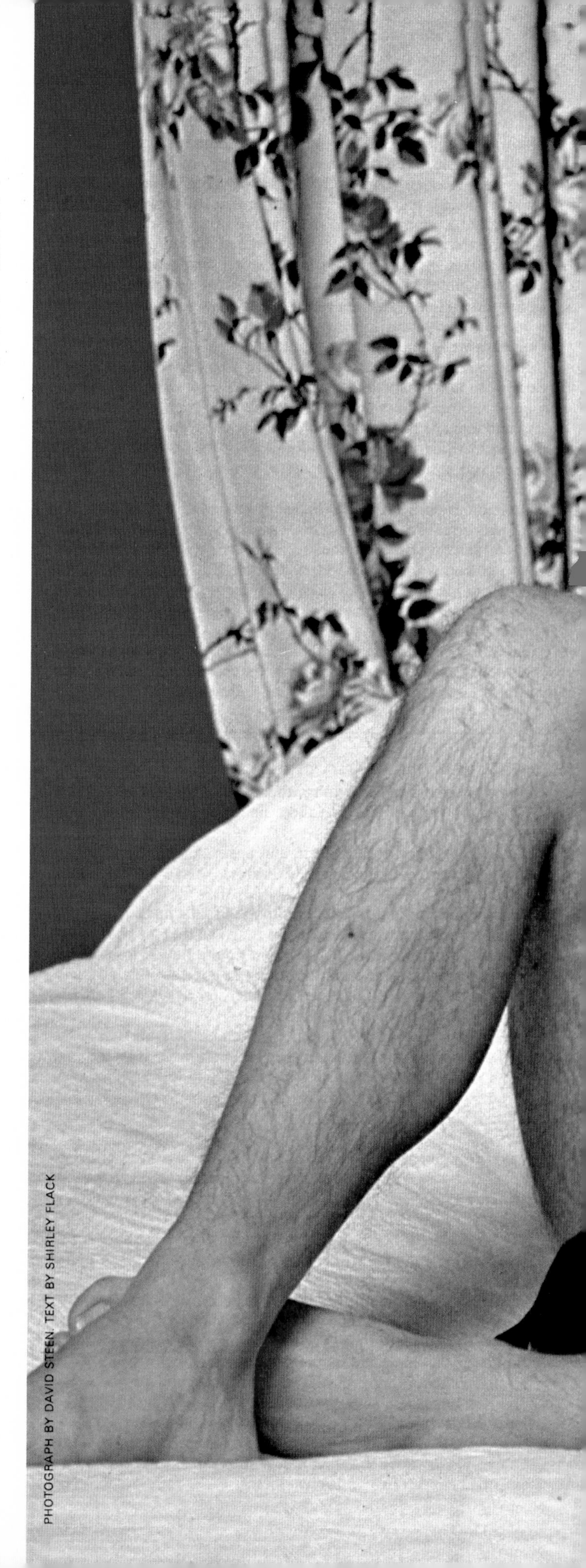

PHOTOGRAPH BY DAVID STEEN. TEXT BY SHIRLEY FLACK

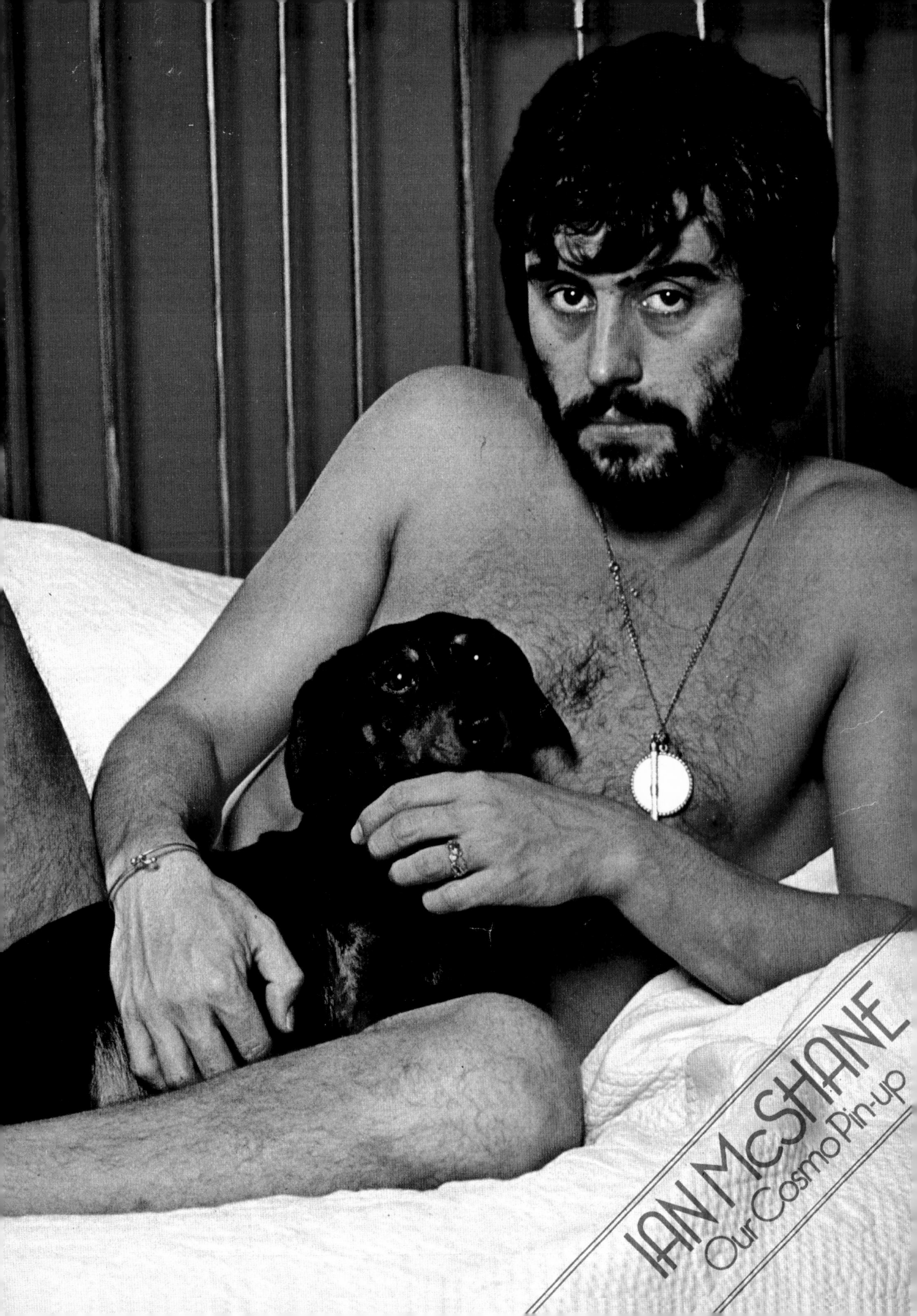
IAN McSHANE
Our Cosmo Pin-up

Give Your Place The Designer's Touch

BY KAREN FISHER

You're not a painter or a furniture designer but you'd love to decorate your flat with something unique. To buy a ready-made "original" would probably cost a career girl's ransom, but if you follow our ideas you can achieve sensational results at a realistic price. And if you're stuck with dreary-landlady furniture, an exciting focal point to your room is not a luxury . . . it's essential survival gear!

The magnificent macramé hanging chair (above) was designed for Cosmopolitan by Gladys Hoisington. If you'd like our free instruction leaflet, send a large stamped addressed envelope to Cosmo Decorating, Cosmopolitan, Chestergate House, Vauxhall Bridge Road, London SW1.

Foam rubber cubes (right), singly or pushed together, make a versatile base for jazzy seating. These can be cut to order by The Pentonville Rubber Co Ltd, 50-52 Pentonville Road, London W1. (Price about £4·50, plus VAT, for an 18in cube.) Decorate with felt cut-outs which can be stuck on with Bostic. Disguise an old-fashioned fireplace by painting an entire wall with bold diagonal stripes (use masking tape to get a clean edge). Stick more felt shapes on a plain roller blind for a highly original wall-hanging.

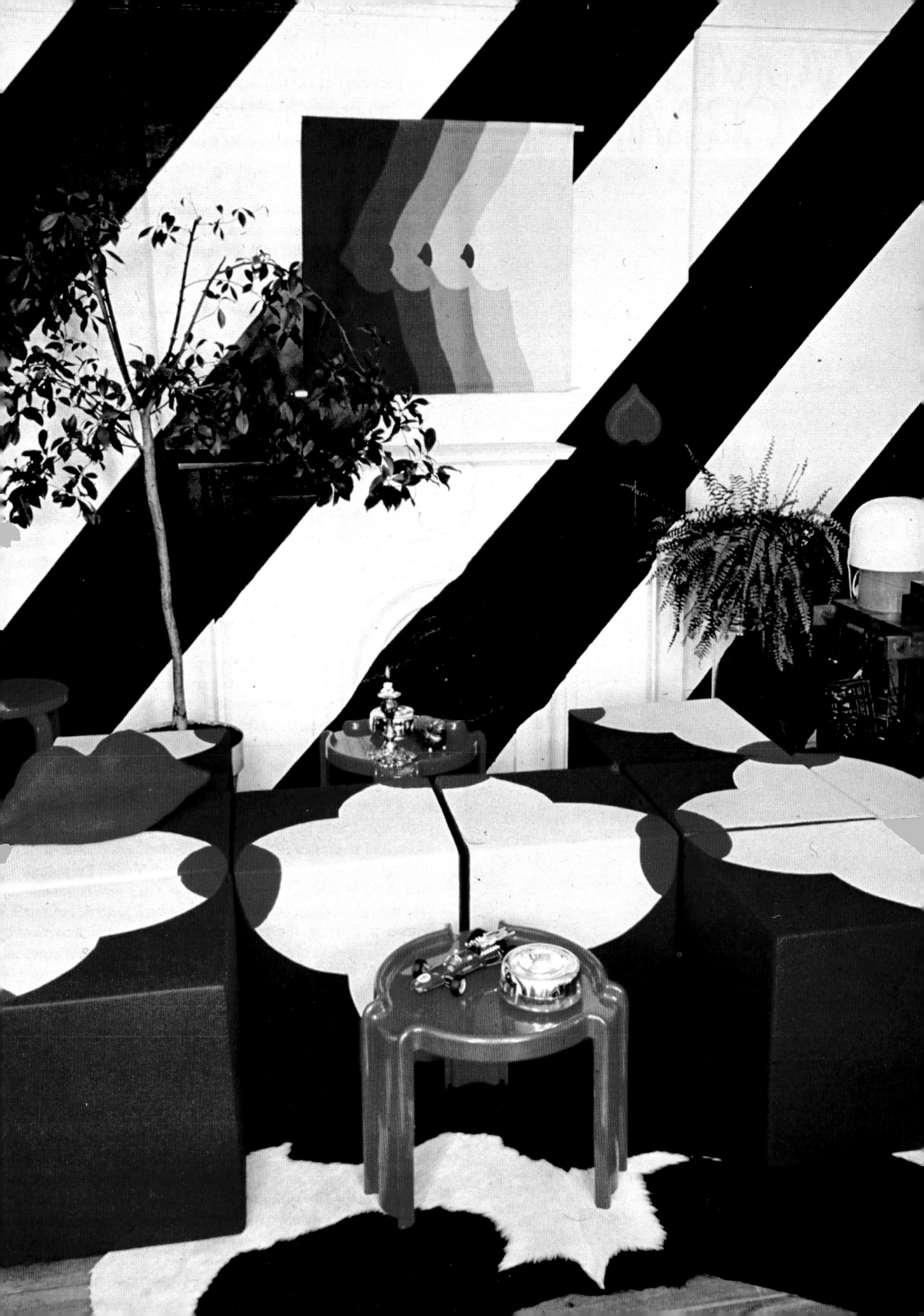

I can't seem to forget you.
Your Wind Song stays on my mind.
Wind Song
Wind Song
Perfume by Prince Matchabelli

Should men do 'women's work'?

Is a man's place in the home? Cosmo asked twenty-six males how they felt about doing housework and generally helping out on the domestic front. We came up with answers from men who ranged from pinny-purring prigs to chauvinists in blinkers, from gods looking down on lesser mortals to tolerant, human and apparently very perceptive people. Before you cast aside the duster with a liberated fling, you might read this survey by ELIZABETH DICKSON.

ERIC CRICHTON *photographer's assistant*
"Housework is absolutely boring, tedious but essential. It's unkind to fob her off with an excuse for not helping, that's pure laziness. Everyone should muck in."

RICHARD GOODWIN *film director and producer*
"I've worn a divided skirt for years. You can't avoid doing women's work if you work from home as we do. Women doing men's work is the complaint I get in our ménage."

TONY JACKLIN *golfer*
"Absolutely not. I'd never help. And I wouldn't expect her to do my work either."

BOBBY CHAPMAN *architect*
"The idea of a man not helping revolts me. You should do things together. When my wife was working full-time we really did share the chores. But now she has taken over most of the organisation. I do things like lay the table and quite enjoy it. I believe children should be a joint responsibility and the major decisions to do with them are joint ones."

HARDY AMIES *couturier*
"Certainly not. Men should give their orders in firm, clear but kindly tones. Meals should be ordered with such precision that it is clear that the best lovers' knots are made by Cordon Bleus."

CHARLES CAMPBELL *restaurateur*
"Yes. I do all the cooking at home. It gives me great pleasure and anyway, women on the whole are incompetent about preparing food. Theoretically I believe in helping about the house, in practice I never do. I can't bear the noise of the vacuum and I like living in a mess."

LEO COOPER *publisher and husband of Jilly Cooper*
Yes, of course. Men are much better at it. I do at least half the cooking. And of course I help with the children and change the nappies. It gets things done. This is what I do—and I don't give a damn what other men do in their marriages."

NICHOLAS SAUNDERS *author of* Alternative London
"I don't see that there's very much distinction between *women's* and *men's* jobs. Helping is a very important part of survival. I'm sure you are just testing out the other side of a relationship if you act helpless. You become helpless if you want attention. You may try and change your way of living, as I do, but basically, deep down, men in our society tend to be more disciplined and organised. So they get things like housework done more efficiently. They'll think it out, whereas women rush into it. I think women are more creative—they produce more feeling about arranging things."

GRAHAM ROGERS *male model*
"I'm quite happy to do housework but I'd draw the line at *having* a brat."

DAVID BAILEY *photographer*
"Absolutely not. Leave it to your servants. Penelope doesn't spend time cleaning the house, and I wouldn't want her too. And I wouldn't want any woman to expect it of me. I've never known that situation. I earn the bread to have someone else do it. It is an unfair question because the answer rather depends on the kind of money you have."

FREDRIC DAVIES *clairvoyant/astrologer*
"If a man's help is needed around the house, he is more likely to be persuaded when the moon is in Cancer. Although, however the stars may be arranged, I get great urges to do the chores when I'm frustrated about something. I can tackle a work problem freshly after I've gone downstairs and cleaned out a lot of cupboards. If I've got a worrying deadline—say I'm giving a lecture—I go to the laundromat. You're a prisoner there. So it's the best place to sort out your problems."

LESLEY RUSSELL *hairdresser and one of the owners of the Salon "Smile"*
"It doesn't enter our relationship not to help. We organise everything between the two of us. There's a certain satisfaction in making things clean. Chores are good therapy. And doing them is one way of showing your affection to your partner."

JUSTIN DE BLANK *grocer and caterer*
"On the whole men should help. There's a curious satisfaction in cleanliness. But the British are a dirty race, slovenly on the whole. I'm amazed by the low standards of hygiene I find in shops. I'm a tremendously fast and good washer-up, and I'm neurotic about dirt. Some chores I enjoy—like using the industrial cleaner. Perhaps I'd take different view if I had to clean all the time. One thing, I know, its best to get things done—I'd leave home rather than live with a nagger."

PATRICK LICHFIELD *photographer*
"It is irrelevant who does it but the army taught me that things must be done well. I require certain standards. I'm easily irritated by sloppiness. I've got a slight hygiene phobia. I clean bath taps. At my London studio we muck in regardless of sex. The place is fairly utilitarian and modern. In the country my staff do all that. A man arranges the flowers there."

NIGEL ANTHONY *actor*
"Its only fair to share chores though there's nothing funny about housework. Men are just as capable, though I don't think you want to get too highly organised about doing it. It's a question of whoever reaches the broom first sweeps. As an actor you are bound to be at home in the day sometimes and you can't expect to be waited on."

APOLLO ROSSIDES *hair-stylist*
"Of course a man should help with the house. A selfish bastard will loll about. But why should a woman be stuck with your kids and the house all day—and most wives are. I love to fix her a meal or pamper her with a hot drink if she's feeling lousy. And I push the sweeper around. It's all part of sharing which is a part of love. And marriage without sharing can't last."

Join the quick set... for the fastest ever party style

BY PENNY GRAHAM

Pin a large roller on the crown to give the hair a lift. Tape the fringe down and carry tape round to the back of the head. Smooth the sides down along the cheeks and under the chin. Keep it all in place with bands of tape wound right round the neck. When your hair dries it should be smooth and straight with ends which flip out. Accentuate the flip by blow-drying the ends over a round brush.

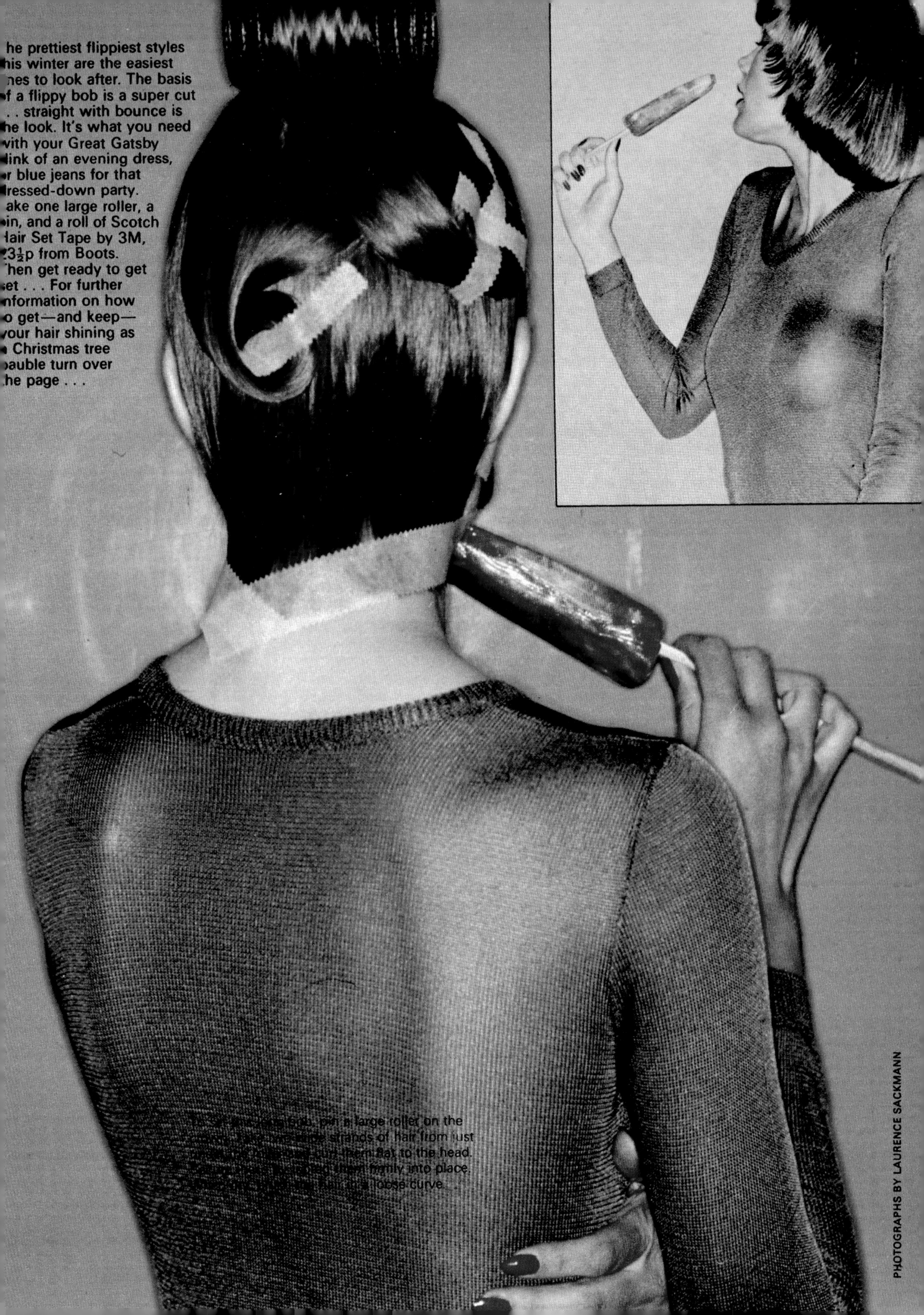

he prettiest flippiest styles his winter are the easiest nes to look after. The basis f a flippy bob is a super cut . . . straight with bounce is he look. It's what you need with your Great Gatsby link of an evening dress, r blue jeans for that dressed-down party. ake one large roller, a in, and a roll of Scotch lair Set Tape by 3M, 23½p from Boots. Then get ready to get set . . . For further nformation on how o get—and keep—your hair shining as a Christmas tree bauble turn over he page . . .

... pin a large roller on the
... strands of hair from just
... them flat to the head.
... firmly into place.
... loose curve.

PHOTOGRAPHS BY LAURENCE SACKMANN

YOU CAN MAKE IT: VALUE ADDED FASHION

KNIT A CLINGY SWEATER from only 91p

You'll need 5(6,6,7) balls Hayfield Beaulon 4-ply in Cream; 2(2,2,3) balls Lipstick; 1(1,2,2) balls in Chrysanthemum; a pair each Nos 10 and 12 needles.
To fit 32(34,36,38) bust sizes.
Tension 7 sts and 9 rows = 1 in on No 10 needles over stocking stitch (1 row knit, 1 row purl).
Abbreviations St(s), stitch(es); K, knit; P, purl; st st, stocking stitch; patt, pattern; inc, increase; dec, decrease; C, Cream; L, Lipstick; Ch, Chrysanthemum; cont, continue; beg, beginning; tog, together; alt, alternate; rem, remain; rep, repeat.

FRONT ** With No 12 needles and C, cast on 108(116,122,130) sts and work in K1, P1 rib for ½ in. Change to No 10 needles and st st in colour patt of 8 rows C, 2 rows Ch, 4 rows L. Inc 1 st at each end of 1st and every following 6th row to 118(126,132,140) sts ending on a P row. Change to No 12 needles and dec 1 st at each end of next and every 5th row to 96(104,110,116) sts. Change to No 10 needles and work straight until Front measures 11(11½,11½,11½) in from lower edge. Inc 1 st at each end of next and every 6th row to 112(120,126,132) sts. Cont straight until work measures 17 (18,18,18) in from lower edge. *Shape Armhole and Neck* Cast off 2 sts at beg of next 2 rows.*
Next row K2 tog, K until 51(55,58,61) sts are on right hand needle. K2 tog, turn, leave rem sts on spare pin or st holder. With rem sts on needle, dec 1 st at each end of every alt row until 7(7,8,8) sts rem. Cont straight until work measures 29 in from lower edge. Cast off. Rejoin yarn to rem sts and finish to match 1st side. **BACK** Work as for Front from ** to *. Dec 1 st at each end of every alt row until 62(66,70,74) sts rem. Cont straight until armhole measures 9½ in. *Shape neck* K18(18,19,19), cast off centre 26(30,32,36) sts, K to end. On last set of sts only, dec 1 st at neck edge on every row until 7(7,8,8) sts rem. Cont straight until Armhole edge measures as Front Armhole edge. Cast off. Finish 2nd side to match. **ARMBANDS** With No 12 needles and C, cast on 182 sts and work in K1, P1 rib for ½ in. Cast off in rib. **NECKBAND** With No 12 needles and C, cast on 260 sts and work as Armbands, but decreasing 1 st at each end of every row. Cast off in rib. **TO MAKE UP** Press pieces with a warm iron over a damp cloth. Join shoulder and side seams. Stitch Armbands and Neckband into place. Press. **HEADBAND** Takes just 1 ball Hayfield's Beaulon 4-ply in Cream; 1 pair No 12 knitting needles. *Measurements* Band is 21 in long. *Tension* 10 sts to 1 in over closed rib. **TO MAKE** With No 12 needles, cast on 30 sts and work in rib K2(P2, K2) to end. *2nd row* P2(K2,P2) to end. Rep these 2 rib rows until work measures 21 in from beg, or length required. Cast off in rib. **TO MAKE RING** With No 12 needles, cast on 12 sts; work in st st for 1¾ in. Cast off. **TO MAKE UP** Join the ribbed band together at both ends to make a circle. Place the st st piece with K side to right side over the join in headband, and seam together neatly on wrong side.

ong stripey sweaters with built-in
ling are the new uniform of the
hic Left Bank set. The Cosmo
ling-knit is as curvy as you'll find
nywhere in St Germain—and it
ould cost you as little as 91p—
r, even if you're in the Raquel
Velch class, under thirty bob.
Knit it in team spirit stripes of red,
French mustard and cream to wear
n warm summer afternoons with
ea on the lawn. On cooler days it
ooks great over a sweater or shirt.
And, with matching
eadband to keep your
ob from falling in one
ye, you'll really be
ble to concentrate on
he croquet—and
he spectators.
PATTIE BARRON

PHOTOGRAPH BY TONY BOASE
Hair by David at Michaeljohn
Ivory bangles, rings from Jones

The Naked Lunch

Make the most of flaming June with the kind of picnic you'll always remember . . . one that recreates, perhaps, Manet's famous painting, Le Déjeuner sur l'Herbe *(Luncheon on the grass), which, when first hung on exhibition walls, scandalised all Paris! That was over a hundred years ago when women wore petticoats by the dozen and men carried walking sticks and gloves, even in the heart of the countryside. After this spring's streaking mania, a naked lunch is scarcely shocking but, to keep your picnic strictly private, we suggest you pick a secluded spot by the river or an out-of-the-breeze glade. Abandon yourself to nature, really fresh food and an appetite inspired by clean country air. Now turn the page for picnic ploys and recipes guaranteed to loosen inhibitions . . .*

FOOD BY LINDA KELSEY

PHOTOGRAPH BY JIM LEE

Men's clothes at St Laurent Rive Gauche
Picnic basket and flowery tablecloth at Habitat

Picnic Ploys

Invite your most fun-loving friends—party poopers who moan about dampness underfoot don't deserve a morsel of your home cooking, and you might want someone to cuddle up to in the late afternoon.

Make the atmosphere authentically French with an old-fashioned wicker basket, a flowery cloth with matching napkins and silvery goblets (don't forget a flask of brandy, too). Pack patterned china plates, wrapped in napkins or paper serviettes so they will not break . . . save your paper cups and plastic plates for lunch-hours in the park.

You can take advantage of latter-day inventions without ruining the flavour of picnics past . . . a vacuum flask for soup, aluminium foil or air-tight, see-through film for keeping bread crisp, and screw-top jars and sealable containers for everything from salads to mousses. And, unless you intend to be caviare for the insect population, pop a tube of insect repellent into the bottom of the basket.

Because you'll want to feel frivolous on the day of the picnic, prepare as much food as possible the night before. Only perishable items need to be bought at the last minute before the picnic.

Ensure there's enough food to last till four, wine enough till sundown. Between courses let him decorate your hair with buttercups. Or, if the sun is really scorching, take a dip in the river.

Would you like to break out of the sandwich syndrome and create a little splendour in the grass? Follow our instructions . . .

MENU (for 4)
for a Naked Lunch

Mousse de Jambon
OR
Gazpacho
OR
Pâté with Crusty French Bread

Lamb Cutlets
in Breadcrumbs and Aspic
French Bean Salad
Chilled Courgettes
Potato Salad
OR
Chicken, Rice and Fruit Salad
Mayonnaise Eggs

Lemon Soufflé
OR
Cheese
OR
Fresh Strawberries
To drink:
chilled Blanc Foussy or Mateus rosé

Mousse de Jambon

8 oz boiled ham
4 oz unsalted butter
8 fl oz double cream
salt and pepper
pinch nutmeg, grated

2½ tbsp gelatine
8 fl oz chicken stock
4 fl oz Madeira
2 fl oz brandy

Mince or very finely chop the ham. Combine the ham and butter in a bowl, mixing well. Blend in the cream. Stir vigorously, add salt, pepper and nutmeg. Soften the gelatine in the Madeira. Bring the stock to the boil, remove from heat and add gelatine, stirring to dissolve; cool, add to the ham. Check seasoning. Mix well with brandy and pack into small soufflé moulds. Chill. (Recipe taken from *Feast of France* by Antonie Gilly and Jack D Scott, £5, Cassell.)

Gazpacho

1 lb tomatoes, peeled and roughly sliced
1 small onion, sliced
1 small green pepper, sliced
1 clove of garlic, crushed
1 tbsp wine vinegar
1 tbsp olive oil
chicken stock, optional
1-2 tbsp lemon juice
salt and pepper

Place prepared tomatoes, onion, green pepper, garlic, vinegar and olive oil in a liquidiser and blend well together. If the soup is very thick, add up to ½ pint chicken stock. Turn into a bowl and add lemon juice and seasoning. Chill.

Lamb Cutlets

8 lamb cutlets
beaten egg
breadcrumbs
grated cheese
salt and pepper
powdered aspic
four leaves of mint

Brush four of the cutlets with beaten egg and dip in breadcrumbs and grated cheese, pressing crumbs in well. Melt some dripping in a baking tin and turn the cutlets in the dripping. Bake at 400°F (Regulo 6) for 45-50 minutes. Allow to cool. Season and grill remaining lamb cutlets. Allow to cool. Decorate each cutlet with mint, coat with aspic dissolved in hot water. When cool, chill. Wrap cutlets in foil for picnic.

French Bean Salad

1 lb French beans
vinaigrette dressing with garlic
tomatoes, diced
parsley, chopped

Top and tail beans, cook in boiling salted water until tender—about 10-15 minutes. Toss in dressing while still warm. When cool, garnish with diced tomatoes and parsley. Chill and pack in a container.

Chilled Courgettes

4 courgettes, trimmed
vinaigrette dressing

Cook courgettes whole in boiling salted water for 6-8 minutes, drain. Slice while still warm, toss in dressing. When cool, chill and pack in a container.

Potato Salad

1½ lb small, new potatoes
mayonnaise
small onion, finely chopped
caraway seeds

Peel and wash potatoes, cook in salted boiling water until tender. Drain and allow to cool. Combine with mayonnaise and onion in a bowl. Sprinkle with caraway seed and pack in container.

Chicken, Rice and Fruit Salad

3½ lb cooked chicken
½ lb long grain rice
3 bananas
3 oranges
½ pint mayonnaise
French dressing

Carve chicken into thin strips. Cook rice in salted water, drain and cool. Peel and slice bananas, then marinate in French dressing. Peel oranges, removing white pith, and cut into segments over a bowl to catch any juice that escapes. Add the juice to the mayonnaise. Fold the chicken, banana, oranges, mayonnaise, and a little French dressing into the rice. Chill.

Mayonnaise Eggs

4 eggs, hardboiled
mayonnaise
knob of butter
salt
paprika

Hard-boil the eggs the night before the picnic. In the morning, peel eggs, halve and scoop out yolks. Combine with mayonnaise, a little salt and a knob of butter until smooth. Spoon mixture back into the whites, sprinkle over a little paprika. Sandwich two whites together at a time and wrap in foil.

Lemon Soufflé

4 large eggs, separated
6 oz castor sugar
juice of two lemons, rind of one
¼ pint water
½ oz powdered gelatine
¼ pint double cream

Mix yolks with finely grated lemon rind, sugar and juice (about 3-4 tbsp). Stir well to blend ingredients. Sprinkle gelatine over water in a saucepan. Allow to stand for a few minutes, then place over a low heat and stir until the gelatine dissolves. Remove from the heat and, holding the pan well above the basin, slowly add the gelatine to the lemon mixture in a thin stream, whisking all the time. When the mixture is well blended set aside to cool until beginning to set. Stiffly beat the egg whites and fold into the thickening lemon mixture. Pour into a soufflé dish and chill. Cover with foil, unpack at picnic and serve with cream.

Are you a picnic addict? Then you're sure to have some intriguing tales to tell about your *déjeuner sur l'herbe*. Write to us about your most hilarious, calamitous or romantic picnic memory—we'll give the winner a hamper full of scrumptious food from Fortnum and Mason of Piccadilly. Send your entry (before 30th June) to Cosmo's Picnic Competition, Cosmopolitan, Chestergate House, Vauxhall Bridge Road, London SW1V 1HF.

Things happen after a badedas bath

(they say it's got something to do with the horse chestnuts)

Welcoming waters, foamy, green and exciting. Heady with the mysterious magic of horse chestnuts. A fresh, invigorating sensation. A powerful lust for living. You might call it Lebenslust, if you happen to know the word. (But Badedas says it better.) **badedas**

The most stimulating thing since bathing itself – with extract of horse chestnuts.

What your legs say about you

BY ERNEST DICHTER, PhD

Of course the shape of your legs is important . . . but did you know the way you use them can be telling as well? Though you may never have noticed, each of us has a highly personal style of sitting and standing, and this distinctive "leg language" can be as eloquent as anything we say with words. The way you hold your legs can tell others exactly how you're feeling—shy or aggressive, tired or energetic, anxious or relaxed, embarrassed or proud, apathetic or vibrantly sexy. Legs can also express the manner in which you relate to men—not only lovers but new friends as well. While not a strictly scientific yardstick, "leg analysis", an offshoot of body language, has a fairly solid basis in observational psychology. Learning to translate your "leg language" is simple but you may be surprised by the messages you're sending. Study each picture on this and the following page and decide which best represents the way you use your legs, then read our instant "leg analysis" provided with each of these telling photographs. Recognise yourself?

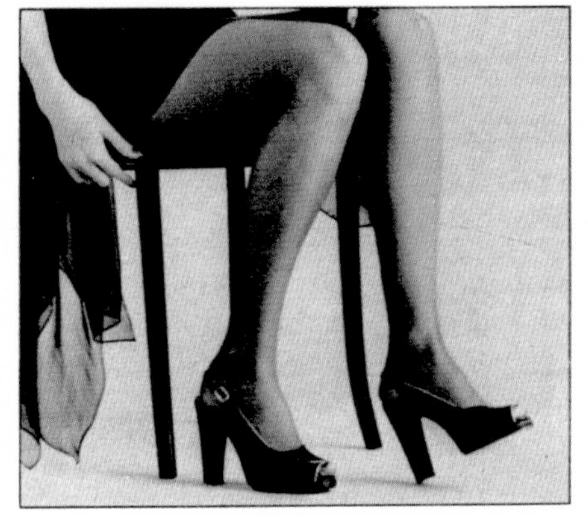

1

Go-Go Girl. You often seem about to spring . . . and you are! Super-efficient, you can do anything—canvass support for a favourite politician, act as hostess at a gourmet dinner for twenty, be director of a company—and do it well. One problem is that you attempt everything at once. Another is that you attract men who tend to lean and can sap your strength. A hint: both career and sex will satisfy more if you'll learn to savour life more slowly . . .

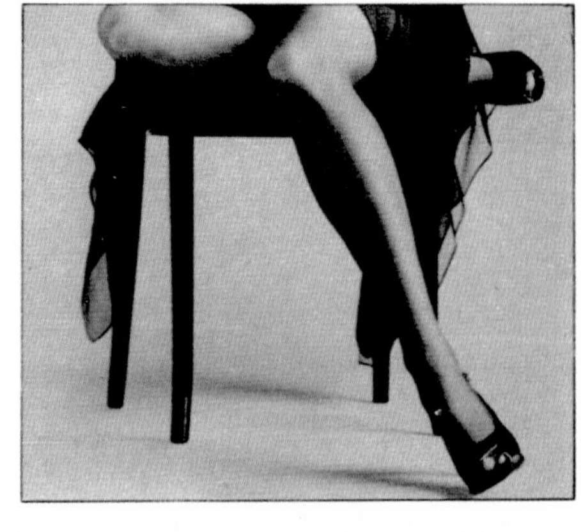

2

The Hedonist. Comfort-loving, individualistic and eccentric, you're the centre of a devoted, artistic circle of friends and can be depended upon at any time to provide some sort of way-out entertainment. You love breaking rules and adore even more the reckless experiment—in love as well as in life. No matter what your age, there's something in you of the precocious little girl; the men you fall in love with are often rather fatherly figures.

PHOTOGRAPHS BY SIGRID ESTRADA

3

Ms Bountiful. You're gracious, self-assured and independent. When male admirers say "you think like a man", you're not displeased. Although you claim you cross your legs for comfort, psychologists say the act of putting one leg over the other is actually an invitation to the opposite sex—"Uncross me!" Always direct, you want who you want when *you* want him . . . and, since you're charming, you practically always get him. He can't resist you.

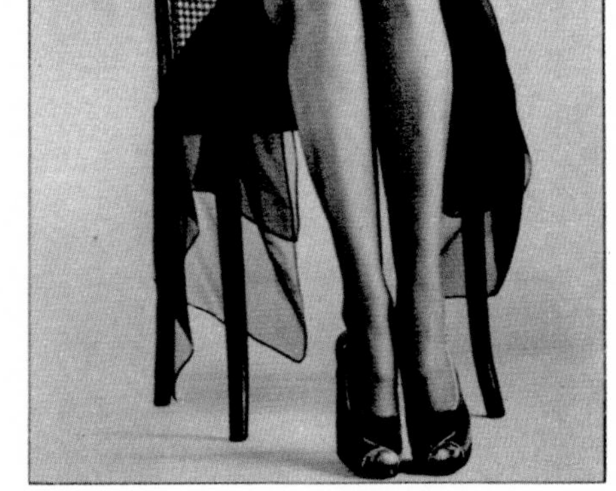

4

Here I Sit. Your tea-party-proper demeanour says, "You won't budge me": no amount of masculine coercion can change your lofty ideals. Since defiance may also be seen as provocative challenge, however, you attract many admirers, particularly king-of-the-mountain mogul types.

What your legs say about you

CONTINUED

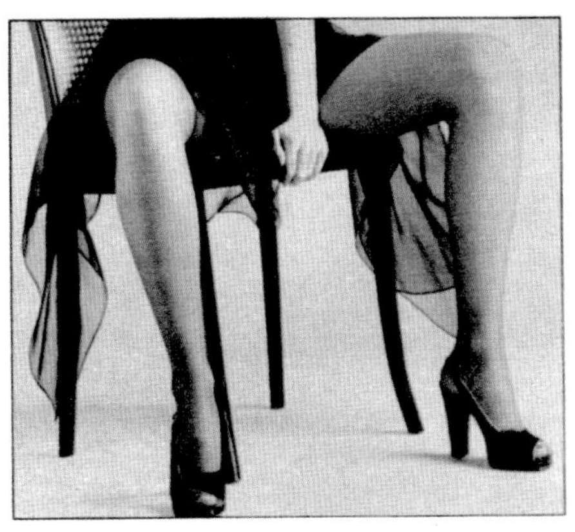

5

To Hell with the Establishment! While the feminine rage for jeans has made this position more common, it has yet to find much favour among men: they're a little afraid of you. Militantly proud of being independent, you thumb your nose at conventional decorum. If someone doesn't like the way you dress or think, or arrange your bookshelves, so much for him! You're also prone to carelessness, however, and a slapdash attitude towards friendships and work could bring chaos to your liberated life. Get yourself organised.

6

Crossed-ankle Lady. Dainty, refined and cultured, you might be inclined to raise your little finger while sipping tea. Your trademark is social propriety: you'd do anything rather than offend. Once married, you play the protocol-perfect lady to your man, whether he's a plumber, a banker or a thief. If he should ever embarrass you publicly, however, he'll suffer your vehement wrath for weeks. Once in a while, why not break out of this strait-laced mould? You'll make yourself—*and* your man—much happier.

7

The Pretzel. Why so worried? Your twisted legs betray insecurity and say in effect, "I'm not alone—I have my legs to keep me warm!" Because of this transparent defensiveness, men tend to keep back . . . which makes you more anxious, which leads to stiffer defences—a vicious, unhappy-making circle. Try to develop more self-confidence.

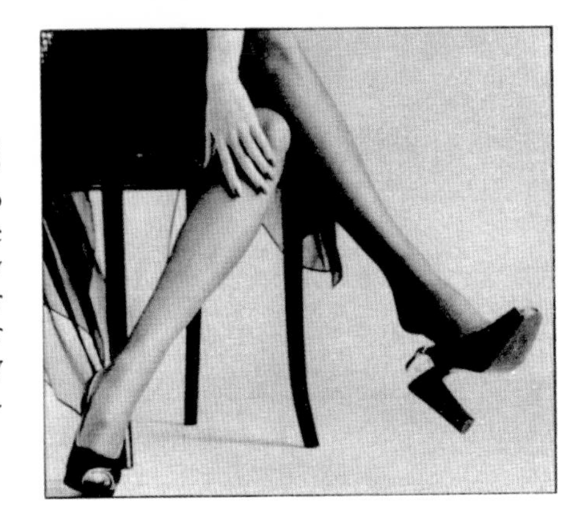

8

The Toe Stripteaser. You're an incurable flirt right down to the tips of your come-hither toes. Well-dressed, attractive and accustomed to playing the princess, you're usually surrounded by a court of admiring males. A clever conversationalist, you're an even wilier listener . . . and flatter men into thinking you're easily seduced. Despite the flighty façade, flirtations end quickly unless you're feeling sexy.

9

The Ostrich. Your nervous habit of rubbing one foot against the opposite ankle tells men you meet you'd really rather hide. It also says, "Forget my legs"—you're not very proud of them. While you claim to shun the limelight, you actually crave attention and are hurt when your aloofness is taken at face value. Sensitive, protective types think you're smashing, but to attract the men you want, put *both* best feet forward.

Note: If you're unhappy with the results of this analysis and wish to change, just pick the position which fits the personality you'd most like to have and adapt it as your own. Remember, though, your "new" legs will be saying things you may never have said before—don't be surprised if your life changes accordingly!

Haven't got a thing to wear..

Don't give up—this could be the year when what goes on underneath could be your major investment. FASHION BY LIZ SMITH. PHOTOGRAPHS BY JAMES WEDGE

The leopard cannot change his spots,
And that's the fix I'm in,
So come and sit by me, my love,
For some highly original skin.

Biba fake-fur bikini, £8. Bangles, Biba. Boots, The Chelsea Cobbler.

When I'm awakened from my slumber
It does seem rather mean—
It's always the wrong number
And never Steve McQueen.

Biba satin bra and panties, £7·75 the set.

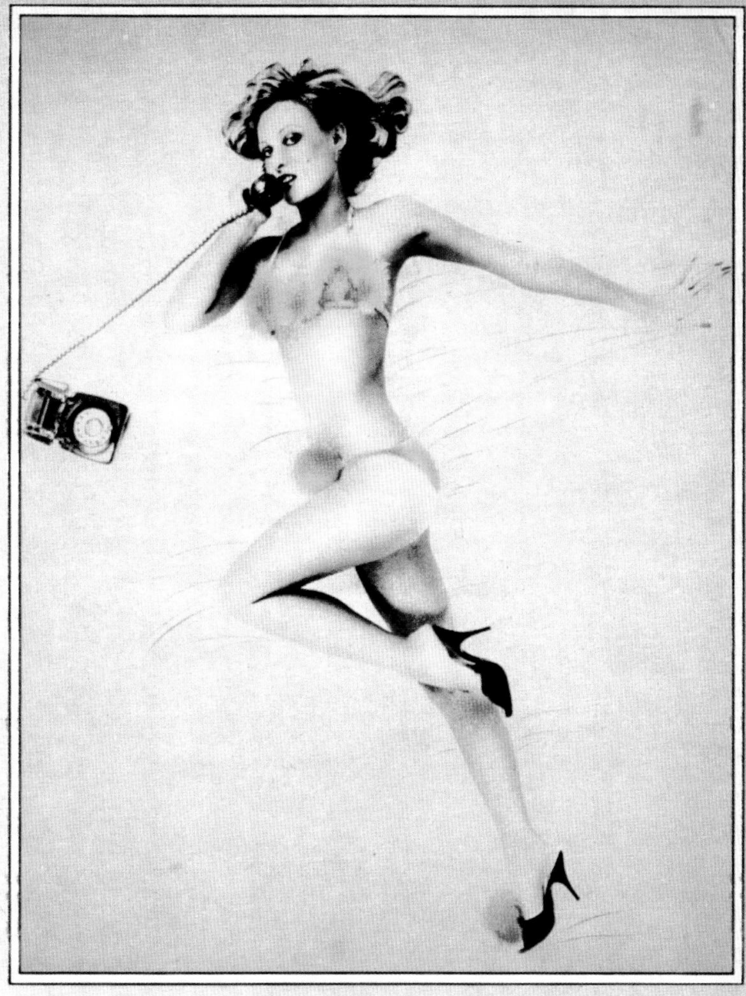

COSMO TELLS ALL

Produced by Linda Kelsey and Pattie Barron

"Fancy bumping into you at a joint like this"
"There's nothing like dancing shoulder to shoulder"
"We're not afraid to face the music"
"Don't turn round till I'm ready, Ronnie"
"Strictly for the grand finale!"

READY, STEADY, BUMP . . .
Next time you see a man you fancy across a crowded room, go on over and bump right into him. If he bumps you back, chances are you've found the perfect partner. No, The Bump is *not* a follow-up to Kung-Fu fighting, but the dance you'll be doing throughout the summer of '75. Model girl Floella and hairdresser Ronnie from Smile are the funky twosome going through the motions for you to follow. So switch on the music, take a stiff drink to loosen inhibitions and let your instincts do the rest . . .

PHOTOGRAPHS BY MONTY COLES

BACK-CHAT
Give them something to talk about when your back's turned: like this cross-stitched masterpiece at Hampstead Bazaar, 30 Heath St, NW3, £21. It's made from olde worlde embroidered table-cloths, but for do-it-yourselfers, reluctant to chop up the family heirlooms, you could get stitching your jeans jacket with Clark's Anchor Embroidery Thread, a crewel needle and a bit of patience.

PHOTOGRAPH BY BARDO FABIANI

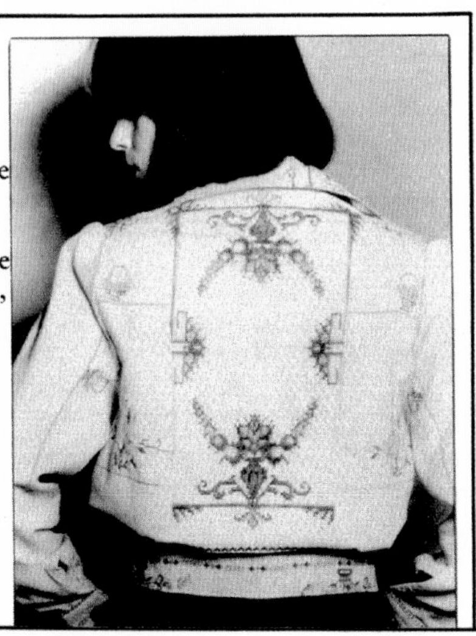

EARLY BLOOMS
Don't wait for the flowers to bloom—fake buttonholes are newer and last much longer. Top left, surrealistic flower in sharp reds with grassy green leaves by Krizia, £2·95; top right, ivory-look plastic posy, Krizia, £1·95; below, Penny Patrick's hand-made ceramic flower spray, £8. At Elle Italian shops, 12 New Bond St, W1 and 21 Sloane St, SW1.

DRAWINGS BY SUSAN BRADLEY

PHOTOGRAPH BY PAULENE STONE

TWENTY WAYS TO MAKE HIM COME ON STRONG

How to put back the sparkle into a love affair that's gone flat

1 Do something totally out of character. If he always comes home to hot dinners at eight, let him find you propped up in bed with a tray of deliciously tactile finger-foods . . . asparagus, giant prawns, mangoes. Provide scented hot towels for mutual mopping-up.

2 Take an evening off each week to learn advance driving, car maintenance, or a new language. Keep quiet until you're skilled enough to impress him.

3 Time for a new smell? Jicky by Guerlain is the sexiest scent around—Brigitte Bardot, Jackie Onassis and Peter Sellers are among those who love to wear it.

4 Brew him a heady cocktail. Try *French '75*: $\frac{2}{3}$ gin, $\frac{1}{3}$ lemon juice plus 1 teaspoonful of icing sugar. Pour over cracked ice into tall glasses and top up with champagne or soda. When he's shed a few inhibitions ask him to read aloud from your favourite poetry book.

5 Force him to *look* at you. Do the vacuuming in bra and pants, wear your old micro-skirt (making sure the legs you flash are brown and smooth) or amaze him by turning up for a date dressed totally in violet—turban, lipstick, dress, tights, shoes . . . with undies dyed to match.

6 Make him laugh in bed—yes, laughter *is* sexy. Wear nothing but enormous bed-socks, or a leotard to invite a fight.

7 Book yourselves into the Ritz for a night.

8 Learn to play chess (well) and challenge him to a game. Distract him by the sensual way you handle the pieces (remember Faye Dunaway in *The Thomas Crown Affair*?). Background music should be subtly insinuating—try something like Adagio in G Minor by Albinoni.

9 Buy him the kitten or puppy he's always wanted—but make sure he's able to look after it. (And don't either of you turn it into a baby-substitute.)

10 Stop clustering up with the girls at parties or going into a trance when the conversation turns to politics, sport, etc. Read the newspapers, subscribe to a literary weekly, listen to the news, absorb enough information to give you a *point of view* on everything.

11 Weekends deadly dull? Talk him into taking up some slightly dangerous sport with you—gliding, ballooning, flying, mountaineering.

12 Just before he gets into bed, put two ice-cold quarter bottles of champagne where he can reach them with his toes.

13 Massage his ego in public by bringing the conversation round to subjects where you know he'll shine; or introducing him to attractive girls (that's the reverse-jealousy technique and though it can be dangerous, it nearly always works in your favour).

14 Find out what's going on in your locality—old movie revivals, theatre clubs, pop happenings. Book the tickets and invite him.

15 Make a habit of cutting out newspaper/magazine articles you know he'd enjoy. When he's away, tape-record radio shows he'd be sorry to miss.

16 Buy him the most luxurious towelling dressing-gown you can afford.

17 Wear shiny rayon stockings—and let him see you straighten them.

18 Make a list of all the things he loves and you can't stand (going fishing, eating Chinese food, horror films, etc). Try them again once more . . . and hope he appreciates *and* reciprocates.

19 Get yourself involved in local politics, conservation or any other cause that interests you. Get a letter published in your local newspaper, even better in *The Times*.

20 As a change from holiday snaps—photograph him in the nude, preferably in the privacy of your own bathroom or bedroom . . . like this jolly snap of designer Christian Christian taken by top model Paulene Stone in her own bathroom. "It makes a nice change to be behind the camera," says cover girl Paulene. "Gives you another point of view." Try that line on your fella! *For a front view of Christian and Paulene see page 162.*

COSMO TELLS ALL

Produced by Linda Kelsey and Pattie Barron

GAMESMANSHIP

The look for your man this summer is sporty . . . but before he makes a grab for that old cricket sweater and rolls up his shirt sleeves, show him these pictures and he'll get the point. Baseball T-shirt (left), £2·95 from Ronnie Stirling, 94 New Bond St, W1; grey hooded sweatshirt, Glynn Manson at Take Six, £6·50, from all branches of Take Six. Baseball cap and visor from Lillywhites.

PHOTOGRAPHS BY BARDO FABIANI

LOVE LABELS

In CTA, January, we asked you to tell us your way of introducing a live-in lover who you're not actually married to. Most of you wrote saying a lover is best introduced by his name—after all, what business is it of anyone else's to know your specific relationship?—but felt that if asked further you'd be quite liberated enough to announce him simply as your lover. Some of the more inventive suggestions included "the beast in my bed", "my votary", "my consort" and "my inmate". But the opener we thought best was: "May I introduce my man about the house."

THUMBS UP: to actress Susan Hampshire for launching the Population Countdown Pennies Campaign by ordering her bank to transfer, on the first day of each month, the pence balance of her current account to Population Countdown which raises funds for world-wide family planning programmes . . . to Hertfordshire County Council's project to set up a network of toy libraries for the benefit of handicapped children . . to Sketchley dry cleaners for offering 25% discount on cleaning prices to customers holding more than fifty shares in the company.

THUMBS DOWN: to butcher George Parlane for refusing to accept pensioners' 20p Government Beef Tokens because he thought they were a nuisance . . . to the National Union of Students' proposal that all schoolchildren over the age of sixteen should receive wages of £845 a year. If parents can't afford to allow children to remain at school, surely *they're* the ones who are entitled to claim any benefits . . . to Art Wallpapers which refused to grant a divorcee credit for a hire purchase transaction of 50p a week unless she told them the probable income of her former husband, plus the address of his place of work.

THIN ENOUGH FOR A THONG?

How to achieve maximum exposure without breaking the law is this summer's fashion message from across the Atlantic. Rudi Gernreich, who pioneered the monokini in the 'Sixties, is now making headlines in the States with his "Thong", without doubt the briefest swimsuit ever. "Only suitable if you have good-looking buttocks," says Gernreich. The thong is not available over here, and if that's a subtle judgement on the shape of the average English girl, now must be the time to cut back on calories, start a rigorous exercise programme, and prove the gentleman wrong!

Monday.
Chinese meal with John.

Tuesday.
At Disco with Bob.

Wednesday.
Meet Peter at the Theatre.

Thursday.
Shopping with Adrian.

Friday.
Introduction to Squash by Alex.

Saturday.
Day at the Coast with Steve.

Sunday. Tennis Club
barbecue with John *(again!)*

It's going to be an exciting life.

How does your week look?

If it doesn't look exactly the way you want, it's time to make a change.

It's time you realised you're free and independent and life is fun. Meet the kind of men you'll find interesting.

Get in touch with the exciting new world of Dateline.

It's the service that gives you the fun in life.

Join us.

Write to Dateline and make the coming weeks more exciting than ever.

Please send me the Dateline brochure by return.

My name is ______________________

____

Age ______________________

I live at ______________________

____

____

ZZ

(PLEASE USE BLOCK CAPITALS)

dateline

23 Abingdon Road, London W8
Telephone: 01-937 6503

MEET DAVID NEWTON—HE IS THAT COSMOPOLITAN MAN (winner of our competition to find *your* quintessential fella!)

Thousands of delicious men, all sitting in the Cosmo office! Well, not exactly, but that's how many photographs and letters you've sent for our delectation since we launched our contest last January. We knew you had good taste, but when we first asked you to nominate the man who, in your eyes, seemed to be the quintessential Cosmopolitan Man—interesting, ambitious, sensitive, witty, and with all the other qualities that make your favourite fellow that extra bit special—we didn't realise just how much gorgeous talent you have to hand. Choosing a winner was one of the hardest, if most enjoyable, tasks we've ever had to cope with. Finally, however, the decision at Cosmo was unanimous. David Newton, twenty-seven, lives in Salisbury, has an open smile and an open mind. Sexy in a believable way—you wouldn't mistake *him* for a shop-window dummy—he's outgoing, amusing, has far-ranging interests and is quite unaware that he's a knockout. In fact David has all the qualities we were looking for, plus the definite advantage of a pretty and intelligent wife to appreciate them.

Here's an extract from the letter we received about him: "Dishy David, as he is known to his friends, is brown, beautiful and gentle. He is an accomplished sailor and water-skier, with ambitions to sail in the Olympics, and is an all-round figure of fitness. David is a real goer at parties, but likes to listen to quieter music at times. I have yet to meet a woman who does not turn her head for a second look when he walks by. Is it surprising?"

Not at all. When *we* decided to take a second look at David, by

David, kitted out in Saint Laurent, has a celebratory drink with his wife, Myrah. Photographed at *La Poule au Pot* restaurant, Pimlico.

inviting him to come to London and meet us, along with the other finalists, we knew we had our man.

Eighteen months ago David had the courage to throw up his job as a computer systems' analyst for a life in the open air as a builder's labourer. And he's healthier and happier now than ever before. David is a man who works and plays hard. At weekends, whatever the weather, he sails his single-handed racing dinghy in preparation for the trials for this year's OK World Championships in Finland. On shore, he plays a mean game of squash.

But the sporting life doesn't prevent David devoting plenty of time to his wife. Says Myrah Newton, who works as a secretary to one of the directors at Debenhams, "David is a great one for the compliments and is never embarrassed to tell me he loves me. He's terrific around the house and does all the decorating himself. We really are compatible, perhaps because we're both born under the sign of Virgo."

David is determined to see more of the world and has plans to visit South Africa and Australia—maybe even to settle there. He loves riding motor bikes (which is why he was so thrilled with the super Honda Fun-Bike, one of his fantastic prizes), dancing, lying in the sun, his two cats—and Myrah. On his own admission he's easygoing and gets on with people instantly.

David is a most deserving winner and here are the magnificent prizes he and Myrah will soon be sharing. Yves Saint Laurent, who produce the classiest clothes and most sensuous perfumes, are sending the lucky winners on a two-week holiday with Club Mediterranée in romantic Marrakesh, and are giving them a collection of YSL *Rive Gauche* and *Pour Homme* scents and beauty products. They are also presenting David with the beautiful Saint Laurent suit, cut as only the French know how, you see him wearing in our first picture.

Honda's prize is the super Fun-Bike David is riding opposite, and Grants of St James's are providing a bottle of French wine for every night of the year—365 bottles in all. No wonder David is

PHOTOGRAPH BY JOHN KELLY

planning a mammoth celebration for his friends in Salisbury! And Grants are also hosts for a celebratory lunch for the winners in the romantic setting of their medieval cellars in London.

Says David of his Cosmo Man title and all the prizes—"I'm overwhelmed!" That's all right, David, because we were pretty overwhelmed by you.

ting on a Honda Fun-Bike is easy. vid tries out one of his fantastic
es. Jacket by Lillywhites.

THAT COSMOPOLITAN MAN [CONTINUED]

Now meet some of the runners-up, each of whom will be receiving *Pour Homme* eau de toilette and bath gel by Yves Saint Laurent.

PHOTOGRAPHS BY JOHN KELLY

Richard Woolford, twenty-eight, is a self-employed surveyor who also renovates old cottages. He lives in Dorset with his girlfriend Shirley and describes himself as a typical Libran. "My ideal life-style is sitting on the beach, swimming and getting a suntan." Says Shirley: "Richard may be a bit of a chauvinist, but women love him for his sense of humour."

Robin Worden, twenty-seven, is a life insurance broker who lives in Norwich. The proud owner of a water-bed and a beautiful Labrador named Samuel, Robin says he will never marry. His ambition is to round up one hundred friends and buy an island in the sun. Says Sue Donoghue who nominated him: "Robin oozes with charm and is *soohh* sexy. I love and hate him like crazy."

An ex-electrician, Chris Pibworth, twenty-five, now works for himself recycling paper and admits to loving the high life . . . he buys all his clothes from Saint Laurent, drives a black Mini and wears beautiful hand-made gold pendants. To keep in shape, Chris does twenty-five press-ups each morning and goes horse-riding with his wife, Denise.

As British Amateur Pair Skating Champion, Colin Taylforth puts in six hours training every day. Aiming to go professional by 1980, in the meantime Colin works at an art shop. Joyce, who entered Colin, says: "His terrific sense of rhythm makes him a wow on any disco floor. It's great to go out with him anywhere, and his popularity is a big ego-booster."

Andrew Seear has a degree in English from Cambridge and is now studying at RADA with an eye to working in films for Morrissey and Warhol. At weekends he plays the university circuit in a band. Andrew loves listening to *The Archers*, drinking Chablis and girls who can match his 5ft 11in. He hates astrology, scientology and the play *Pyjama Tops*!

John Griffiths, twenty-six, is a semi-professional footballer—he plays for Dorchester Town in the Southern League—and teaches games at a primary school. Lexie, his wife, says: "John is helpful round the house—but immensely butch with it! He likes women to be volatile and independent and hates me to wear a lot of make-up. Spear-fishing and backgammon are his favourite relaxations."

Lawrence Rocca, 6ft 3in tall with green eyes, is a successful American banker who loves the English countryside. Despite his weekday "City" image, Lawrence is happiest jogging with his Irish setter, playing squash and rugby. His girlfriend describes him as "a combination of Robert Redford and Donald Duck! He's also very lovable and unpredictable."

QUIZ

HOW MALE DOMINATED ARE YOU?

You may think you're liberated, but have you really managed to break away from the traditionally passive female role? Try this quiz and find out.
By Paula Smith

1 *A girlfriend says she has no intention of ever getting married. You assume:*
a she's temporarily disillusioned with men.
b she doesn't like men.
c she's discovered satisfactory alternative life-styles to marriage.
d she's a career woman.
e she's frigid.
f she doesn't want children.

2 *A man asks you out. You assume:*
a he's paying.
b you're paying.
c . . . oh, it's not important who pays.
d you'll go halves.

3 *Your best friend has six boyfriends (at the the last count), at least two of whom are her lovers. You are her only close female friend. You are:*
a surprised because she has so few female friends.
b pleased at her good fortune.
c envious of her.
d amazed at her disloyalty to her lovers.
e convinced she is ruining her chances of finding a man willing to marry her.

4 *You buy your round at the pub:*
a always.
b sometimes.
c never.
d depending on whom you're with.

5 *A friend of yours, who is unmarried, tells you that she is pregnant. You:*
a ask her what she would like to be given as a wedding present.
b feel embarrassed and quickly change the subject.
c ask her whether she will be able to manage on Social Security payments.
d ask her whether she wants a boy or a girl.
e ask her whether she is going to terminate the pregnancy.
f lecture her on birth control.
g heartily congratulate her.

6 *You see a woman standing by the side of the road beside a car with its bonnet up. You:*
a presume that the driver has gone for help, and, therefore, drive on.
b stop and ask if you can do anything.
c assume that she would probably rather have a man stop to offer help.
d decide her problems don't concern you.

7 *Your mother wants you to get married. You regard her attitude as:*
a only natural.
b unreasonable— she should accept that not every woman wants to get married.
c selfish.
d incomprehensible.

8 *A girlfriend announces her plans to postpone her marriage until she has finished college. You tell her:*
a she should marry now in case her fiancé changes his mind.
b she is sensible not to mix serious education with the responsibilities of marriage.
c she may find someone better at college.

9 *You ask a man out:*
a sometimes.
b never.
c frequently.

10 *What do you think of women bosses?*
a It makes no difference whether your boss is a man or a woman.
b Women bosses have no real control over their staff.
c Women are good at managing women, but not at managing men.
d Women are good at managing men, but not at managing women.
e Women tend to understand people better, so make better bosses.

11 *You have as friends:*
a more men than women.
b more women than men.
c about the same of each.

12 *When it comes to male/female IQ, you think:*
a men are, on the whole, more intelligent than women.
b women are, on the whole, more intelligent than men.
c there's not much difference in intelligence between the sexes.
d Men and women have a completely different type of intelligence.

13 *Your boyfriend suggests going to a film that you don't want to see. You usually:*
a state your point of view but go anyway.
b find something you both want to see.
c automatically defer to him.
d argue with him until he agrees to see the film you want to see.

14 *You think that day-care centres for young children are:*
a generally a good idea.
b a threat to organised society.
c harmful from the child's point of view.
d absolutely vital for female liberation.
e a good idea but not practicable.

15 *Your boyfriend wants to make love to you but you just don't feel in the mood. You:*
a tell him you have a headache.
b tell him to get lost.
c make an effort to feel in the mood.
d firmly, but sympathetically, tell him he's out of luck.
e make love but rather apathetically.
f tell him you don't feel very sexy but encourage him to continue.

NOW CHECK YOUR SCORING . . .
1 (a) 0, (b) 1, (c) 5, (d) 2, (e) 1, (f) 2.
2 (a) 1, (b) 0, (c), 2, (d) 3.
3 (a) 3, (b) 2, (c) 1, (d) 0, (e) 1.
4 (a) 3, (b) 1, (c) 0, (d) 2.
5 (a) 0, (b) 1, (c) 4, (d) 3, (e) 2, (f) 2, (g) 5.
6 (a) 0, (b) 3, (c) 1, (d) 1.
7 (a) 0, (b) 3, (c) 1, (d) 2.
8 (a) 0, (b) 1, (c) 2.
9 (a) 0, (b) 3, (c) 5.
10 (a) 3, (b) 0, (c) 1, (d) 4, (e) 5.
11 (a) 1, (b) 2, (c) 3.
12 (a) 1, (b) 5, (c) 4, (d) 3.
13 (a) 1, (b) 4, (c) 0, (d) 5.
14 (a) 4, (b) 2, (c) 0, (d) 5, (e) 1.
15 (a) 3, (b) 5, (c) 0, (d) 4, (e) 1, (f) 2.

PHOTOGRAPH BY GUIDO CEGANI

HOW MALE DOMINATED ARE YOU?

Having added up your scores, now is the moment of truth, read on. You might be surprised . . .

Score 55-60: You are a true radical, but tend to be rather domineering with people—especially men. You know what you want out of life and tend to strive for it regardless of popular opinion. Beware of going to extremes.

Score 40-55: You assess each situation on its merits with little or no male/female bias. You would have been able to tell Freud what his stumbling blocks were in trying to analyse the female mind. You like men as human beings but do not accept that they are naturally superior to women in any way. You recognise unfair male advantage when you see it, and stick up for your rights in a very positive way. You have no preconceptions about what marriage should be like, in fact you positively reject some of the more cherished ideals of your contemporaries. Male domination would be forgotten if you had your way.

Score 20-40: You tend not to think very carefully about the everyday situations you experience. You take life as it comes and are not particularly interested in analysing or trying to improve the lot of women, whether for yourself or for others. You are content to believe that women are less capable than men and, although you may have your doubts at times, you shy away from having to say so in public. Some of your ideas are modern and rational but this is largely due to fashion rather than your own thought-out opinions. Try to have more confidence in the capabilities of yourself and your women friends.

Score 0-19: You seem unaware of the inferior status given to women in so many walks of life. You see the natural ambition of every woman as being happily married to a sensible husband. And if you have children, you consider their care totally your responsibility. You do not even try to understand women whose ambitions are different, but regard their actions as somehow unrespectable. You are quite happy to allow society, and men in particular, to dictate to you. Try to be more positive and self-assertive; make an effort to be more self-reliant and flexible—otherwise you'll wake up one day and wonder why life is so dull.

"CAN I CALL YOU BACK, MOTHER, I'M JUST SEEING THE LAST OF THE GUESTS OUT."

Charlie
A most
original fragrance
Charlie
he gorgeous, sexy-young fragrance. By REVLON
oncentrated cologne, concentrated cologne spray, concentrated perfume spray and other original Charlies.

"I dress to look sexy and to raise a laugh. I wear stockings and suspenders, not tights. I hardly ever buy *new* clothes. When I do, I can't resist chopping hunks off and adding bits of my own." Actress Helen Mirren's years in the theatre have inspired her to design, or at least put together, her own funky style. She elaborately embroidered a co-star's jeans during the run of one play. And here she wears a flounced cotton skirt that got the Helen Mirren treatment. She first dipped the skirt in dye, then embroidered birds in bugle beads and silk threads, and later added extra flounces of brightly flowered cotton and antique lace. Tiny lace bodice from a jumble sale is fastened with a *diamanté* bird brooch she unpinned from a hat in a Red Cross shop.

Inset: Helen wears new flowered cotton shorts, £4·50, Van Der Fransen, Waterford Rd, London SW6, with satin cami-knickers (a present from a friend), scarlet stockings rolled down to above the knee, and shoes from Terry de Havilland, King's Rd, SW3. Hair by Christine of Mane Line.

PARTY SWINGERS...

FOR CHAIN DRINKERS!!

Look – no hands! The glass that you don't have to put down. Ideal for parties, picnics, races, etc.

£1.95 plus 25p p & p or
£9.50 plus 35p p & p for six.

Black, red or mixed.

Cheques/Postal Orders to: –

Carolyn Morgan Designs Ltd.
92 Godstone Road, Whyteleafe, Surrey

Also available from [illegible]rod's Hospitality Shop

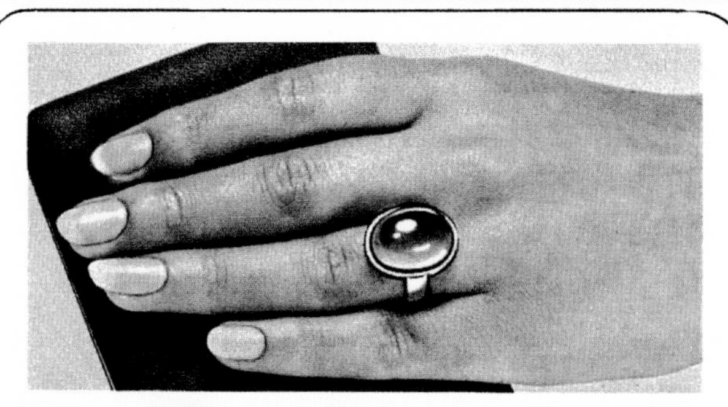

The Mood Ring tells all–

The Mood Ring tells all – as featured in the Sunday Express October 5th, 1975. The ring is black, it's amber, or turquoise or violet – depending on your mood. Taking the U.S. by storm – the latest fashion accessory worn by film, stage and T.V. stars.

The Mood Ring is named as a "portable biofeedback aid" that supposedly monitors different levels of tension – it changes colour, theoretically, as your mood changes. It is made of quartz crystal according to the Gemological Inst. of America over an opaque changeable colour material.

The "Living Colour Crystals" are in the opinion of scientists encapsulated liquid crystals, activating at different temperatures, at which time, reflecting light and colour. Created by Josh Reynolds, said to be a descendant of Sir Joshua Reynolds the famous painter, the ring is oval, set in sterling silver. Your Mood Ring can alert you (and anyone who knows the secret) to your inner changes, whether it be relaxed, passionate, tense, inhibited or harassed. Adjustable size for both men or women – give your loved one a present – even yourself.

The Mood Ring – Available at **£9.50** Only from
Belgrave Direct Supplies Ltd.
(Dept. C)P.O. Box 41, Humberstone Road, Leicester.

Full refund if not satisfied.

AutoDate

Dating
for 'out-of-town' people

Details from your nearest local office:–

NORTHERN ENGLAND	SOUTHERN ENGLAND	GREATER LONDON and HOME COUNTIES
Autodate	Autodate	Autodate
Hazel Drive	Locks Road	Marsh Lane Taplow
Poynton	Park Gate	MAIDENHEAD Berks
MANCHESTER	SOUTHAMPTON	
Tel: Poynton 4665	Tel: Locks Heath 4821	Tel: Maidenhead 20388

THE TIE FOR THE MAN YOU LOVE TO HATE.

If your man believes that a woman's only place is in the home, he deserves a surprise.

Like being given this Male Chauvinist Pig Tie.

It's a top quality navy blue tie patterned with small white pigs and with the letters 'MCP' in sky blue beneath.

Just £4.50 pays for the tie and postage.

If he's half the man he says he is, he'll love it.

To: MCP Tie, 24-26 Telford Way, London W3 7XF.

To: MCP Tie, 24-26 Telford Way, London W3 7XF.
Please send me............tie(s) at £4.50 each.
I enclose cheque/P.O. for £..................payable to MCP Tie.
Name________________ (BLOCK CAPS PLEASE)
Address________________

C15

The T-shirt & sweat shirt

Rock Follies is coming back. Great, new T.V. series, fabulous L.P....and NOW, from Mr Wadsworth's Clothing Co.,– the sensational T and sweat-shirts. Produced under exclusive licence from Thames T.V., in stay-fast, metallic neon type on superb quality cotton T-shirts and sweatshirts.

T-shirts £2.30 + 20p P&P, sweatshirts £4.20 + 30p. Cap sleeves £3.30 + 20p P&P
To: Mr Wadsworth's Clothing Co., 65a King Street, Knutsford, WA16 6DX.
Tel: Knutsford (0565) 52007

Sizes: S–30-32," M–34-36," L–38-40."

To order, fill in boxes with size and quantity	T-shirts	Sweat shirts	Cap sleeves
Gold on navy			
Silver on black			

I enclose cheque/P.O. £________ Tick for poster ☐
Satisfaction or money back
Allow 21 days for delivery

Name________________
Address________________

To: Mr Wadsworth's Clothing Co.
65a, King Street, Knutsford WA16 6DX CO3

CAREER IN GAMING

Want to combine your working life with glamour *and* good career prospects?

Are you attractive, intelligent and between 18 – 25 years (with a basic knowledge of maths)?

Do you enjoy working with people?

Then apply to Ingrid Seward on –
629 6666

Anytime with a view to training as a Croupier Bunny for Playboy Club Casino.

COSMO TELLS ALL

MOVE OVER, FERRY

Beautiful Bryan Ferry, lead singer of Roxy Music, has a dedicated following of male fans who copy his sartorially elegant style. *This* Ferry freak, spotted at a recent concert, must have been disappointed when his idol appeared on stage in GI uniform rather than his usual tie and tails. Not to be perturbed, when asked to pose for our picture, he put his best Ferry face forward (he tells us he has other faces, too). The high priest of Biba rock, as Ferry was once described, would have been amused to discover that his fans have difficulty keeping up with his changes of style.

PHOTOGRAPH BY TONY McGEE. CARTOON FROM "NEW BEHAVIOUR"

POETIC JUSTICE

Judging by our postbag, inside every Cosmo reader is an ambitious poet fighting to get out. We don't have much space for poems, but if you long to see your work in print, The Poet's Yearbook could help you. It's hardly riveting reading, but then that's not the aim. For a directory of poetry publishers, complete with their latest publications, details of all poetry magazines, poetry groups and money-making opportunities for poets, you won't do better. Published by The Poet's Yearbook Ltd, 1 Herbert Rd, London N11 at £1·95.

"MY PSYCHIATRIST TOLD ME THAT IF I WATCH MUCH MORE OF KOJAK, I'LL REMAIN ORALLY FIXATED FOR EVER."

TELLY DATES

For those of you whose idea of a good fantasy is 365 dates with Telly Savalas, we present the 1976 Kojak calendar. It measures 60cm by 87cm and costs 95p plus 35p p&p from Athena Reproductions Ltd, Bishop's Stortford, Herts. Hang it on the wall above your bed for sweet dreams. And if you're hooked on the supercop television series, a warning, in the shape of this clever Paul Pearson cartoon, about what an overdose of lollipops can do to your health! Now turn to pages 76 and 77 for Cosmo's very own version of Kojak and see if you can spot the difference.

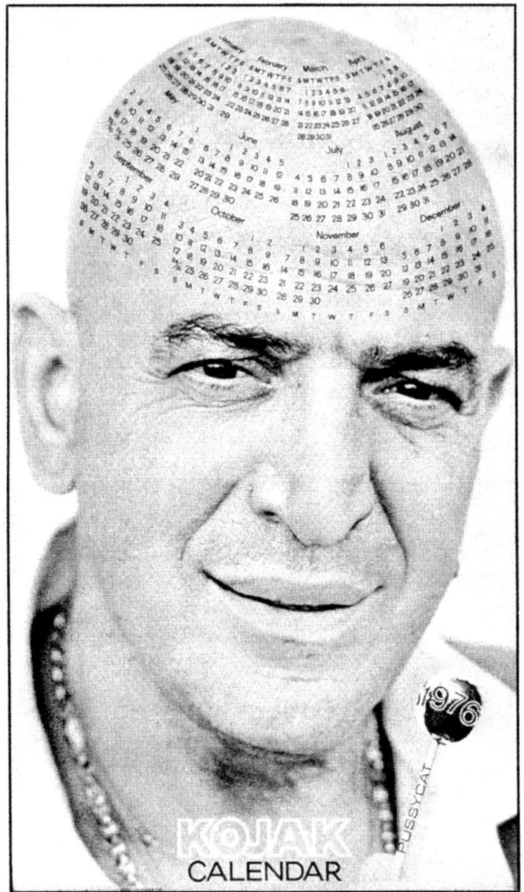

THUMBS UP

... to the "pictures to take home" schemes which enable local library users to borrow prints and original paintings for up to three months ... to Marks and Spencer for launching a £65,000 private scheme to give jobs in community work to fifty unemployed school-leavers for a year ... to the six "nude" models who good-humouredly posed dressed for a week to protest against cuts in their wages ... to Rodier's fashion advertising (see below) showing real girls who look surprised, not smug, about being photographed.

THUMBS DOWN

... to National Panasonic for the patronising ad for portable cassette players which appears in their brochure: "Soft rounded styling that's ideal for the fair sex and children, too. Operation is child's play" ... to the United States Marine Corps for court-martialling Second Lieutenant Mary Niflis on the grounds that she has had eight affairs with enlisted men (would they have minded if the men had been officers?) ... to some doctors who dub working-class wives as too daft to be trusted to take the pill.

The Agony Column

Irma Kurtz helps

We know this page is needed because of the letters which pour in asking for help about every kind of problem . . . depression, shyness, marriage/job conflicts, sexual boredom or inadequacy, loneliness and a hundred others. If you've read Irma Kurtz's articles in *Cosmopolitan*, you'll know she's just the sort of warm, compassionate and outspoken person we'd all like to bring our problems to. And although Irma cannot give private answers, she will try to cover as many different situations as possible on this page. Your letter will be treated in the strictest confidence so don't be afraid to be honest.

Q When I started going out with my boyfriend ten months ago, I let him assume that I wasn't a virgin. He is experienced, but we decided to wait until we are engaged before making love. Now that we are getting engaged, I am frightened; I have lied to him and one thing we respect in our relationship is that we have no secrets from each other. After previous heavy petting with another boy, I know that intercourse will hurt and I will bleed heavily. Can I stop this happening?

A You're not only frightened, you're also confused. How do you know from previous heavy petting that being deflowered is going to hurt and you will bleed heavily? If it hurt, and you did bleed, you're no longer a virgin. Virginity does not grow back again. If your lover is quite as experienced as you believe him to be, then being deflowered will not be the excruciating experience I suspect you've been reading about in some silly books. Worry less about defloration and more about contraception.

You say you have no secrets from each other; will it alarm you to hear that everyone, even your fiancé, has some perfectly justifiable secrets? Why are you getting engaged? To make love? If making love is only one aspect of the union, then what earthly difference is there if he, in the past, has made more love than you? Believe me, you will catch up. Simply tell the man immediately that you are a virgin, that you were embarrassed to tell him before, and you are glad he is to be your first lover. Men react to virgins in different ways but if he is as experienced as you think, or if he loves you, he should be able to face the prospect of your purity with courage and fortitude.

PHOTOGRAPH BY ELIZABETH ELY-HUXLEY

Q Every time my boyfriend phones to say he's working late, I'm compelled to ring back and check on him. I can't relax at parties unless I'm absolutely glued to his side, and recently when he came back from a weekend with his parents, I asked so many leading questions that he finally lost his temper. I don't think he's two-timing me but I suppose I think he might one day, and I'm determined not to be made a fool of. What can I do?

A Physical jealousy is an allergic reaction to romantic love; everyone suffers from it at different times and to different degrees. Jealousy and fear of loss are always in proportion to your own insecurity and I suspect that you are possessive because you feel inadequate with him. Why? Does he make you feel incomplete emotionally, sexually, intellectually? Is your extreme jealousy peculiar to this union, or are you always possessive about your friends and lover? If you are, then rummage through your personality and pull out whatever terrible secret about yourself you fear someone close to you can discover, reveal and broadcast to others. You see, I'm worried when you write that you "are determined not to be made a fool of". Apart from this phrase's unloving and threatening sound, it shows that you see your relationship as it looks to others and you're hardly concerned with how it looks to you. Is your man a lover or a status symbol? What you really fear is that you will be seen by *others* to lose a man because you weren't good enough, sexy enough, clever enough to keep him. And, you know, you will lose this man soon; you're tying the ropes so tight he'll have to stretch them or break them in order to breathe. What do you do? Find out what you fear, and face it.

Q At twenty-six, I have had a successful career as a model, and four years ago I married Terry, a good-looking architect in his thirties. Our flat in Chelsea is the one Terry had in his bachelor days. We go to parties and have a holiday each year in the South of France . . . But I long to be a cabbage. I love cooking. I like domestic bliss. I want to live in a house with stairs and I long to have a baby. Terry likes his free life, he is terrified of a mortgage, and hates the idea of a sensible family car. But I want to settle down and grow up. I know he loves me and won't leave me if I do get pregnant—which is what I am determined to do. Do you think he will ever come to terms with the ordinary life I hanker for?

A No. Why should he? Four years ago when you were a successful model and he married you, did he know that what you really, really wanted in life was a house with stairs and a mortgage? Did he promise to provide them? If he did promise, then he has failed you. If he didn't, then you have failed him. Why did you marry a super-glamorous bloke like Terry in the first place? If you wanted steak, why did you order caviare? You say you now want to compound the felony of that initial deception by having a baby your husband does not want and then relying on his love to make him grit his teeth and keep you. That would be very silly and very self-centred; silly, self-centred impulses are not the best ones with which to begin motherhood. You have a number of healthy child-bearing years left; Terry, on the other hand, has not got much longer to be a playboy. Before you start a baby, you'd better start him wanting one too, or I'm pretty sure you'll cease being a trendy wife and become a trendy single-parent. Trim the sails of your dream if you expect him to trim the sails of his. Be patient. What do you do with yourself? Why don't you find an irresistible house to show him, or a big, appealing vintage car? If he likes display, then start acquiring the decorations of a family before you present him with a baby. Tailor your dream to fit him and *then* sell it to him.

You long to be a cabbage? Are you sure you aren't already a cabbage who thinks it might be nice to be a ratatouille? What ever gave you the idea that bringing up children and looking after a house was easy or passive. I promise you that smiling into a camera is infinitely easier and less active than smiling at a baby with colic; I assure you that the round of fashionable restaurants is much less tiring than a pile of wet nappies; holidays in France are nowhere as demanding as coping with a toddler's nightmare, or a husband who fears his youth is passing. You'll find that a growing family will make demands upon your emotional resources and your generosity beyond any you have ever known. Growing up means learning to consider the needs of others before those of yourself. You say you want to "settle down and grow up"; listen, love, *you'd* damn well better grow up before you settle down.

If you have a problem write to Irma Kurtz, Cosmopolitan, *Chestergate House, Vauxhall Bridge Road, London SW1V 1HF.*

Special offer

SMOCK AROUND THE CLOCK

BECAUSE OF THE TREMENDOUS DEMAND FOR THESE SMOCKS, THE MANUFACTURERS HAVE REPEATED OUR OFFER.

fantastic any-wear cotton drill top for only

£4.50

KENNETH BIEBER

Casting around for a different top to team with your jeans for a super-comfy casual look—a cover-all to shrug on for shopping in town, walking in the country, everywhere you go? Then it's a good bet you'll fall hook, line and sinker for our super fisherman's smock — specially when you can net it for just **£4.50.** There's no end to its wearability. Looks great with slacks for sightseeing, golfing, walking—or just lazing. Go gardening in it, or wear it when you're cajoled into car-washing. On the beach you can slip it over your bikini when it's back-to-the-hotel-for-drinks time. Birds with super legs can wear it as a cute micro-dress! Great for a holiday twosome (looks just as good on a bloke, too) and boating or fishing, of course! Then there are those jobs around the house like cleaning and tidying up. What better cover than our versatile smock? Available in four super colours: emerald green, tomato red, khaki and navy—in bust/chest sizes, **small** 81cm–86cm (32 in.–34 in.); **medium** 91cm–96cm (36 in.–38 in.); **large** 102cm–107cm (40 in.–42 in.). Made of tough, hardwearing drill in 100% cotton, the smock is fully washable. Word of warning though—the red should be washed separately as the colour may run a little. It's got three-quarter sleeves, a beautifully-detailed stand-up boat neck and two roomy patch pockets. And you won't have to fish for compliments – they'll come naturally . . . ●

Please note: The smocks are generously cut to allow room for thick sweaters underneath.

We regret that the offer at this price is open (until November 30th, 1976) to UK readers only. Please order as soon as possible, and allow up to four weeks for delivery. If demand is exceptional, there may be further unavoidable delay. Any inquiries to Cosmopolitan Advertisement office, please.

Proprietors: National Magazine Co Ltd. Registered Office: Chestergate House, Vauxhall Bridge Road, London SW1V 1HF. Registered No: 112955 England.

To Smock Offer, Crown Works, Jasmine Road, Old Basford, Nottingham NG5 1JQ.

Please send me (state number in appropriate boxes) smocks at £4.50 each.

Small 81-86cm (32"-34")

	red	khaki	emerald	navy
1st choice				
2nd choice*				

Medium 91-96cm (36"-38")

	red	khaki	emerald	navy
1st choice				
2nd choice*				

Large 102-107cm (40"-42")

	red	khaki	emerald	navy
1st choice				
2nd choice*				

*** Alternative colour will be sent only if 1st choice is not available**

TOTAL £ ....

I enclose cheque/PO No ....

Value ....

(Made payable to National Magazine Company and crossed/& Co/). Please write name and address on backs of cheques.

NAME ....
(capital letters please)

....

ADDRESS ....

....

............**TEL NO.** ....

Mark number of smocks ordered here

NAME ....
(capital letters please)

....

ADDRESS ....

....

....

....

....

If undelivered please return to Smock Offer, Crown Works, Jasmine Road, Old Basford Nottingham NG5 1JQ.

This label will be attached to the parcel containing your order.

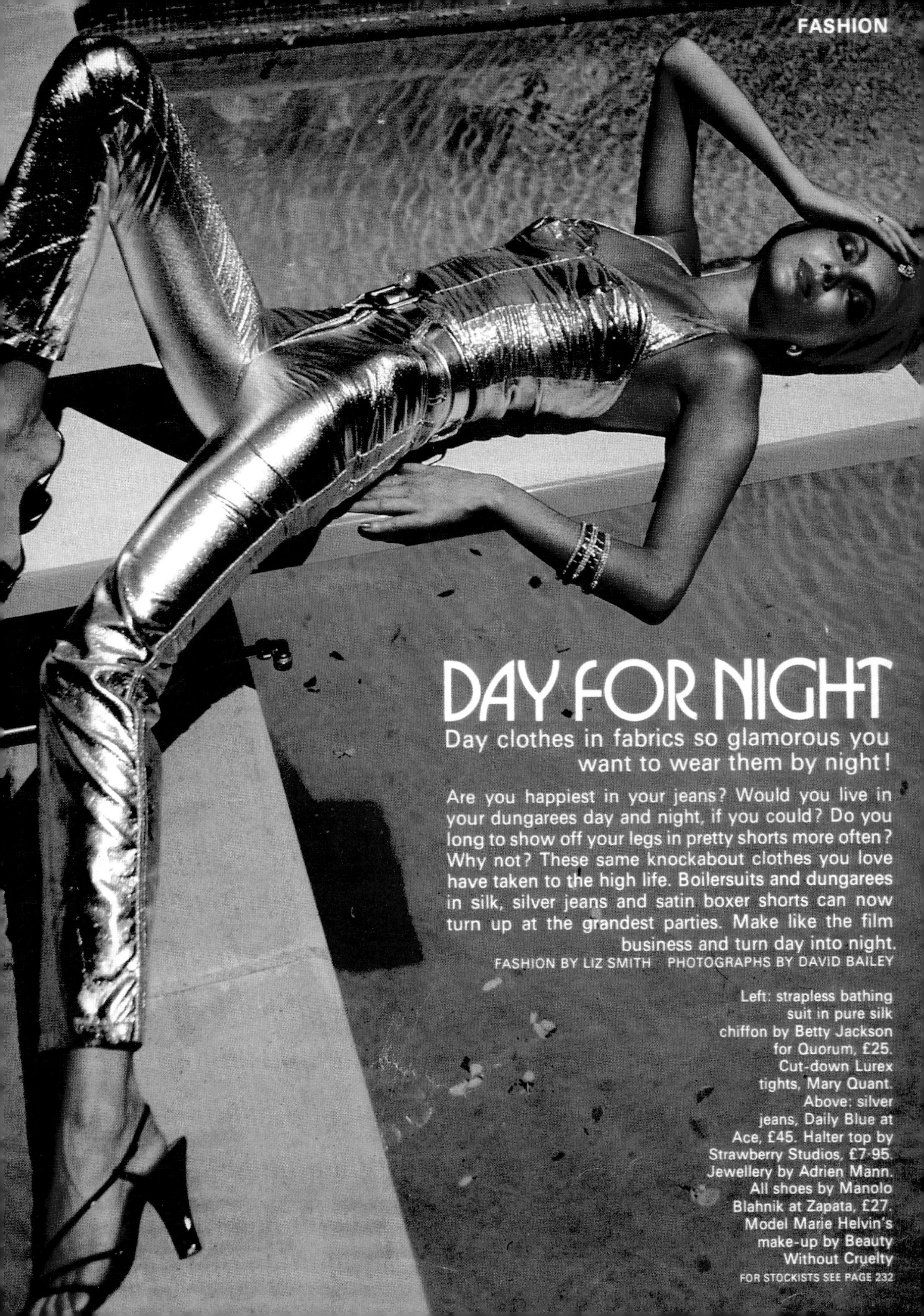

DAY FOR NIGHT

Day clothes in fabrics so glamorous you want to wear them by night!

Are you happiest in your jeans? Would you live in your dungarees day and night, if you could? Do you long to show off your legs in pretty shorts more often? Why not? These same knockabout clothes you love have taken to the high life. Boilersuits and dungarees in silk, silver jeans and satin boxer shorts can now turn up at the grandest parties. Make like the film business and turn day into night.

FASHION BY LIZ SMITH PHOTOGRAPHS BY DAVID BAILEY

Left: strapless bathing suit in pure silk chiffon by Betty Jackson for Quorum, £25. Cut-down Lurex tights, Mary Quant. Above: silver jeans, Daily Blue at Ace, £45. Halter top by Strawberry Studios, £7·95. Jewellery by Adrien Mann. All shoes by Manolo Blahnik at Zapata, £27. Model Marie Helvin's make-up by Beauty Without Cruelty

FOR STOCKISTS SEE PAGE 232

HE'S STINGY IF...

You can forgive a man almost anything except meanness. Is your man a tiny bit close? A little on the careful side? Look out if he . . .

○ Returns the towelling dressing-gown you bought him for his birthday and deposits the money in a savings account.
○ Does all repairs himself—only nothing ever works properly.
○ *Itemises* who owes what when you're going Dutch, rather than splitting the bill.
○ Washes plastic cups to re-use them.
○ Steams stamps from envelopes that haven't been post-marked.
○ Prefers eating meals at your house to anywhere else.
○ Insists on seeing old films at the local cinema instead of taking you to a West End theatre.
○ Would love you to make him a shirt or knit him a sweater—you buy the basic materials.
○ Throws a bottle party and doesn't contribute a single bottle himself.
○ Disappears at Christmas every year.
○ Re-shapes bent paper clips.
○ Pales at the sight of diamonds.
○ Arranges to signal you with two rings on the phone when he's coming over, so he won't have to pay for the call.
○ Can *always* get it for you wholesale.
○ Is thirty-four, has a good job, and still borrows his father's car.
○ Looks *hard* for small change he drops.
○ Brings flowers that never survive more than a couple of hours.
○ Waits right until the car is running out of petrol before refilling.
○ Tips *exactly* ten percent of the bill in restaurants.
○ Always asks you to collect his suits from the cleaners, his shoes from being repaired, and never "remembers" to pay you back.
○ Reads your newspaper and never buys one of his own.
○ Waits until March before buying a diary—when it's reduced in price.
○ Says he doesn't believe in sending postcards on holiday.
○ Fusses about leaving lights on and turns on heating only when it's *freezing* cold.
○ Has always *just* run out of cigarettes and has to smoke yours.
○ Is wearing open-neck shirts until narrow ties come back into fashion.
○ Reverses the charges when he phones you.
○ Asks you to cut his hair.
○ Tells you he's a spontaneous person who considers giving gifts for Christmas, birthdays, Valentine's day, *un*spontaneous and hypocritical (the only spur-of-the-moment present he's ever given you was a six-can pack of beer).
○ Never orders a second brandy.
○ Sends you home on a *bus* at night.
○ Keeps a three-minute egg timer next to his telephone.
○ Accepts the fifty pence you offer when he goes out to buy your cigarettes.
○ Brings his dirty washing over to do with yours at the launderette.
○ Burns only twenty-five watt bulbs in his flat.
○ Splurges . . . and takes you to an international motor show.
○ Orders Coke all evening—and then pours his own rum in it.
○ Drives twelve miles to a shop which has washing powder on special offer, so he can save five pence on a box.
○ Just happened to forget his cheque book twice and *never* carries cash.
○ Suggests you go away for a romantic weekend together—at his parents' cottage in the country.
○ Redistributes presents people gave him last year.
○ Gets sore thumbs from squeezing the last of the toothpaste out of the tube.
○ Thinks all heiresses are beautiful.

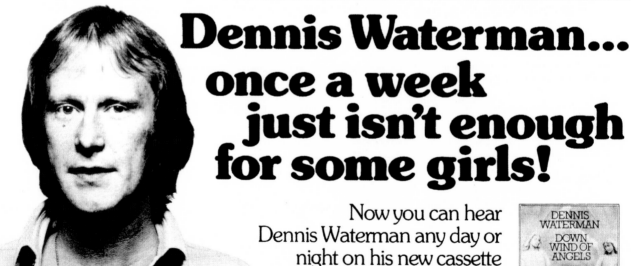

If these are your PROBLEM AREAS Just 5 minutes a day could put you in GREAT SHAPE

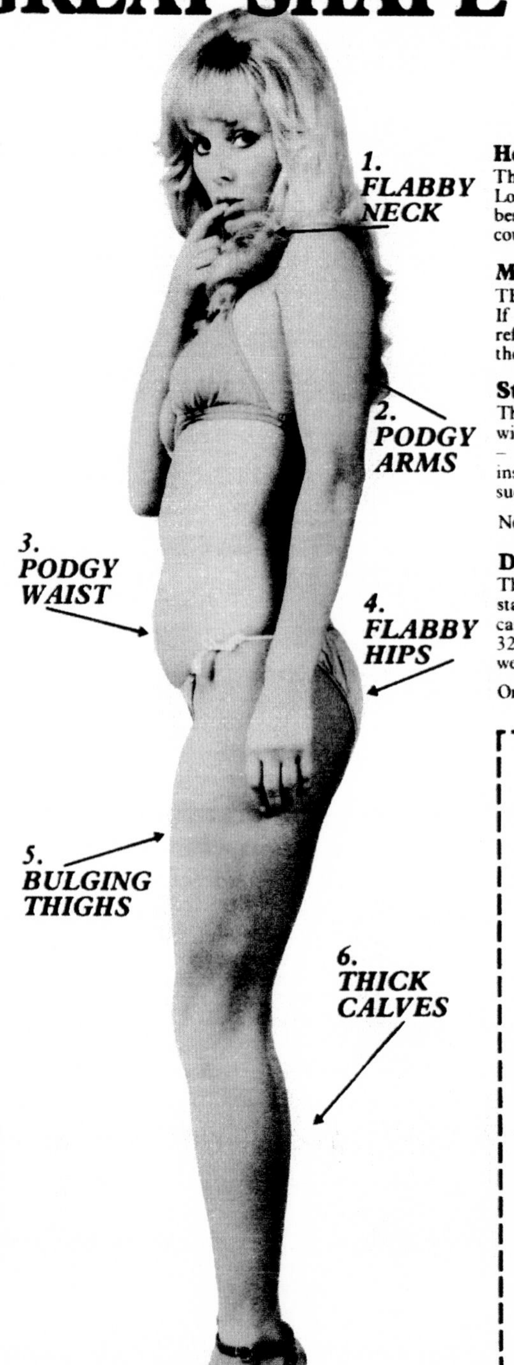

Right weight but wrong shape?
At some time or another, all of us have seen charts in magazines which gave us a 'right' weight for our height and frame size, yet many of us are still dissatisfied with bits of our figures – the bits that bulge. Most of us would like firmer, tauter, trimmer figures. Exercise is one answer. But most women find exercises time consuming, boring and aren't sure which exercises to do, or if they're doing them correctly. But don't despair, there is a way to fight the flab round your hips. It's called the 5 minute Figure Shaper.

Now exercise need not mean physical jerks
We all did P.E. at school and very good for us it was, with carefully planned exercises for every bit of us. Now that we're big girls we've forgotten what they were. With Figure Shaper you needn't worry. It's a new exerciser that helps to shape firm and taughten your total figure, or the areas that need most attention. The 5 minute Figure Shaper makes it possible to do specific exercises properly, regularly and in the comfort of your own home. It's easy and fun to do and you can even use 5 minute Figure Shaper whilst watching the telly or listening to your favourite 'beat' music.

More than just another exercise gimmick
Figure Shaper was developed in America and is quite unlike anything you've tried before. It takes all the jerk out of physical jerks. Like all the best ideas in the world, 5 minute Figure Shaper is dead simple. A clever arrangement of nylon cord, pulleys and hand and foot grips – it is especially designed to take the hassle out of exercise. Just hook the end over any convenient door knob, lie on the floor, put your hands and feet in the grips, and in five minutes you're on your way to a firmer, trimmer, tauter you.

How does the Figure Shaper work?
5 minute Figure Shaper can be used to perform a variety of exercises, but essentially, all movements consist of the arms and legs moving in unison. The clever design of the Figure Shaper (co-ordinated arm and leg movements) means that exercise can be continued after local muscle fatigue would have set in under ordinary exercise conditions. Which is why we have called it the 5 minute Figure Shaper and why we say that 5 minutes with Figure Shaper can't be compared with the old-style hands, knees and oops-a-daisy gymnastics.

Will it work for me?
Make an honest appraisal of your figure and its faults and determine which areas need the most work. Promise yourself that your aim is worthy of your very best effort. Then use Figure Shaper with the instruction booklet supplied. You won't be disappointed.

CRAVEN HOUSE (Dept C10) Ham Common, Richmond, Surrey.

How do I get started?
That's what Figure Shaper is all about really. Looking and feeling better. When we look our best we feel happier and more confident. Post the coupon today – you've nothing to lose but flab.

Money-back undertaking
TEST AT HOME AT OUR RISK.
If after 14 days you are not delighted we will refund your money in full provided you return the Figure Shaper to us undamaged.

Standard model
The original standard model has been a great hit with beauty conscious women for over two years – the famous exerciser and fully illustrated instruction leaflet combine with your personal success chart.

Now only ***£3.99*** plus 45p post and packing.

De luxe model
The deluxe unit has all the same features as the standard model plus its own pocket sized travel case in simulated leather finish and a colourful 32 page instruction leaflet including height weight charts, posture guide etc.

Only ***£4.99*** plus 45p post and packing.

YOUR ORDER FORM AND PROBLEM AREA RECORD
(STRICTLY CONFIDENTIAL)

To assist in establishing which areas are your problem and to ensure that the course we supply with the Body Shaper is just right for you please indicate which areas you wish to trim.

1. Neck ☐
2. Arms ☐
3. Waist ☐
4. Hips ☐
5. Thighs ☐
6. Calves ☐

Post this order to:
Craven House
Ham Common, Richmond, Surrey.

Yes I want to firm and shape up my total figure. Please send me the 5 minute Figure Shaper Plan and instructions. If after 14 days I am not delighted I may return it post paid for a full refund of my money.

Tick which model you wish to order:
Standard at £3.99 plus 45p p.&p. ☐
Deluxe at £4.99 plus 45p p.&p. ☐

I enclose Cash/Cheque/P.O.'s for £..............
Please send under plain wrapper.
NAME ....
ADDRESS ....
....
....
(A division of D & A Exports Ltd. Reg. No. 1139024)
C10

Orders from OVERSEAS welcome.

A stocking snagged looks very sad,
To me there's nothing sadder.
My window-cleaner's just a lad—
But can he climb a ladder!
Sleek soft bra, Gossard,
£1·99. Lace panties,
Marks & Spencer, 69p.
Pure silk
stockings, Funn, £5·50.

In a knee-deep-in-water emergency,
My plumber's undoubtedly great.
And he works with appropriate urgency
When I act as plumber's mate.

Flower-printed lace bra and pants, Marks & Spencer, £1·75 the set. Silky knit wrap, Bif Boutique, £19. Pure silk stockings, Mary Quant, £3. Ankle-strap Perspex shoes, Russell & Bromley, £22·99. Plumber's overalls, Badges & Equipment.

Dudley Moore

Manolo Blahnik

Amanda Lear

Nigel Dempster

Jerry Hall

WHO ARE THE FLIRTS?

Flirting is a game of charm with little to do with overt sexuality —Mick Jagger is not a flirt, Jack Nicholson is. Guiding signs are twinkling eyes rather than sexy pouts. Because it's attractive, flirting is always a come-on, although a true coquette will make sure a flirtation is never consummated.

THE BONA FIDE FLIRTS
The people who flirt because it's in their nature . . .
David Hockney, painter
Wayne Sleep, Royal Ballet dancer
David and Marie Bailey, husband-and-wife photographer and model
Dudley Moore, comedian
Rebecca and Flora Fraser, daughters of Lady Antonia
Miriam Stoppard, medical pundit
Prince Charles
Barbara Daly, make-up artist
Peter Firth, actor
Harold Evans, editor of *The Sunday Times*
Tina Chow, wife of restaurateur Michael (Mr Chow's)
Jimmy Connors, tennis star
Christopher Ward, journalist
Tina Brown, *Punch* columnist
John Cleese, actor
Helen Mirren, actress
Ryan and Tatum O'Neal, actor father and daughter
Lord Snowdon
Andy Fairweather Low, musician

. . . AND NON-FLIRTS
Princess Anne
Linda McCartney, musician
Tom Stoppard, playwright
Angelica Huston, actress
Rod Stewart, singer
Mia Farrow, actress

THE FUN FLIRTS
Teasers who flirt for the fun of it, although it never leads to anything else . . .
Bill Gibb, designer
John B Fairchild, publisher
Pat Harmsworth, wife of Vere
Barney Wan, art director
Lord Dufferin and Ava, Patron of the Arts
Manolo Blahnik, shoe designer

THE VETERAN FLIRTS
They've never lost the knack . . .
Jean Rhys, novelist
Sir Ralph Richardson, actor
Sir Frederick Ashton, choreographer
John Huston, director/actor
Sir John Betjemen, poet

THE ESOTERIC FLIRTS
So subtle, only those in their coterie understand . . .
Andy Warhol, artist
Rudolph Nureyev, dancer
David Bowie, singer
Charlie Maclean, novelist
Bianca Jagger
Prince Michael of Kent
Michael White, impresario
Amanda Lear, model

THE PRACTISED FLIRTS
Flirt with panache; often media people and party-goers . . .
Jerry Hall, model
Mara and Lorenzo Berni, restaurateurs
Russell Harty, TV personality
Peter Langan, restaurateur
Lord George Weidenfeld, publisher
Lady Antonia Fraser, writer
Tom Maschler, publisher
James Hunt, racing driver
Michael Parkinson, TV personality
Mark Boxer, cartoonist
Bruce Oldfield, designer
Warren Beatty, actor
Martin Amis, novelist
Nigel Dempster, gossip columnist
Glenda Jackson, actress
Myna Bird, model
Claire Tomalin, author
Aldine Honey, party-goer
Tessa Dahl, actress
Geshi Fengler, model
Pat Booth, photographer
Gully Wells, Weidenfeld publicist
David Frost, TV personality

Julie Kavanagh

THE "LADIES" OF LONDON

A selection of Ladies' loos compiled for your convenience. * denotes a pleasing atmosphere; X (crossed loo brushes) the standard of hygiene.

First Prize "Atmosphere"* ** XXX**
The Garrick Club, Garrick Street, WC2. Famous club, frequented by legal and theatrical persons, maintains a noble aura of culture in the Ladies; the attendant, noticing that my hem was slovenly secured with Sellotape, ministered with a needle and cotton.

***Good Loo for "Overhearing Things"* (1) *** XXX**
Fenwick's, New Bond Street, W1. Ground floor, off "Separates". Clean and pretty. Frequented by jolly nice gels who say "actually" a lot, eg "Actually, Fiona, are you wearing your new one to Nigel's cockers P [cocktail party]?" Fiona: "Actually no, actually."

***Good Loo for "Overhearing Things"* (2) ** XX**
The Cartoonist pub, Shoe Lane, EC4. Ribald jokes, *bons mots*, Fleet Street gossip overheard from the Gents, adjacent to Ladies.

***Romantic Loo* *** XXX**
"Ladies", Southampton Row, Theobalds Road Underpass, WC1. Capture the scent and sound of pinewoods and Alpine streams. Much evidence of pine disinfectant and rushing water in this well-supervised loo.

***Useful Loo* ** XX**
"Ladies", Victoria's BR Station, SW1 (near Continental platforms). For 5p you get a ticket, a hand towel and the freedom of tiled precincts. Here, loos and wash-basins parade, orderlies bustle, Muzak plays; 35p will buy you a bathroom and, for 5p, a machine will spray you with French perfumes. (A cocktail of Quadrille and Je Reviens not advised.)

Trendy Loo* * XXX**
Zanzibar, Great Queen Street, WC2. Much evidence of designer: pretty colour scheme, German door furniture, violets in vases, inscrutable graffiti.

Exciting Loo* * XXX**
The Connaught Hotel, Carlos Place, W1. On each occasion, I have observed ladies in distress. The first time, a young woman was sobbing into the folds of a capacious mink coat. The second time, I could not help but see an American woman, *d'un certain âge*, cantilevering her bosom, with the help of Elastoplast strips, into the skimpy top of her dress, which had failed her.

Posy Simmonds

WHO LOOKS OK? WHO LOOKS KO?

Our candid camera strikes again on the streets of London. Bear in mind that this is a *subjective* assessment of style.

Jackie O look: dark glasses, shiny boots and soignée hair-do. Conservative but can't-fail chic.

The Vamp lives—Biba still has a lot to answer for.

This girl made her outfit herself. It works.

These girls made their own outfits, too. They're fun.

The right way to wear jeans and a big sweater. Fantastic!

Who's been reading all the fashion magazines lately?

Some people have style, some have looks. This girl has both. We really could spit.

This is the fur jacket that doesn't go with the denim skirt. Separately, they'd look fine.

Very classic. Very Italian. Terrific.

Chick in chap's clothing—could be catastrophic, but this girl has the cheeky style to carry it off.

THE COSMO GIRL'S GUIDE TO FASHIONABLE TELEVISION VIEWING

	IN	FADING	"PSEUD"	OUT	NOSTALGIA
American series	*Starsky and Hutch*	*Kojak*	*Police Woman*	*Cannon*	*Dragnet*
Arts	*Read All About It*	*Aquarius*	*Arena*	Anything called *The Lively Arts*	*Late-Night Line-Up*
Children's television	*The Muppets*	*Dr Who*	*Six Million Dollar Man*	*Blue Peter*	*Muffin the Mule*
Comedy	*Rutland Weekend Television*	*Fawlty Towers*	*The Generation Game*	*Monty Python's Flying Circus*	*That Was The Week That Was*
Current affairs	*This Week*	*World in Action*	*Weekend World*	*Panorama*	*24 Hours*

	IN	FADING	"PSEUD"	OUT	NOSTALGIA
Music	*Pop Quest*	*Supersonic*	*So It Goes*	*Old Grey Whistle Test*	*Juke Box Jury*
Quizzes	*Mastermind*	*University Challenge*	*Face The Music*	*Call My Bluff*	*University Challenge* (the year you appeared)
Science	*Horizon*	*Chronicle*	*Don't Ask Me*	*Tomorrow's World*	*Your Life In Their Hands*
Serials	*When The Boat Comes In*	*The Sweeney*	*Crossroads*	*Z Cars*	*Compact*
Sport	*Match of the Day*	*The Big Match*	*Pot Black*	*It's A Knockout*	*1952 Cup Final*

DIETER'S NOTEBOOK

HOW I LEARNED TO STOP WORRYING ABOUT BEING FAT AND GOT THIN

The story of Susie Orbach by Mary Kenny

Between the ages of thirteen and twenty-three Susie Orbach was obsessed by one thing—her weight. She was, she felt, horribly fat. Actually she weighed only nine stone, but she is short and small-boned so those nine stones made her feel round, and those ten years were dominated by the fluctuation of her weight.

"I must have tried every diet ever invented," she says. "And they all worked. I lost weight very successfully. And then I gained it again."

She knew the calorie count and the carbohydrate value of every piece of food available. She lived by the bathroom scales. She would deprive herself for three weeks, lose weight and feel she was "good". Then, feeling deprived, she would fall to stuffing herself for weeks, and feel "bad". She had three kinds of clothes in her wardrobe: oversized clothes for when she was "bad", undersized clothes for when she was "good", and what she calls "carrot clothes"—clothes that would act as an inducement to be good and beautiful, which meant just one thing: being thin.

Susie (pictured above), a Londoner, is now thirty and a beautiful, sylph-like seven-and-a-bit stone (she *thinks*—she never weighs herself any more). A kind of miracle happened to her when she was twenty-three. She was teaching in New York City and became involved with a feminist group there. A woman called Carol Munter said to her: "Look, Susie, do you realise that fat is a feminist issue? I mean, all this obsessive dieting and compulsive eating really only means one thing—you have not accepted yourself as a person. You have not accepted the balance of your own body, but you are allowing yourself to be tyrannised by rules made for you by alien criteria."

She started to talk to the feminist group about her feelings and soon realised how oppressed she felt by a society which yelled "thin, thin, thin" at her. When she thought about it, she realised she was very angry about being made to feel that she should have to be thin: she was angry that she had accepted the idea that you could only be a real woman if you fitted into a size eight dress; and she had, she realised, turned that anger against herself.

This was Susie's road to Damascus. She threw away the bathroom scales, flung out all the calorie-counting books, cleared her wardrobe of everything that she didn't feel comfortable in and resolved from that day that her relationship with her own body would primarily be one "of harmony". And this miracle happened. "From the moment I stopped worrying about it, my

metabolic rate changed, quite spontaneously. I started to eat anything I wanted to eat and I found that when I relaxed, my body naturally regulated its own needs. I stopped being compulsive about food and started to look on it as something to enjoy whenever my body told me to enjoy it." From that day onwards, she has weighed (she thinks) seven and a bit stone.

Any woman who has been on the compulsive eating/compulsive dieting yo-yo—probably three quarters of us—will recognise what Susie went through. "The compulsive dieter/eater does not eat one Kit Kat and enjoy it," Susie says. "She has to eat *six* Kit Kats and doesn't enjoy any of them. The reason why she does it is a complex mixture of deprivation and addiction, of reward and punishment. What we have to get over to women is that there is nothing wrong with eating a bar of chocolate. If you fancy a bar of chocolate, eat one and love it. Don't imagine that it's such a terrible sin you must then eat six."

If you can get to a point of genuine relaxation about food, she says, you will eat only what you really want, and the body will adjust itself accordingly. And what the heck if you do weigh ten or twelve stone anyway? "Other cultures, other times have and still do regard stout women as handsome. Learn to love yourself as such."

Women who consider themselves overweight usually have a completely distorted view of their own figures. In the therapy classes for this very problem that Susie organises, women who are obsessed with their own sense of grossness will remove their clothes and say to the others, "Aren't I horrible? Look at my great hanging thighs"—and the other women will say, quite truthfully, that the woman is seeing herself completely out of focus. Certainly, compulsive dieters—at the extreme end of the spectrum, people with anorexia nervosa—can never see themselves in a realistic light. And anyway, says Susie, what is a realistic light? Who says the classic British pear shape—small top and big bum—isn't lovely? The male media, that's who.

Susie Orbach is now an evangelist in her own cause, and with a colleague, Luise Eichenbaum, she has set up a Women's Therapy Centre at 19 Hartham Road, London, N7 (01-607 2864) to help other women to be serene about their bodies. Seventy women a week attend the Centre for counselling, much as women attend shrinks and psychotherapists all over London. The difference is that the Therapy Centre is cheaper (between £1 and £8 a week according to income), and feminist. No woman going there with a problem about the menopause or work/family conflicts or whatever is going to be told that she suffers from penis-envy or that she subconsciously feels inadequate as a mother.

The Centre sees all the problems in the casebook, but the most common of all is that of obsession about weight. Women so frequently feel unhappy in their own bodies. As Susie says, women did not endlessly go on about dieting in Jane Austen novels, and they don't endlessly go on about it in Arab countries or Eastern Europe. It has to be, in great part, the pervading culture that is oppressing them. Often, she notices, a woman really wants to be fat in order to protect herself against her sexuality. A teenage girl who can't cope with sex will often become fat so that men won't make passes at her. Why does a woman feel the need to assume a coating layer of protection? Why should she have to? If only women could learn to have confidence in the substance of themselves they would mostly be neither very fat or very thin, nor feel upset about being either, nor drive themselves to compulsive eating or compulsive dieting, but settle down in a happy rhythm with their souls.

But it is hard for anyone—man or woman—to free themselves from the mirror image of the culture around them, and our culture is enormously tied up with the camera, which likes thin people. However, a movie which was showing in London recently may signify hope.

It is a love story called *Cousin, Cousine* and both the hero and the heroine are perceptively overweight. She has quite a little tummy, he really ought to be worrying about heart attacks. Yet both seem utterly insouciant—indeed, part of the idyllic tale shows us the comforting spectacle of this pair of fatties indulging in Danish pastries.

It just might be a cultural breakthrough. It just might be the start of a wave which breaks through the idea that a woman is lovable only when she's slim.

The Packaging Of Farrah Fawcett-Majors

She's America's Number One Pin-Up (her posters have outsold Marilyn Monroe's five times)—her face and figure have launched a thousand fantasies. Here's why FF-M can't fail. By Alan Cartnal.

Dear Mrs Farrah Fawcett-Majors:

I'm a great fan of yours. I think you are super. You are very pretty. I like your series and commercials. My whole family likes you very much. My father stays up just to see you.

Would you please send a picture of yourself. I would like to know how tall you are, your age and your measurements. Is it true that you are going to leave your series? Are you going to leave Lee Majors? If so will it be on TV? Please tell your husband I think he's cute.

Your greatest fan,
Pauline Snider,
Hicksville, NY

The love has been pouring into Beverly Hills. Not illicit love or lustful love—but phenomenal pure-of-heart love from Middle America's Farrah-loving adolescents, and it takes the form of 40,000 letters a week delivered to the William Morris agency. What is going on in America? From out of the world of corny television series and the *real* fantasyland of TV commercials, a Kewpie-doll attraction Hollywood had turned away, a dish with a name that sounds like a corporation or an English duchess gone mod, Farrah Fawcett-Majors, is demanding at least one million dollars a shot as the nation's new sex symbol.

We are all grown up here, so news that an actress is demanding a million dollars for a commercial is similar to American football players demanding, and getting, $300,000 a year for five years, guaranteed. Besides, Farrah sells a commodity more basic than that of a footballer—sexual fantasy. That in itself is nothing new, but what is interesting about Farrah is exactly how powerful she is in merchandising her sexual power. To measure the message of Farrah, you would have to uncover the corporate secrets of Wella Balsam, of Mercury Cougar cars, of Ultra Brite, to find out how many people are washing, driving or brushing *because of Farrah.* Those numbers are hard to come by, since corporate advertising directors who gamble millions on a pretty face are loath to admit the gamble doesn't work. Representatives of all three products say Farrah has done a good job for them. But it is easier to measure Farrah's powers when she is used to sell magazines. In the American supermarket tabloid sweepstakes, one magazine reports that Farrah on the cover has meant eleven percent more purchasers; and a national newspaper says that with the Farrah cover its sales went up "five or six percent", which represents between 250,000 and 300,000 extra readers.

The real question to be asked about Farrah, however, is *why?* Why Farrah? Farrah *is* whatever Raquel Welch was supposed to be (but Raquel has hidden herself away, tired, she says, of just being sexy), or perhaps Lauren Hutton (but Hutton's too high fashion and, therefore, too clever), or surely Catherine Deneuve (but she's too French). What the Farrah phenomenon seems to tell us is that Venus, in America in 1977, can rise up out of the pages of *TV Guide*, pages in which the primary concerns seem to be overweight or terminal itching. The nation, her message seems to say, is starved for a positive ointment of the soul, an "up" heroine. If she is wholesome—a word often used to describe her—it is because that is what she *has* to be, because we don't much care to have unwholesome people in our living-rooms. Our TV-inspired lust can be real, but it must not be down and dirty. It is worth noting that our societal lust came from the pin-ups/movies in the 'Forties, from the men's magazine centrefold in the 'Fifties, from the fashions and liberation of the street in the 'Sixties and now from the biggest sales medium of all, TV in the 'Seventies.

PHOTOGRAPHS BY SCOPE, TRANSWORLD, GAMMA

It must be a cosmic joke. Farrah Fawcett-Majors—Miss Bland—as the girl most likely to succeed in the New Hollywood of pot and promiscuity? The successor to such historic hot stuff as Rita Hayworth, Betty Grable, Marilyn Monroe, Raquel Welch and Lassie? Why Farrah? Why not? She certainly has the glandular magic required for American myth status, that ideal, perfect-woman guise like a *Playboy* centrefold before it went pubic.

The legend, as told by Farrah, is that she is our new Miss Up. As she tells it, men who are coming home from a hard day's work can catch her on TV and suddenly be transformed back to the good-old-days. According to Farrah, we're tired of having all our fantasies and heroes destroyed, tired of "conversations in the raw" and the Jane Fonda and the Gloria Steinem Women's Lib heavies as female role models. We're turning to TV, not the cinema, to bring us back to clean and cuddly. Farrah, thirty and super-fit, reigns as a giantess of all-Americanism and upstanding morality against the forces of doom.

Faye Dunaway, this year's Oscar-winning best actress, couldn't even rise above fifty-seventh place in the US national TV ratings when she appeared in Arthur Miller's *After the Fall* drama on NBC. But Farrah—who offers nothing but sweetness and light on a dumb cop show—has an audience reaching an estimated fifty million souls a week.

Farrah will not be just a star. She will be a legend, say the wizards who cloister her from the cruel, cruel press and feed her myth to the hungry folks in TV land.

"Farrah Fawcett-Majors is a terribly pretty girl," reads the Jay Bernstein press release. "She stands five-five and would take your breath away were you to come on her unexpectedly. Even being warned that you're about to meet an exceedingly attractive young lady, you might get palpitations when introduced. She has that effect on males of all ages." The entire release sounds as if it were written after visiting Disneyland on diet pills.

Reality: Farrah is the biggest snoozer of an interview in Hollywood since Mary Tyler Moore. Ms Moore is honest enough to admit that "I'm not colourful. If you want great quotes go to Tallulah Bankhead." Intent on keeping herself an old-time Hollywood legend and guarding her privacy, Farrah has babbled on about "cooking for Lee is more important than my career" and how "as a little girl I believed in fairy tales and felt that if I did I would overcome any challenge". Writers come out of her "limited" interviews in an almost comatose state. When they reach their typewriters, it is in a state of panic to wonder if such Hollywood hype will still go down with Farrah fans. (Note: it does).

Her life is touched, you might say, with a marvellous averageness. Born 2nd February, 1947, in Corpus Christi, Texas. Daughter of James and Pauline Fawcett, who now reside in Houston, her father is an oil field contractor. We are led to believe by the Farrah myth-makers that she is pure Middle America—never touched by the protests, the lib marches, the pot parties, the panty raids, or anything else that wouldn't go down with the new mass uprising for "happy endings" and "hopeful stories".

The Bernstein release tells us about Farrah's college years in verbiage that hasn't been attempted in press agentry since the heydays of such once-towering stars as Jeanne Crain and Sandra Dee. Farrah was, it says, an art major at the University of Texas:

Farrah Fawcett-Majors

"During her early days she devoted most of her time to art while she quickly developed into a beauty who would inspire an artist." Nifty, huh?

We can also imagine Farrah, the innocent, unknowledgeable girl from Corpus Christi, confronting Hollywood for the first time in 1968. But, frankly, once Farrah arrived in Hollywood—which, after all, is not exactly a religious capital—the realities took over. Those were the days of Farrah Fawcett Minor.

"Farrah was luckier than most starlets," reports Marge Shicktanz, the William Morris agent responsible for putting Farrah into the Wella Balsam, Mercury Cougar car and Ultra Brite toothpaste TV commercials and, in her own words, a good Farrah friend. "Within a week here she met Lee Majors. He already knew the ropes in Hollywood. He guided her away from the usual starlet routine. She never had to go the, shall we say, risqué route."

Nonetheless Farrah didn't always have an easy time. Take, for instance, one screening of *Myra Breckinridge*, the campy Twentieth Century-Fox film about a transvestite who is played by Raquel Welch, in which Farrah had a minor role as the sweet young thing who dates Myra's male stud dream. At the screening, Farrah, who appeared in one scene in the film in a see-through fabric that showed too much of her herbal essence, was yanked bodily from the cinema by Majors while he yelled insults at the producers for spoiling the image for the future Mrs Majors.

"Those weren't good times for Farrah professionally," says Jane Feinberg, an independent casting director who brought Farrah into countless interviews knowing that her glamour and clean-cut image were not exactly the thing for the time. "She was always nice. Always very co-operative. And she never got uptight about the refusals. If you live in Hollywood you get pretty used to rejection. Producers would take one look at her and laugh. She was like something out of another time. The Old Hollywood." Even up to a couple of years ago, Farrah was hardly considered a Hollywood heavy. "She was up for the role of the girl in *Young Frankenstein*," reports Feinberg, "and she got all the way to Mel Brooks, the director. She looked all right for the role. But the part required a German accent. And, well, let's put it kindly—Farrah is just not that type of actress. She couldn't hack it."

But Farrah is the dream for TV commercials. Soft and smooth. Long and silky. The kind of girl who got a kick out of clean. A girl who never had to worry about every-other-day hair, but had 25-inch screen hair the likes of which women hadn't seen since their days studying cave paintings in school.

Even when *Charlie's Angels* was being cast, the producers couldn't see anything extraordinary in Farrah. "She is a sweet girl," explains Leonard Goldberg of the Spelling-Goldberg (*Starsky & Hutch*) production company, who reportedly got Farrah for $5,000 a week for the series. "She was just what we needed. But we had no idea that the series was going to be a landmark. We just looked around and figured that what the tube needed was a complete fantasy with three beautiful women." Goldberg also assures us that Farrah fanatics will be continuing their dial-a-goddess sessions in front of the home screen next season. On 9th March, the *Hollywood Reporter* headlined that Farrah had made it official that she would not return for a second season of *Charlie's Angels*. Goldberg says that the production company is proceeding with a court challenge on the issue, pointing out that there is a binding contract. A similar contract kept Carroll O'Connor playing Archie Bunker on *All in the Family*, so it might be thought that Farrah's threat is a ploy to get her price up.

"My God, I don't know what all this fuss is about," whines designer James Reva. "Farrah buys my clothes all the time. And she's awfully nice. But pah-leeze! This girl is not a goddess."

Fashion editors are clogging up switchboards to get her on the phone. Hairdressers are battling each other and throwing their blow-dryers to the chandeliers in their posh salons trying to get recognition as the first to have created Farrah's mane. Hugh York, a Beverly Hills shampoo king, swears it is he and he alone who rinses out the white hairs in Farrah's spectacular mop. Allen Edwards, one of the owners of the Beverly Hills salon named after Jon Peters, graciously accepts the honour of creating one of the most trend-setting hair sensations ever to come from TV.

And who cares? Certainly not the lesser lights in the hair field who watch the stars come and go in the big salons. "Farrah has very average hair," says Betty Pehrson, Barbra Streisand's haircutter at Jon Peter's. "To tell the truth, I am sick of cutting the Farrah cut. I mean, it's been out for five years. I wouldn't wear it myself. Who wants to look like somebody else?"

But businessmen in the instant fad biz—the kind of men who make their livings by rushing into children's bedrooms and pleading with them to find out who's the latest TV whiz—are flying to Los Angeles by the legions. Only a few get to Farrah. There is an incredible screening process and at least a day's indoctrination before they are ushered in to meet the pin-up queen who has sold more posters for Pro-Art, Inc, than anybody in the history of the craft. (Trailing Farrah's six million are Raquel Welch at two million, Marilyn Monroe and Betty Grable at 1·5 million and Lindsay Wagner, the Bionic Woman, at 400,000.)

"I just spent three hours with her," pants Stan Weston, who signed the deal for Farrah dolls for his Leisure Concepts firm. "She's the most powerful woman in the world today. A talent. The superstar of all superstars. Gorgeous. I never heard her use one word of show-biz slang. Not one off-colour word came from her lips. She is a real lady." Weston also mentioned that in one *day* at the New York Toy Fair last month the new Farrah doll (which will hit stores later this spring) billed nine million in orders (larger than the Barbie doll's initial order). Since the entire expected gross was ten million, the accountants are gleefully re-adjusting their figures to fit the appetite for Farrah statuary which the buyers hope will exist in the bedrooms of the young.

Why? Why? The public wonderment of adults who are attacked by eight-year-olds with questions about Farrah at family get-togethers has even caused the media to consult our most trusted metaphysicians—high-paid analysts.

Professor Ray Brown psyched-out America's fixation with Farrah's hair this way: "It's sort of wind-blown and free-spirited. But it is a safe sort of free spirit because the role she plays on TV represents law and order. Innocence and bold abandonment are the wildest sexual combinations to a man," he reasons. "She's the boom, bang, hot dog, cop lady," analyses West Los Angeles psychologist Irene Kassorla, a woman with an inside track on the awareness quotients of the biz, since she has seen many stars on her couch. "The kids turned to her because she has a pair of great legs, lovely-placed boobs, flowing hair and is a good-guy cop at the same time. Who wouldn't prefer Farrah to bald-headed Kojak or gruff-mannered Karl Malden?" Sniffing a trend, Dr Kassorla says, "This Fawcett lady smells like the new lady. Angie Dickinson is too old. But I can definitely see Farrah in short skirts with boots and a whip in her hand." Besides, Farrah has what doctors call "mommy acceptance". Kassorla says, "Today's housewives are bored with soft-blend margarine and toilet bowl cleaners. They want a new fantasy to assure them that there will be champagne and black lace nighties around the corner. They identify subconsciously with Farrah because she is the perfect papier-mâché woman. The tragedy of Farrah for men and women is that her phenomenon tells us that we are still terrified, as a culture, of meaningful, authentic, straightforward sex symbols."

Finally, consulting the spirit world, we find that even they have been getting vibes from the angelic Farrah. The word from Madame Sophia, a Los Angeles seer who advertises as a "spiritual reader. Advice on love, marriage and business. Past. Present. Future", is that she sees what is coming.

"She the blonde on TV?" asks Madame Sophia, speaking in a thick foreign accent. "Yah, I pick up vibrations from the television set. She gonna be big. She gonna be big movie star. This girl have spiritual powers. Big ones. I predict—and what Madame Sophia says is usually true—that she will be around all this year."

FIRST VIEWS

That our readers are literate and articulate is not news to the staff of this magazine. That the writers and reporters of tomorrow are among our valued readership makes the hours—nay, days—spent reading through the entries for our Young Journalist Contest absolutely worth while and, in many cases, an illuminating, heartening and even chastening experience. So many of you can really write, and with style and wit! A sense of the comic is a sadly uncommon quality, so when some new writing makes us laugh, it's cause for celebration. Which is what we are doing on these pages. The editor and judges of the Young Journalist Contest, which we launched in our April issue, are delighted to print the first of the new writing, six pieces which will give you a taste of the talent to come. In our next issue we will print the work of the winner and the five runners-up, plus comments by judges Mary Kenny and Christopher Ward. In the meantime, here is a selection of answers to the question, write on any subject you feel strongly about.

WHERE HAVE ALL THE BOSOMS GONE?

By Nell McDuff

Those soft, sensuous, womanly curves which are irreverently referred to by a variety of unsavoury synonyms, not least objectionable of which is "breasts" (which to me evokes surreal images of pre-packed chicken at my local Marks & Sparks) are being discriminated against.

We are again informed that the "pencil-slim" shape is in. Great!—for Jane Birkin, Bianca Jagger and Julie Christie. What about those of us whose patron saint is Di Dors? Those of us who frantically swaddle our female protuberances into Tennessee pancake shapes, cram them into Laura Ashley bodices and pray that the zip won't zap before we turn purple because we can't breathe any more.

It's impossible for us to go bra-less because our bosoms jog down the street, leaving us behind while we walk. Also, my nipples refuse to stand out and so there's really no point. I was recently obliged to explain to my husband that no, I hadn't started bed-wetting; the damp sheets had been caused by ice cubes which had expired on the summits of my sierra as I endeavoured to create something which might remotely resemble volcanic activity. I had a brief love-affair last summer with a stunning, strapless top in a Chelsea boutique and, convinced in the blindness of my passion that it might soon enfold my willing body, I ransacked the local stores for the answer to my prayer—a strapless bra! But alas—and, indeed, alack—each one that I tried stayed, like an obedient puppy, while I held my breath, but as soon as I exhaled and began to move, it would wriggle enthusiastically down to my waist.

To add to these mortifications, an "eminent" boffin—whom I would dearly love to disembowel—claims that his vital statistics of a cross-section of the community (I'm a very cross section who wasn't consulted) conclusively prove that large-chested ladies are less intelligent than flatties. All that the man's spurious speculation proves—if anything—is that the skinnies had to find something to do after school while we voluptuous sirens were out courting during the good old days when we were in vogue.

MOTIVES FOR MARRIAGE

By Helen Fielding

Over the past year, seven of my friends have come into a state of marriage, engagement, obsession with rings, or—horror of horrors—the "we might get married some time, but *don't tell anyone*" complex. The result is that I'm filled with gloom at the way in which women persist in looking at marriage, despite its no longer being seen as a sanctuary to be attained at all costs. It is generally accepted that marriage is no longer the be all and end all for a woman any more than it is for a man; that it is also her right and duty to develop her personality and abilities. Moreover, modern thought abandons the romantic view of marriage as a magic state of bliss, and sees it as an agreed relationship between two people, who are ultimately separate but who agree to be together, aware of all the problems that it may bring.

You'd think that women would jump at the chance to let marriage play a much healthier part in the shaping of their lives, and I'm sure that many do, but among the women I know best—all young, intelligent, educated—far too many retain the ridiculous attitudes that others have fought to destroy: "We've been going out since we were fourteen. If he's not prepared to marry me now, there's no point in carrying on"; "I've got past the stage of being independent, I just want to settle down with a nice house and nice things", etc, etc. As if marriage is more than the relationship! As if it could stop you going on the rocks!

And what a waste! Marriage should be the greatest source of comfort, fun and satisfaction. It stems from the strongest of our animal instincts—the urge to mate—and the continuity of any society depends on it. We have to recognise the desire for marriage as such—but we must also recognise that there is more of us to satisfy than the mere urge. We must learn to wait, wait until the "mate" is right in every sense, and till we are ready to make this change in our lives. Then let marriage become an adventure, a stepping out into uncertainties and problems, mingled with the highest of pleasures and not a cowardly creeping into a world of dullness, a fortress of matching pillowcases and tea-sets.

Right: learn to recognise a Maxfield Parrish at one hundred paces; this one came second in a poster contest.

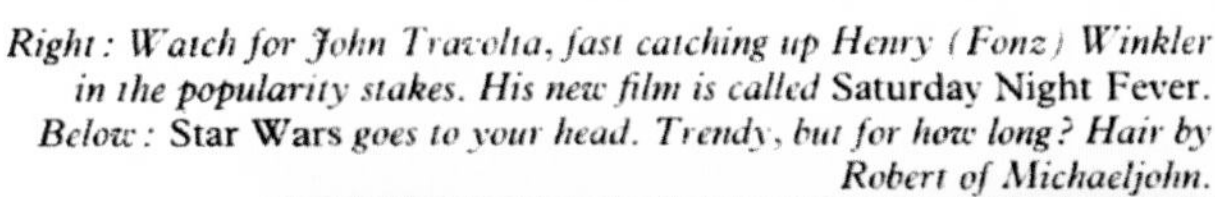

Right: Watch for John Travolta, fast catching up Henry (Fonz) Winkler in the popularity stakes. His new film is called Saturday Night Fever. Below: Star Wars goes to your head. Trendy, but for how long? Hair by Robert of Michaeljohn.

Right: Aussie kitsch is in. Below: Movie-star mules spell class.

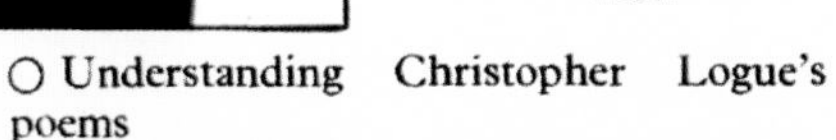

ILLUSTRATION BY CHARLOTTE BARNES

- ○ Japanese lunches
- ○ Silk pyjamas from Sulka in New Bond Street
- ○ Boots cosmetics and Clarins eye gel
- ○ Regular pedicures
- ○ Mules from Frederick's of Hollywood
- ○ Not being surprised by anything you read in *Private eye*
- ○ Carrying a girlie magazine with the *Financial Times* inside
- ○ Liking the National Theatre
- ○ Not being intimidated by taxi drivers
- ○ Philip Sayer in *Censored Scenes from Hong Kong*
- ○ A painting by Derek Boshier
- ○ Being a tennis freak
- ○ Understanding Christopher Logue's poems
- ○ The limp edition, as distinct from hard, of *Dame Edna Everage's Coffee Table Book* (Harrap, £1·95)
- ○ Frank Langella in the New York stage production of *Dracula*, coming to London soon, and John Travolta in the film *Saturday Night Fever*
- ○ Knowing that Frank Langella and John Travolta will be the next big stars
- ○ Not fantasising in print about film stars you're never likely to meet
- ○ Never complaining about tourists or the cost of living
- ○ Travelling really heavy
- ○ Not appearing in your own photographs like Lord Lichfield
- ○ Having always liked punk
- ○ Framing the grandest invitations you've ever had
- ○ Buying your books at Hayward Hill
- ○ Pretending to know Woody Allen
- ○ Ralph Richardson
- ○ Hot-water bottles
- ○ Not being irritated by Bernard Levin's reviews or Angela Rippon's legs
- ○ *The Encyclopaedia of Chess*, all 352 pages of it (Batsford, £7·95), *Lady Ottoline's Album* (Michael Joseph, £7·50), Bruce Chatwin's book of travel, *In Patagonia* (Jonathan Cape, £4·95)

HOW TO CUT YOUR OWN HAIR

If you've always wanted your hair cut by a top international hairstylist but could never afford it (or the air fare), take a lesson from Bruno, the professional who has snipped locks off the famous such as Brigitte Bardot, Sylvia Kristel, Jane Birkin and Raquel Welch. Cutting your own hair as short as this need not be a formidable experience if you follow Bruno's clear instructions and diagrams (asking a reliable friend to help you where appropriate), use proper hairdressing scissors and cut hair wet. And even if you are happier with your hairdresser holding the shears, Bruno points out, "These pictures will help you to understand the art of hairdressing and how to communicate with your hairdresser,"—a lesson all can benefit from. Professional stainless steel haircutting scissors 15 cm (6 in) long, £7·35 inc. of p & p, are available from J & T Gorney, 16 Oakwell Mount, Leeds 8, Yorkshire.

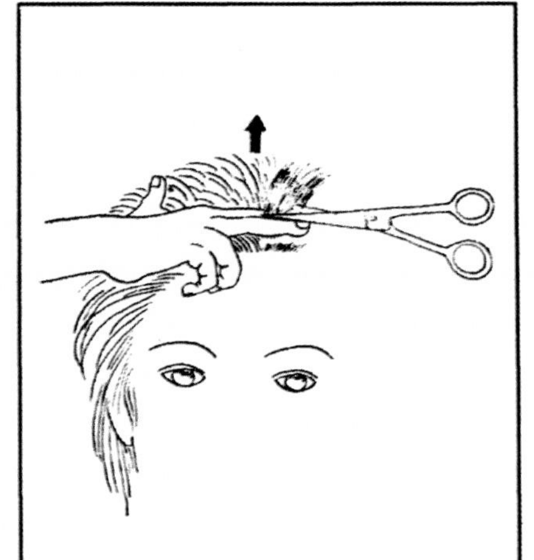

Starting at the front, cut the first layer to the length you want—it can vary from $\frac{1}{4}$ to $1\frac{1}{2}$ inches.

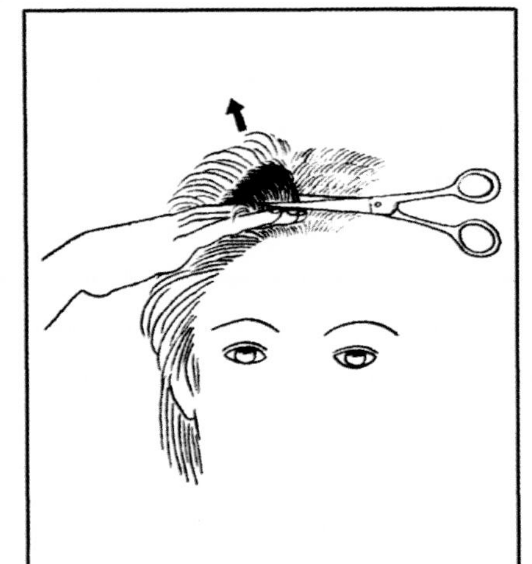

Continue cutting, using the hair you have just cut as a guide for length.

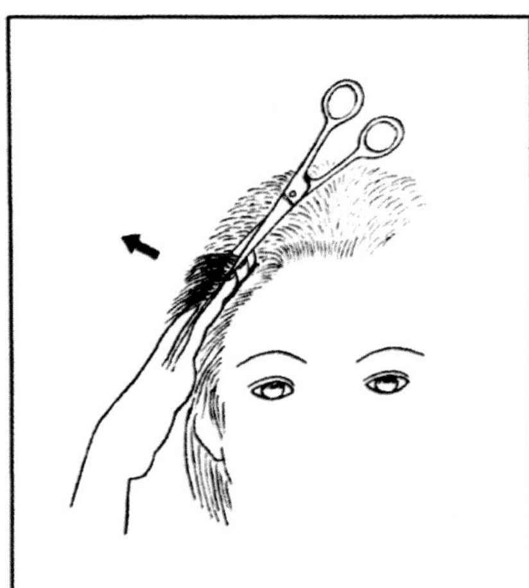

Follow the order of cutting indicated by the diagram in order to keep the hair very even.

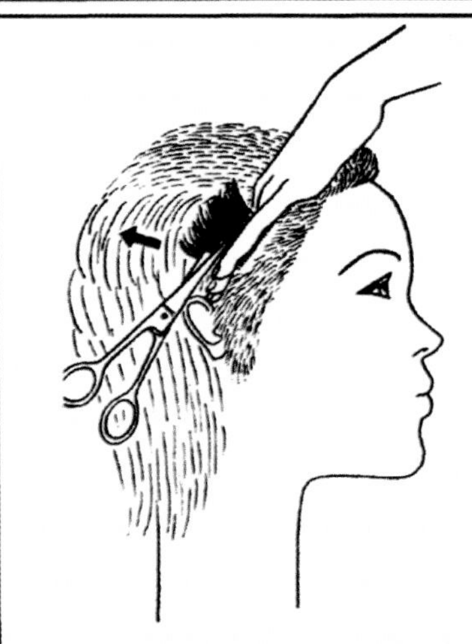

Cut around the sides, continuing to keep the length the same all over.

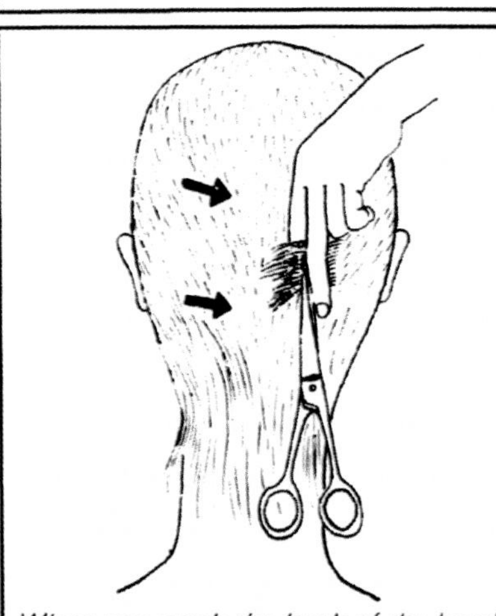

When you reach the back of the head, continue cutting in the direction indicated by the hand, scissors and arrows.

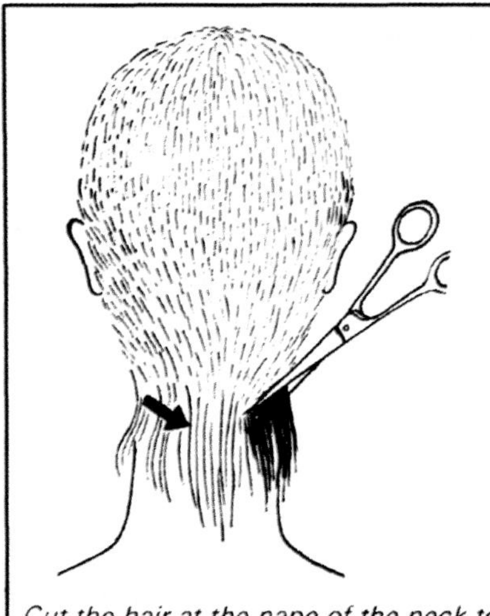

Cut the hair at the nape of the neck to taper gently to the centre as shown.

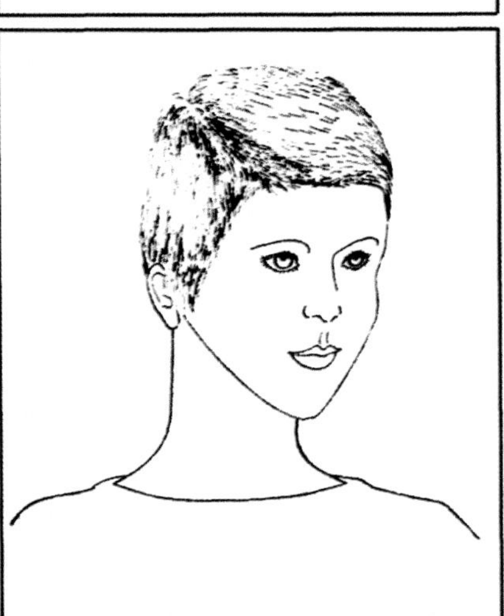

Final result is a versatile cut giving a gamine look when brushed forwards . . .

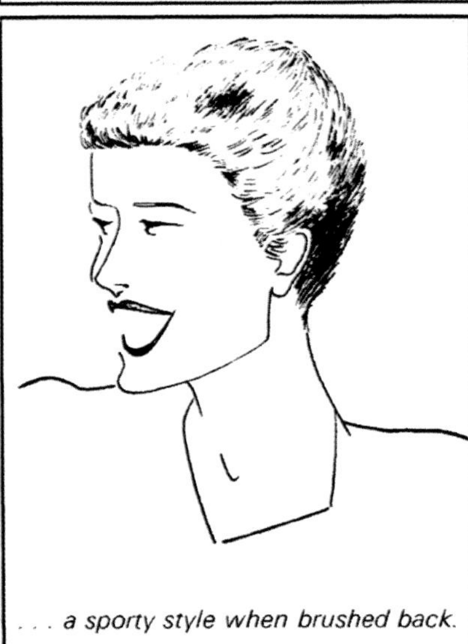

. . . a sporty style when brushed back.

Gentlemen prefer Blondie

Debbie Harry, lone woman in the rock group Blondie, explains why bump-and-grind music sells better than the moon-and-June variety. By Bart Mills.

What kind of woman would get up on a stage in front of twenty rows of drooling guys and sing lyrics like, "I will give you my finest hour—the one I spent watching you shower"?

Debbie Harry, vocalist of New Wave group Blondie, is the first white female rock star who isn't coy about being sexy. She's got it, she knows it, and she flaunts it. "I wish I had invented sex," she says. "Sex is everything. It's number one."

Sex sells. In contrast to the soft eyelash-fluttering songs offered by the Linda Ronstadts and Olivia Newton-Johns, or the phony moanings of a Donna Summer, Debbie Harry purveys down-to-earth lyrics like, "All I want is a photo in my wallet, a small remembrance of something more solid." Jumping up and down on stage like a pogo stick in heat, Debbie leaves no doubt exactly which portion of her lover's anatomy she remembers best.

Debbie Harry and Blondie have had three big hits in Britain, though they have yet to rise above cult status in their native America. Their songs, like "Picture This", generally use what Debbie calls a "bump-and-grind beat", and are far more to the point than the usual Top Ten ditties of the June-moon-spoon variety.

"We're more, uh, sophisticated than the old-style groups," says Debbie. "We're closer to what kids really think. Teenagers do watch each other shower, and other things too. They get together real young today."

Aside from their songs' frankness, the gimmick that sets Blondie apart from others in the tell-it-like-it-is New Wave is their Brigitte Bardot-ish leading lady. Other groups in the genre are pursuing Slum Chic, but Debbie will pose for a glamour photo (like our cover) at a moment's notice.

"I didn't create the situation," says Debbie, who is sometimes forthright, sometimes defensive about being a pin-up. "My face seems to sell. I can't help that. When you come to watch a group play, you normally watch the vocalist, unless you have a mad infatuation for the drummer.

"You want to know what I really wish? I wish I got more money for it, that's what I wish. There are all these posters out, and there's only one of them that I get the money from."

Debbie's image on all those posters is of a sex-crazed nymphet, innocent yet experienced, a Miss America candidate who went to bed with all the judges. Unfortunately, little of this image is true. Her real age? Mid-thirties. Her actual availability? Nil. She's been settled with Blondie's guitarist for over five years.

However, her saving grace as a sex queen is her background, which does indeed have a few lurid aspects. Her father was a salesman of woven labels for clothing and commuted to the New York garment district while Debbie grew up in a New Jersey dormitory town. She still has some of that Joisey accent, which goes so well with chewing gum. "It was always my dream to live the bohemian life in New York and have my own apartment and do things. I didn't like suburbia. I always had my own secret, private ideas."

PHOTOGRAPH BY TERENCE DONOVAN

What were they? "To do what I'm doing now. I always knew I would be involved with entertainment somehow."

One of the stories she grew up hearing was about the time she'd missed a chance for fame as an infant. "My mother was offered a contract for me to become a Gerber Baby." A Gerber Baby is a little gurgler who goo-goos happily in advertisements while being fed America's most popular baby food. "But my mother told them there was no way. She wouldn't be a showbiz momma.

"So maybe that's why it took me so long to get my music thing together." What happened to Debbie's twenties? Why wasn't she a star long ago? It was only when she met guitarist Chris Stein five years ago and formed Blondie with him that she "got her music thing together".

"I started in the music business right after college. I was too idealistic. I got disillusioned. I went into other fields. I tried painting and writing. I was never satisfied." She was a druggie as well as a hippie. "I lived in the East Village in New York, which was the mecca of the *avant-garde*." Her friendly neighbourhood bands were groups like the Velvet Underground and the Fugs. She had boyfriends with professions like drummer-sculptor. She was a secretary, a saleslady, a waitress. She lingered on the fringes of the Warhol pop-art crowd. She sang in a variety of groups with names like the Wind in the Willows and the Stilettos, in a variety of styles. She drank the bohemian life to the dregs, trying a little of everything. "I kept changing. I was always experimenting. I wanted to see what the big wide world was all about. And it really was everything it was cracked up to be. I had a good time. I still do."

One of Debbie's problems used to be the fatal attraction dirty old men feel for her. She'd like to think her present audience doesn't contain many of them. She was extremely incensed last year to discover that one of Blondie's songs was being plugged by their record company with the catchline, "Wouldn't you like to rip her to shreds?"

"It was a sexually exploitive advertising manoeuvre. They thought it was the hippest way to advertise us, to capitalise on our identity that way. It was a mistake. Aside from that, I don't think Blondie or I are sold as sex objects," she says.

"I happen to have a sensual nature, and I suppose it comes out in pictures. I've always had that kind of response as a female. I know, because I've always been followed by perverts. Always the sick kind. In public places, flashers. I remember once when I was a child. It was at the zoo, and I was with my mother. This man came over and whipped open his coat. Disgusting.

"I think about the whole thing differently every day. Sometimes I think it's so silly. Inevitably, if I meet someone, they find me not what they expected. When I was a fan and I fantasised about the singers, it was a really great feeling to adore them. Really nice. It must be the same for the people who like me and Blondie.

"So what? I can only be what I am. Big deal."

CHRISTMAS DAY IN THE MORNING

BY PAT GARRATT

Christmas is a time for doing all those mad, bad things perhaps you shouldn't. Like dancing on the rooftops, drinking till dawn or breakfasting in bed, with crumbs in the sheets, honey on your fingers and your favourite man popping the champagne cork. So this year, forget your usual breakfast routine, and *live* a little!

Lay the tray the night before, and come morning, surely the most chauvinistic male couldn't refuse to heat the rolls, make the coffee, and squeeze the oranges for a reviving Buck's Fizz? (All that vitamin C plus a hair of the dog can't *fail* to phase out a hangover.) Proportions are two-thirds chilled champagne to one-third orange juice and don't let a swizzle stick near it. Would the French spend years putting the bubbles *in*, if they knew you were going to pop them *out*? Keep the food simple. Buy petits pains, brioches, croissants, poppy-seed or cottage loaf, and pile them high. Choose fresh, unsalted butter, runny honey in a jar or comb, the most alcoholic marmalade and jams (peach with brandy, plum with rum or add your own booze to your fruitiest preserve). Use your fanciest china, laciest cloth and a sprig of mistletoe for romance. Now you're ready to unwrap the most generous, enjoyable day of the year.

Our crazy Christmas was photographed at Homeworks, London's latest palace of decorating ideas. The tree comes from Selwyn Davidson; the food is from Justin de Blank; the champagne by Moët et Chandon; glass and cutlery from Heal's; china and hen from Homeworks; and toy tiger, gift-wrapped presents, tray and pretty boxes from Harrods. The television comes from Rumbelow's, the red-boxed gold pen from Les Must de Cartier and the Christmas tinsel from Paperchase and by Swan Decorations. We took perfume from Penhaligon's, one perfect orchid from Interflora and pyjamas by Sulka (his, but even better on her).

PHOTOGRAPH BY JOHN CARTER; hair by Christine at Mane Line

MOET
MOET

Into the 'Eighties with men at our side

Who wants liberation? Do you? Does the man in your life? We asked these questions in *Cosmopolitan*—and the answers you sent us are pretty surprising. If you want to know which men want to marry virgins, who thinks women are handicapped at work, and whether men are happy to stay at home and look after the babies—read on! By Virginia Ironside, Dr John Nicholson and Brenda Jones

COSMOPOLITAN FEBRUARY 1979

Sex

Most women believe a woman should be as sexually experienced as a man before settling down—but half the men disagree.

Facts: *64 percent of women aged 16-24 approved of women being sexually experienced before marriage and the figure rose to nearly three-quarters among women over 25. But only half the men aged 16-24 approved of a woman having equal sexual experience with the figure rising to 60 percent for other men.*

Obviously, most women think it's important for them to be sexually experienced before marriage—nearly three-quarters of women over 25, who presumably know what they're talking about, agree.

"I do feel strongly that a girl or woman needs some sort of springboard from which to dive—unless she and her partner have a very frank relationship," wrote one young woman. "I don't think there are a great number of couples who can readily express views and desires explicitly.

"I left my husband after four years of marriage. I met a man who was considerably more experienced than my husband and I began to enjoy sex again. I have had two or three lovers since, and things get better all the time.

"It may be that my husband and I just weren't suited, yet how many first relationships are strong enough to stand that sort of thing? I feel very sad when I think of two very young people groping about in the dark. I am a good example of the need for a woman to be experienced before settling down. I would also like to see more sex education in schools and at post-natal clinics—and to hell with embarrassment."

But men are less certain. Only just over half of them agree that a woman needs early sexual experience, and almost a third of the younger men actually disagree, while 18 percent weren't sure about it. Does this mean that *half* the younger male population (16-24) still wants to marry virgins? Apparently so.

"I'd like to marry a virgin, but I know I won't. I can't help it, I think it must be the way I was brought up, but I would prefer my wife to be a virgin. *I'm* not, but I would like her to be. I just would not like the idea of marrying a second-hand woman," said one male student.

As they get older, however, men become keener on the idea of women being experienced: 60 percent of men over 25 approved of women having varied sexual experience before marriage, which may be the result of a realism gained from experience, in the knowledge that ignorance may not be a good foundation for long-term happiness within a relationship.

But one couple wrote to provide a salutary reminder that there's room for more than one view on this subject. "We both agree that some degree of sexual experience before embarking on marriage or a long-term relationship is a good thing for anyone, regardless of his or her sex.

"However, if what you mean is that every woman and every man should have umpteen partners, then no, we don't agree, any more than we agree with those members of our church who would say that the only place for sex is within marriage. Both attitudes are far too narrow. Some people will be happiest with many partners, others with a few, others with only one. No single sex-life is going to be right for everybody."

Women should be free to take the same sexual initiatives as men.

Fact: *Over half of all the people questioned thought that women should be free to make the first move: 58 percent of women and 65 percent of men.*

This seems to represent quite a major shift of opinion from the old idea that women should confine themselves to a passive role in the sex game, and it's interesting that men are in the vanguard of this revolution. Should women be pleased by this or is it just that men are getting lazy? Or, dare we suggest, a bit frightened by the new breed of women? Women like a twenty-one-year-old beautician who said, "I do take the sexual initiative. I'm not blatant about it, but I always return signals if I'm interested, and make sure I return

Will you marry me, Michael?

them very strongly." Such forthrightness may be making men a little withdrawn, tending to leave it to women, now, to make the first move. As one male reader put it: "Before I met my wife, I was completely off women for about two years. You could have put a nude buxom blonde in front of me and I would just have turned round and got on with my pint. It was she who made the initiative to get me out of that frame of mind."

But women's fear of taking the sexual initiative is shown in a letter, this time from a woman. "How many men would really welcome a blatant first grope in car or cinema before they'd got around to making a pass at the woman themselves? (Yes, of course, there are more subtle ways of doing it, but we're talking of women being free to do *exactly* the same as any man, aren't we, including this not infrequent crude type of male?) I fear many men would run a mile at this sort of approach—and bang would go another promising encounter."

Not if it was an encounter with one of our male *Cosmopolitan* readers, it seems!

Feminine wiles are out of date.

Fact: *Two-thirds of our respondents thought the days when a woman used her feminine wiles to seduce a man have gone. Only a third of all women and even fewer men were still in favour of this approach.*

Men, even more than women, seem to have tired of the idea of trickery, deceit or play-acting having any role in the mating game. A straightforward, honest approach is more popular, especially with more experienced men and women.

Some women, however, still seem to enjoy the devious approach. As one reader put it: "Feminine wiles are part of the whole fun of getting a man."

Women should no longer wait to be asked.

Fact: *Fewer than 10 percent of either sex thought a woman should wait to be asked out by a man, with special contempt coming from the 25-34 age group where 95 percent rejected it.*

Obviously the whole idea that a nice woman waits to be asked out, or at least pretends to, makes no sort of sense to the present generation. Men and women now seem to accept that since both of them enjoy sex, both of them should make some effort to get to know each other, and not put the whole responsibility on to the man.

Couples should try to share all their important interests and their friends.

Fact: *Over half our respondents thought that a couple should play together if they are to stay together: 55 percent of all women and 60 percent of all men advocated this approach, though women over 35 were less sure, with fewer than half of them certain they wanted to share all their interests and friends with their husbands.*

It's encouraging to find that friendship seems to be the basis of partnership for so many. The old idea of the man having a regular night out with the boys while the wife stayed at home obviously doesn't appeal to our readers, especially the younger ones. The change of heart in older women perhaps represents a change of circumstances towards greater domesticity as family demands increase and women become more involved with chores which husbands don't share. And this is also the age when women who have missed out on education return to night school or the Open University and need to spend more time on their own pursuing their private studies.

Many women believe they should be free to spend an evening alone with a male friend after they marry, but men are not so keen on the idea.

Fact: *41 percent of young women believe that married women should have this freedom, with support rising to 52 percent in women over 35. But only about a third of the men agreed with them.*

It's not surprising that men are less keen on the idea than women. But it *is* surprising that older women are even more in favour than younger women. Are the older women getting bored with their husbands? Or do they feel they're less likely to get into a sexual entanglement than a young woman and therefore find the idea more practical?

Perhaps younger women believe that their partners will cater for all their needs, while older women realise that they have interests their husbands don't share and so need other friends.

Our male respondents are clearly worried about this one. One man said: "If my wife assured me that a relationship with a man was purely platonic, and it was someone she met prior to meeting me, then I would let her go out with him. But should I catch the merest whiff of rumour that something was going on, I'd be after them with a shotgun. I'd break their necks. Or at least try to." And another admitted: "I wouldn't like the idea of my wife going out with another man, even if it was for business reasons. I know I'd still get jealous."

But a more rational attitude is expressed in this letter from a young male medical student: "I am friends with females and it would seem to me that to have a sexual relationship with them would be as ludicrous as a sexual relationship with my male friends. If or when I do marry, I would not suddenly drop my friends like hot potatoes, and of course my wife would have the right to be out alone with a male friend."

Men can no longer expect to be allowed a bit on the side while their wives remain faithful.

Fact: *Only seven men and one woman in every hundred were prepared to accept the double standard. And not a single woman under the age of 25 in our sample would stand for it.*

While the people we talked to seemed to accept that extra-marital affairs will still happen, no one suggests any more that this is, or should be, a purely *male* phenomenon. Instead they believe that affairs may involve either party, and that they will probably cause trouble. As one man put it: "If a man's going to have a bit on the side, then the woman should be allowed to have a bit on the side. Since I've been married I haven't done so, but if a girl came up to me now and she had a pad round the corner and she said, 'Do you want to come back, like?' I'd probably go. Know what I mean? I'd probably regret it and feel guilty, but if you can give a dog a piece of meat, he'll eat it. It's a case of what the eye doesn't see the heart can't grieve over. I think my wife would most probably do the same in that situation. But as long as I don't know about it I don't get worried."

One woman made the distinction between sex on the side and love on the side. "If my husband had an affair and it changed his feelings for me I'd be livid. I'd be hurt. I'd be angry. I'd want to throw a fit. If it was just sex, it wouldn't matter. I don't *approve* of the zipless fuck, but I'm realistic enough to know that it happens."

Although a steady 7 percent of men of all ages wanted to keep the privilege of extra-marital sex as a male prerogative, this young male student's attitude seems to sum up the general feeling that what's sauce for the goose is now sauce for the gander: "Providing nobody finds out, yes, I suppose when I'm married I will have affairs. It's a bit deceitful. If there was a definite chance of having a bit on the side without anybody finding out I would take it. And as long as I didn't find out she would be entitled to the same."

ILLUSTRATIONS BY POSY SIMMONDS

How do I hustle through my period?
That's my secret.

If you've always wanted the kind of freedom tampons give, but want the confidence only a towel can offer, then Fancy Free by Dr. White's is good news for you!

Fancy Free is the softest, most compact stick-on towel ever made. And it's just as safe as normal-sized towels. Fancy Free has a unique Hydrosorb filling specially developed by Dr. White's for full absorbency right through your period.

Fancy Free has rounded ends to suit your body's shape and a special backing. It's completely flushable too.

When you're having your period, that's your secret. Share it with Fancy Free and be free to do what you like, when you like.

Write for a free sample to Dr. White's Fancy Free (HCO5), Birmingham B8 3DZ (UK only).

FANCY FREE
New from Dr. White's
The first compact towel that's fully absorbent.

Cut-Price Chic

Take a colour, a shape and a T-shirt. Then take a look at a painting by Kandinsky or Malevitch and construct . . . By Deb McCormick and Dinah Hall.

► Straight long-sleeved dress, £16.95, Joseph; socks, £2.25, Miss Selfridge; shoes, £22.50, Plum; luggage grips worn as belt, 29p, Greenfields; sunglasses, £2.90, Last Resort; earrings, £4, Detail.

▼ Sunshine yellow dress, £19.90, Elle; belt, £3, Miss Selfridge; earrings, £4, Detail.

Scoop-neck dress with spag-etti straps, £20, Elle; add a little riental promise in the shape of fan for 59p from Woolworth nd chopsticks painted red, vailable from Chinese upermarkets. Spiral a racelet up your arm, 1, The Last Resort.

▼ Next Sunday afternoon make yourself this T-shirt dress (instructions on page 204). Dress it up with poodle bows and high heels. Dress it down with string ties, extendable shower hose worn as a belt (available from hardware stores). Cotton jersey, £2.95 a metre, John Lewis; ankle socks, Miss Selfridge, £1.25; flat suede shoes, £22.50, Plum; blue wriggle earrings, £2.50, and silver shell necklace, £4.50, Detail.

▲ Climb into a soft look T-shirt lress, £12.99 Snob; elasticated belt vorn back to front, £3 Miss Selridge; spaghetti necklace £2.50 and anodised, aluminium bracelets £1.20, Detail.

PHOTOGRAPH BY PETER JAETH

The things that make life worth living

Near the end of his film, *Manhattan*, Woody Allen lists the things that make his life worthwhile. Our Cosmo crowd decided that the spice of life is. . .

- ○The latest Woody Allen film.
- ○Someone you fancy telling you "they haven't anyone special."
- ○Finding the book you're dying to read is out in paperback.
- ○Warm, fresh wholemeal bread and cheese.
- ○Glossy magazines with that "new" smell.
- ○Listening to Radio 4's *Hitchhiker's Guide to the Galaxy*.
- ○Riding pillion on a fast motorbike.
- ○Hearing a dedication on the radio for somebody you know.
- ○Discovering a book or a song that exactly describes something you've experienced but never knew how to express.
- ○A hot bath when your body aches.
- ○Morecambe and Wise repeats.
- ○Chocolate éclairs.
- ○Answering correctly a question that a Mastermind contestant says "pass" on.
- ○Reading Graham Greene's latest novel (*The Human Factor*) and liking it.
- ○Peeling a price tag off something you've just bought to find a higher price underneath.
- ○Open fires, strokeable cats, hot toddies.
- ○Seeing Bob Dylan live, and realising that behind the myth and legend the *person* is even more mysterious.
- ○Seeing the clothes you couldn't bear to throw away come back into fashion.
- ○An electric blanket when it's freezing outside.
- ○The Sunday papers in bed with breakfast.
- ○Making a surprise visit to someone and finding they've been trying to get in touch with you all day.
- ○Guessing whodunnit.
- ○A cold lager after a long, hot day.
- ○Wimbledon fortnight.
- ○Cool, clean sheets.
- ○The smell and the sound of the sea.
- ○Meeting someone for the second time and finding they remember what you talked about at your first meeting six months ago.
- ○Not being recognised by an old-schoolfriend in the street because you've lost so much weight.
- ○Giving a dinner party where no one leaves until two in the morning.
- ○Getting a sun-tan over a weekend in Britain.

"Why are women such sluts?"

By Peter Lewis

To judge by magazines like this one, you might think that all problems between women and men arise from sex. They don't. They arise from gender, a more mysterious source. As an example of one of the overlooked gender problems in many a relationship, let me pose a stark male question: Why are women such sluts?

I write this sentence after clearing a space on what I thought was my desk between a pile of unpaid parking tickets and unclaimed cleaning tickets, hair slides, two cups of cold tea, a shoe, half a Munchie bar, a tennis ball and a jar full of pointless pencils and exhausted felt pens. None of them is mine.

Is "slut" the word I want? Looking up the dictionary—or rather having rescued the dictionary from the kitchen and cleaned the butter off it (crosswords should be forbidden at breakfast)—I find this definition: "Slut: slovenly woman, slattern, hussy; (joc) girl." I thought so. Sluts are exclusively female. If there is a word for a male slut I suppose it is a sloven—and how often do you hear anyone use that? Before this begins to sound smug, let me admit that slovenly, untidy men, who are no cleaner than they should be, do exist. But they make a different kind of mess. They are not true sluts.

For example, they don't leave make-up around in any of the six basic places for keeping make-up, other than the dressing table or the handbag: namely the bathroom shelf, the kitchen windowsill, the hall drawer, the car floor, beside the telephone and inside the typewriter. They tend to keep their shoes on their feet instead of in the bathroom, the car, on the hall seat, under the coffee table and, in extreme cases, in the fridge. This tells you something about gender: women like to keep things handy. Ask a woman why she left her shoes in unlikely places and she will probably explain: "Because my feet were hot." When her feet have recovered, she will have shoes available wherever she is. In the meantime, she just doesn't *see* them.

The law of women's and children's clothes is that tabs for hanging up their coats are always broken (which is why so many of them end up hanging on the handle of the Hoover). A similar law applies to the fasteners of handbags which burst open disgorging lipsticks, gap-toothed combs, false eyelashes, exhausted cheque books, cracked mirrors, foreign coins, old air tickets, and empty envelopes. Only women keep empty envelopes. Nearby there is a wastepaper basket. It will be empty too.

This brings us to the dressing table and its mysteries. One can understand the presence of twelve kinds of lipstick, four hairspray aerosols, two boxes of dried-up mascara and sundry deodorants. The artist has a right to her palette. But why the cups of dried-up coffee, the empty glasses that smell of something stronger, the used cotton wool balls like dead chicks, the grey paste composed of spilt cleansing milk, talcum powder and cigarette ash?

Deliberate ignorance comes to the aid of women where cars are concerned, and I speak as a man who has been asked "just to pick up" a car which turned out not only to be occupying a no-parking space but to be out of petrol and needing a wheel change. "It's making a funny noise and it smells of burning I wondered if it needed oil or water or something . . . Well, there was a clanking noise for a bit but it stopped. Oh, was that what it was . . . the exhaust fell off?"

Any man is familiar with this conversation, which demonstrates the different things cars mean to women and to men. To a man, a car is an extension of his mobility. To a woman it is a place to live in. Hence the bra, shoes, tights, jacket—enough for a quick change —in the bottom of it and on the back shelf. And have you ever seen a glove compartment with gloves in it? Of course not. The thing exists to hold make-up, Tampax, broken sunglasses, change, old apples and boxes of dead matches. The ash-trays are stuffed with wrappers, tissues and cherry stones. The ash is kept on the floor. The sunshield is pulled down permanently because of the mirror on the back of it. Women work on the run-it-till-it-melts basis with cars. Then they borrow mine. If you apply the same principal to houses they would let the chaos accumulate until it is waist high—then move. But this does not seem to happen. There comes a point beyond which selective blindness does not work. Even a slut from time to time decides enough is enough.

"We must get this place straight"—this means *you* must get it straight, while *she* sticks as much of it as possible in the nearest drawer. Why don't they throw their junk away? Or, if it isn't junk, why not put it in the *right* drawer? Here we approach the very nub of the difference between the genders.

Not all women are sluts. Of course I am prepared to admit it. There are exceptions. And there are men—even myself—who leave something to be desired in the way of orderliness. But we make a different kind of mess. A man making a cupboard or writing a book will leave the bits around, messing the place up. But that is Work in Progress. Mentally he has drawn a chalk-line round it, until he finishes or abandons it. Everything, to a woman, is Work In Progress. Nothing is ever over, done with, put-awayable. Suitcases are an especially poignant example. Never unpack completely—that is to admit that the trip is over and you are not currently expecting to go anywhere.

"*But I might want it again.*" This form of logic comes out in many ways. Ironing boards, for example. Put them away and it will be the very devil to get any more ironing done. You wonder why women are incapable of putting a record back in its sleeve? Because they might want to play it again, Sam. Their implication is that all this getting out and putting away is the mark of a phlegmatic, uncreative, inferior mind, unable to seize the inspiration of the moment.

"*But I know where everything is.*" This is a transparent lie. Every female exit is a desperate hunt for missing belts, umbrellas, keys, gloves, purses, watches, hairbrushes, safety pins or dark glasses. And when they can't be found in time, what is the solution? They take yours, my friend. Can you get through the dry season on less than three pairs of sun-glasses? Not if there is a woman around.

"*But I have a tidy mind*". In a curious sense of the word tidy, this is truc. Women do not seem to be distracted by surrounding chaos. It does not impair their concentration, paralyse their ability to act until order has been restored, or at least until the floor is visible again. Take the matter of telephone numbers. Perfectly good pad for writing them on by the telephone, but will women use such a thing? Scarcely. What are directory covers for? And if you ask what good are numbers scrawled on directories with no names attached, they will claim they know whose number it is when they see it.

Perhaps millennia of raising children amid constant interruption have made women proof against being distracted by things. Only people can distract women. And, of course, a ringing telephone . . . have you ever met a woman who can let a telephone ring because she is busy? But men are easily panicked by the thought *that things are against them.* They seek to master their environment, or at any rate knock it into some sort of temporary order. Women will play it as it lies. Chaos is their natural element. Besides, they can't see it.

PHOTOGRAPH BY ALEC MURRAY

Catch the spotlight wit[h]
Fantas[y]

This is the season when nothing succeeds excess. Forget that little black dress and the stage in an orgy of colour, improvising masses of chiffon and imagination. Take inspiration from Bakst, the brilliant desig who created sensational costumes for Diaghil Ballets Russes, and enjoy the fun and the fant

Skirt, £250, (incl blouse, no shown), Anna Beltrao. Matching swathe, sequinned fabric for top, from a selection at Liberty. Shoes, £57.50, Walter Steiger. Jewellery, Adrien Mann.
Opposite: dress over net petticoat, Emanuel. Shoes, £67.50, Charles Jourdan. Hat, £75, Alan Couldridge. Children's costumes, Emanuel. Ruff, £10.95, Strawberry Studio. Ballet shoes, (sprayed gold), £5.30, Dance Centre. Girl's hat, £3.50, Ally Capellino.
STOCKISTS ON PAGE 250.

Fashion

JILLIE MURPHY
OTOGRAPHS BY JAMES WEDGE

ir and turbans by
line at Clifford Stafford
ke-up by Linda Mason
Helena Rubinstein

DYNAMIC AND DEMANDING
the shape of jobs to come

Secretarial work could cease as a major job for girl school-leavers. But don't despair—in spite of increased mechanisation, the 'Eighties will also see an increase in technical, communications and personnel jobs. So grab your training now! Edward Fennell tells you how.

For all of us, as individuals and workers, the next decade will present a challenge. A challenge to move with the times, to note the trends and to flourish. It will be a decade of loud debate with only one thing undisputed: the 'Eighties must be a time of deep change in employment. The transition to an industry run by microprocessors will spark off a relay of developments whose tentacles will extend into every corner of our lives. Some people, already, are becoming pretty bored by the omnipresent electronic chip. That's understandable, but dangerous. To ignore the chip would lead, according to Colin Leicester of the Institute of Manpower Studies, to a future of "chaotic failure", a country stranded in the past. The alternative, he argues, is to embrace the inevitable, to become instead a "turbulent success". But that needs people with a "go and invent it" mentality who can develop and sell to the world a terrific range of fresh products and services.

And that's where the potential lies for a range of *new* jobs and careers. But it is, still, only a possibility. A lot of the decisions which will influence our future have yet to be taken. Most politicians and business managers are so preoccupied with present problems they find it difficult to take a long-term view. One fear is that, as usual, we will try to "muddle through". But muddle will not be enough. It is already clear that in the decade to come more and more people will be wanting to work. A recent report shows that during the 'Eighties an extra two million people will be looking for jobs. And it will be women, and married women in particular, who will cause the greatest impact. Increasing numbers of women are working, and continuing to work after marriage. By the end of the 'Eighties women will form a *majority* of the workforce—and the implications of that, socially, politically and occupationally, may be considerable.

But statistics like these only add to the questions. What about a few answers? Well, many jobs will change, especially in the service sector. Some jobs will disappear, but most of these will be the kind people don't really want anyway—the routine, the boring, the unskilled. And then there will be the new jobs. Demanding and dynamic, they will be in the sciences and technologies. If you are looking for growing opportunities, this is where you should turn your gaze.

To bring into action the new technology (which, frankly, in America is already the old technology), we shall need **electrical engineers, production engineers, mathematicians, physicists,** and **computer scientists.** Quite a formidable list! And these are all careers requiring high-powered skills, not the sort you can pick up in a term or two of evening classes. It means O-levels, A-levels and often a degree.

People with these qualifications are in short supply. Last year Roger Hilbourne, the development manager of one of the few British companies producing silicon chips, went head-hunting for six newly-qualified engineers. He ended up with two. Not because he pays badly or was too choosy, but simply because his firm, and all its rivals, were chasing the same small number of final-year students. The result now is that design and development staff are overworked, and the new knowledge is, quite simply, not being exploited rapidly enough.

In fact, demand for all these specialists will mushroom as microprocessors find more sophisticated applications. A new specialist will appear, the "microprocessor" or "programmer", who will combine the jobs of electrical engineer, systems analyst and computer programmer—a real scientific wiz! Undoubtedly there will be an increasing number of these élite technological jobs, and for those qualified to do them it will be a seller's market on an international scale. Roger Hilbourne's fear, in fact, is that his hard-won recruits will stay only a couple of years before being lured to the States where the shortage is almost as bad.

So engineers who work on computer hardware are becoming human gold-dust, a glittering attraction to talent-seeking employers. But the obsession with electronic gadgets should not obscure a more pressing need. Energy starvation stares at us from the fuel gauge, and if you're an oil diviner, then you're in business. To get fossil fuels out of the ground and into the economy we need **chemical** and **mining engineers,** as well as **mechanical** and **electrical engineers.** And as oil prices rise there is a strong chance that there will be new exploration in the tougher parts of the North Sea. That means **geologists** and **geophysicists** being dusted down and brought back into demand. And again there is a shortage of skills: according to Esso there is little chance of the company meeting its manpower need, particularly for petrochemical and chemical engineers. It is resigned to getting by, permanently short-staffed.

So what can be done to increase our education of engineers? The latest university figures show that applications for electrical and production engineering courses are consistently rising more than almost any other subject. And, interestingly, there was an eleven percent increase in university applications by women—three times more than by men.

The Engineering Industry Training Board is about to start giving fifty annual undergraduate bursaries, worth about £2,000, to women entering engineering degree courses. And this year, for the first time, there are 250 special grants for women entering training at the "technician level".

The National Advisory Council on Courses for Women feels that most women still have not grasped the impending changes in the employment field. Even when girls do take physics and maths at O-level and start on a technical career, they too often remain unwilling to take the professional training courses, which is a sure handicap to them later on. In future, just doing the job well won't

PHOTOGRAPH BY SACHA/TRANSWORLD

be enough—the employer will want to see paper qualifications—certificates, diplomas or, best of all, a degree. More and more women *must* take professional training courses, but it can be an uphill struggle, and the lack of ambition among young women is not the only problem. For employers need a new set of priorities for women as well. Last year, for example, the Chemical and Allied Products Industrial Training Board invited employers to apply for twelve grants for the sponsorship of women employees on postgraduate management courses. Only one of these was taken up—a clear case that more "affirmative action" is needed on the part of employers.

Increasingly, though, the 'Eighties will see more action to help women make up lost ground in education and training. Recent initiatives like the New Opportunities for Women and Wider Opportunities for Women courses point in the right direction, but each individual must still make her own struggle through the tangle of conditioning and prejudice to pick up what's on offer. This can mean a hard slog through O-level courses in tough subjects—maths and physics, for example, are the most important.

Designing and developing the new "high technology" will be the biggest expanding areas of new jobs in the 'Eighties. But once manufactured, who will operate it? There has been a famine of **computer programmers** and **systems analysts** from the start, and the boom in demand will go on. Some Sunday newspapers seem to devote whole supplements to advertisements for computer vacancies.

The government is convinced that still not enough people are being trained to keep pace with the introduction of computerised systems, so to plug that gap the Training Services Division has recently decided to spend £11 million over the next three years to pay for 9,000 computer training places. But even that won't be enough. By the mid-'Eighties industry and commerce are expected to take the scheme over so that it becomes a permanent feature. These courses have the advantage that you don't need to be a scientist to get on them, in fact it has been said that people with language ability make the best computer programmers—because it is a form of translation. So computers are not entirely the preserve of the mathematical genius—again O-level maths and English are a help, but above all else it needs "trainability"— that is, people who are capable of being taught and eager to learn.

Making and using hardware and software is where the biggest growth in jobs will be. The actual number depends on political and economic decisions about the speed of innovation. Automation will probably see the end of the more routine jobs in both factories and offices. According to Muriel Turner of the Association of Scientific, Technical and Managerial Staffs, women will face the greatest threat: "Despite equal rights legislation, most routine office work is done by women and they are very vulnerable. With thousands of office jobs advertised every day of the week they may find it hard to believe, but their jobs are going to be drastically reduced, and within a very short period of time. What is more; secretarial work could soon cease altogether as a major work-outlet for girl school-leavers."

Not everyone is as gloomy as this, however. Julian Smith, the banking manager of IBM thinks that although **secretaries** will see a change in their work, it will probably be for the better and they are still very much needed. Admittedly typing will gradually disappear, but few will mourn its passing and the **"personal assistant"** function will grow. In fact most managers will need a personal researcher of their own to tackle the vast volume of information available to them in their decision-making. The secretary will then become involved in sifting out this data—a pointer, in fact, to more, better qualified secretaries, trained in basic computer skills.

These changes will happen, probably, in the decade's second half. But, again, there is no clear prediction on the rate of change. Jonathan Slay of the Manpower Services Commission reckons that it will be slow: although the know-how is there, the cost and complexity of implementation means that the transition will be gradual, certainly nothing violent.

But the fact that substantial change has already arrived cannot be overlooked. Habitat, for example, now has automatic warehouses, and by installing a centralised computer linked to all its cash tills, has relieved staff of many tedious chores, like marking and remarking prices. The effect has been to change the nature of the **sales assistants'** work: they now spend more time advising, helping and informing the customer—assisting the sale, in fact. Staff numbers have remained the same and their responsibilities, in some respects, have grown. They have had to improve their knowledge of the merchandise and the knock-on effect of that is that more training is required, which means more teachers. Although Habitat has always had a strong training policy, it is only recently that a full-time training section has been established at their head office, and Chris Turner, Habitat's personnel chief, explains: "We don't just use our own trainers, we also bring in the Distribution Industry Training Board, who provide an excellent service." The DITB confirm that throughout the retail trade, the number and importance of **training jobs** is growing, and this will offer many opportunities to people who have a flair for teaching.

The experience of the distribution industry is only a reflection of a general trend. In a tough, competitive world, success is dependent on efficient, trained staff. Added to that is the disappearance (because of industrial relations legislation) of casual hire-and-fire policies. Even inefficient staff have got to be made more productive. In consequence, the whole field of **personnel management** and **industrial training** is set to grow throughout the 'Eighties.

Alastair Evans of the Institute of Personnel Management has witnessed the pattern emerging: "Increasing trade union legislation and the greater complexity of jobs inevitably leads to more people being involved in the personnel field. As computers take over some jobs, the growth areas are bound to be in human relations, management and decision-making. And the **managers** definitely need to be formally qualified. Certainly here at the Institute of Personnel Management we are aware of an increasing number of people who are coming forward to take the professional exams."

All of which means even greater opportunities for people with teaching ability, and those with a flair for handling people and running a department.

Logically, the best areas of advancement for non-scientists must be those where it is not possible for machines to function. People with problems won't get their solace from a telephone answering service: sympathy is still essentially human. But whether or not the **social services** expand together with related fields like nursing, youth work and counselling, depends on political decisions and for the moment it looks as if the emphasis will be on reduction rather than expansion.

Two decisions, taken recently which are clear markers towards the "careers escalators" are, first, that independent local radio is set to triple in size; and second, that the fourth TV channel (ITV 2) is now a certainty. Together these mean jobs and more jobs for **communicators.** According to James Conway of the Independent Broadcasting Authority, we can reckon on about 2,000 new jobs in independent local radio alone.

Presenters, producers and **journalists** as well as **technicians** will be needed. Some will transfer from existing stations and the BBC, but so great is the expansion that even outsiders will get a look in. And ITV 2 is to be based, in part, on an "open access" concept to allow small, independent producing companies to get air time; a deliberate attempt to open the field to newcomers.

Broadcasting is, in fact, one of the few definite winners in an area full of ambiguities. Journalism and advertising, for example, hang in the balance while the wrangle goes on in Fleet Street and elsewhere about the introduction of computerised type-setting. If it is introduced, a wide range of new publications are likely to appear on the book stands producing in their wake a multiplying number of jobs. Without it the number of jobs will stay the same and might even decrease.

So, standing back from this welter of trends and predictions, one is struck by the ambivalence of it all. Some skills will become more mechanised; others more humanised. And the more the corporate state takes over, the more some people will want to go off into a smaller, private world of individual enterprise and neighbourhood co-operatives.

While researching this article, I was told by one educated career woman: "It's all so frightening! I hope by 1990 I have a home and a baby and a man to look after me." How many other women will respond like that? Or will it be like a recent French advertisement for energy conservation: "Every time there is an energy crisis, we become more efficient. Every time there is an opportunity, we seize it"?

GET EQUIPPED FOR THE 'EIGHTIES

To prepare for the "jobs of the 'Eighties" you will need qualifications and training. Here is a summary of some of the most important requirements.

Careers for Professional Engineers, Scientists and Technologists

These are based on Degree courses at universities and polytechnics. To get in you will need five GCEs, two of which should be at A-level. These A-levels should be in: Mathematics and Physics for most Engineering subjects; Pure Maths and Applied Maths or Physics or Statistics for Mathematical subjects. Overall, Physics, Chemistry and a Mathematical subject is the best possible combination of subjects at A-level. It opens up a great variety of choice at Degree level, including Computer Sciences and Geology.

Insight 80 is a scheme for Professional Engineers approved by the Engineering Industry Training Board and run by various engineering firms such as Marconi. Girls aged 16-17 who are A-level candidates and interested in graduate level training go for a week to one of several universities throughout the country to see what is involved in becoming an engineer. Details from EITB, PO Box 176, 54 Clarendon Road, Watford, Herts WD1 1LB.

Careers for Technicians

GCE O-levels are normally required. Mathematics and Physics are the most important subjects, together with English Language.

Most careers

To get a sound foundation, try to get about five GCE O-levels including Mathematics, English, two Sciences (preferably Physics and Chemistry/Biology) and a literate or language subject (History, Geography, French, etc.). For computing there are in-company training and City and Guilds courses.

Some useful addresses

Women's Engineering Society, 25 Foubert's Place, London W1V 2AL.

Council of Engineering Institutions (for general information on professional engineering), 2 Little Smith Street, London SW1 3DL.

Engineering Careers Information Centre, 54 Clarendon Road, Watford, Herts WD1 1LB.

Technician Education Council (for advice on technician training), 76 Portland Place, London W1N 4AA.

National Computing Centre (for advice on computer training), Quay House, Quay Street, Manchester M3 3HU.

National Advisory Centre on Careers for Women, 251 Brompton Road, London SW3 2HB.

The following are pamphlets available free from the Department of Education and Science, Room 2-11, Elizabeth House, York Road, London SE1 7HP: *After O-Levels, On From A-Levels, Becoming An Engineer, Science At Work.*

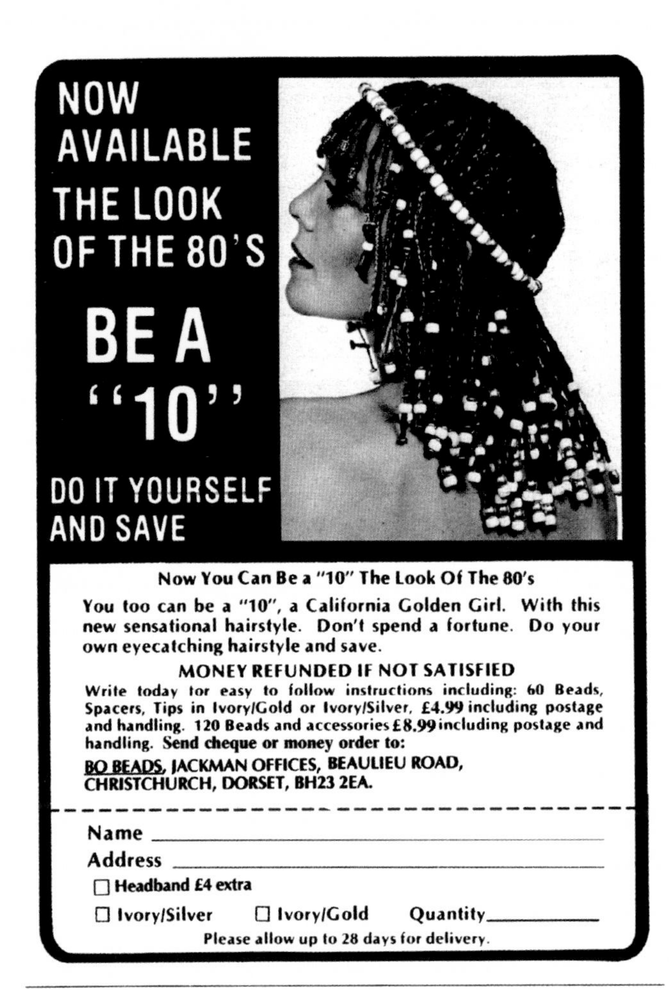
NOW AVAILABLE
THE LOOK OF THE 80'S
BE A "10"
DO IT YOURSELF AND SAVE
Now You Can Be a "10" The Look Of The 80's
You too can be a "10", a California Golden Girl. With this new sensational hairstyle. Don't spend a fortune. Do your own eyecatching hairstyle and save.
MONEY REFUNDED IF NOT SATISFIED
Write today for easy to follow instructions including: 60 Beads, Spacers, Tips in Ivory/Gold or Ivory/Silver, £4.99 including postage and handling. 120 Beads and accessories £8.99 including postage and handling. Send cheque or money order to:
BO BEADS, JACKMAN OFFICES, BEAULIEU ROAD, CHRISTCHURCH, DORSET, BH23 2EA.
Name
Address
Headband £4 extra
Ivory/Silver
Ivory/Gold
Quantity
Please allow up to 28 days for delivery.

Now a Full-Size UVA Sunbed
for only £399 inc VAT, plus £12 delivery
Until the present, most sunbeds have carried jet-set price tags. Now Alpha, after careful research, offer a superb, solid pine sunbed giving the home-owner everything required at a volume-production price. Like Ford's famous Model T, the Alpha Caribbean comes in just one form—at one unbeatable price.
*Providing your skin tans with normal sunlight
The Caribbean measures a full 7'3" and, with nine 6' Wotan tubes, has greater capacity than any other single bed available at this price and to buy a comparable bed elsewhere you might expect to pay up to 40% more. Get tanning fast* and safely with Alpha—at a price you can afford. Small additional delivery charge for Northern Ireland and UK islands.
For full details of how to enjoy exotic, year-round tanning simply complete the coupon.
Alpha Health & Beauty
Dept. 82, 87 Fore Street
St. Marychurch, Torquay TQ1 4PZ
Telephone (0803) 33800
(Personal callers welcome)
Alpha
NAME
ADDRESS

Introducing the sensational NEW
SAUNA SUIT
Everyone will want to benefit from the amazing NEW suit that creates its own SAUNA ATMOSPHERE when you do your EXERCISES
ONLY £7.95
GREAT NEW WAY TO HELP SHAPE UP. Here's an exciting new design in exercise suits - it's based on a method that sportsmen have developed over the years - many footballers and athletes have discovered the amazing benefits of using this type of suit whilst training. They found that this speeds the build up of heat and causes strong perspiration, whilst you exercise - NOW a figure culture expert has taken this method and designed the complete SAUNA SUIT - as our illustration shows the suit has airtight cuffs and neckband and is made of soft, pliable, waterproof fabric (which will keep in and build up the heat around your body, waist, thighs, arms and legs). If you're on a training course wear the sauna suit and see the difference - girls can wear it while they do the housework or other exercise - men whilst they do the gardening, wash the car or do other physical work or exercise. SIMPLE, COMFORTABLE AND SUPER EFFECTIVE.
TEST IT AT HOME ON OUR 12 MONTH 'NO RISK' GUARANTEE.
We invite you to test the SAUNA SUIT in the privacy of your own home, wear it around the house - try a little jogging or skipping - within seconds you'll start to feel the temperature rise inside the suit - you'll experience the pleasant sensation of a SAUNA around the body.
If you are not completely satisfied with this super SAUNA SUIT you may return it to us for a full cash refund. We Know you'll be delighted but should you wish to return it for any reason it may be machine washed first - it's easy to wash and dry. Universal size. Fits anyone.
CRAVEN HOUSE (DEPT. CM03SU),
22, CHURCH STREET, GODALMING, SURREY, GU7 1JD.
AIR TIGHT NECK BAND
BODY HEAT BUILDS UP AND CIRCULATES
AIR TIGHT BAND
AIR TIGHT WRIST BANDS
AIR TIGHT ANKLE BANDS
POST TODAY FOR YOUR SAUNA SUIT
CRAVEN HOUSE (DEPT. CM03SU).
22, CHURCH STREET, GODALMING, SURREY, GU7 1JD.
Yes, I want to experience all the benefits of a sauna suit.
Please send me .... Sauna Suits at the low price of only £7.95 each plus 75p post and packing. If I am not delighted in every way I may return them anytime within 1 year for a full and prompt refund of the purchase price.
I enclose cash/cheque/postal order value .... made payable to 'Craven House'. Access or Visa welcome.
Card No
Signature
NAME
ADDRESS
Phone your Credit Card order on Teledata 01 200 0200 ANYTIME!
Please allow 14 to 21 days delivery

FEBRUARY OFFER

Stretch a leg

long lean trousers only £15.50

For the longest, leanest look of all—leg it from morning to night in high sheen stretch fabric pants. Made of 94 percent nylon and 6 percent Lycra, they'll stretch as much as you do, and spring right back into shape. They come in red, blue and black, in sizes 8-16. The length is 84 cm (33 ins) but we left the hems unfinished so you can turn them up to suit.

PHOTOGRAPH BY NEIL KIRK
Hair by Steve at Schumi
Make-up by Patti Burris
Red top by Secret Ingredient
Blue top by Quorum
Red shoes and black shoes by Midas
Belt by Trimfit

HOW TO ORDER: Fill in the coupons below with your name and full postal address in BLOCK LETTERS and send with a crossed cheque or postal order (name and address on the back, please) made payable to The National Magazine Company Limited. Please allow four weeks for delivery. If demand is exceptional there may be a further unavoidable delay. This offer is only available to readers in the UK, and closes 30th April 1980, or until stocks are exhausted. Any queries to *Cosmopolitan* Offers Dept. please. If you are not completely satisfied, please return within 14 days, with a covering letter, and your money will be refunded in full.

COSMOPOLITAN STRETCH TROUSERS OFFER COUPON
Send to: Cosmopolitan Stretch Trousers Offer,
Belton Road, Loughborough, Leicestershire, LE11 0XL.

Sizes:	8	10	12	14	16
waist: cms	56	61	66	71	76
(ins)	(22)	(24)	(26)	(28)	(30)

unfinished inside leg length: 84 cm (33 ins)
Colours: Red, Black, Blue
Price: £15.50
I enclose cheque/PO value ....

Number required	Size	Colour 1st choice	*Colour 2nd choice

*Alternative colour choice will be sent only if 1st choice is not available.

NAME
ADDRESS

COMPLETE BOTH COUPONS TO ORDER

NAME
ADDRESS

If undelivered please return to Cosmopolitan Offer,
Belton Road, Loughborough, Leicestershire, LE11 0XL.

CUT ALONG DOTTED LINE

CUT-PRICE LIVING

Bold Brushwork

Enough of tasteful restraint—excess costs less and looks more! See what a little imagination, a few pots of paint and some colour non-sense can do for the most ordinary whitewood furniture. Whether you think in glorious technicolour or black and white, think extreme: take brush and courage in hand, enjoy breaking the rules . . . and let art take its place in your home. By Dinah Hall. Photographs by John Carter.

Main pic, left. Pay homage to Kandinsky on a self-assembly (no, it doesn't need a man, just a hammer and screwdriver) ottoman chest, £13.75 and storage unit, £34.75. Prime the wood first and apply two coats of paint—we used Dulux Matchmaker Silthane Silk. Geometric designs don't require a steady hand—mark shapes with masking tape, paint area, and when dry remove tape. Pine chair with painted shadows, £8.95.

Main pic, above. Asymmetrical black and white blocks give drama to the combination wardrobe, £29.95, and chest of drawers, £25.50. Rocking chair, painted half and half, £12.95.
1 *Painted legs take the rustic out of pine stools, £12.95 for two, and table, £23.95.*
2 *Clash coloured spotlights, £9.50, London Lighting, with curly cable, £3.95, Spectrum.*
3 *Mix and mis-match plastic and paper tableware from Habitat and Paperchase.*
4 *Too lazy to do-it-yourself? Black and white mesh chairs, £45.00 for four, Habitat.*
5 *Pristine white china and tray, Habitat.*
6 *Star in your bathroom—black and white Teti lights, London Lighting, on Pilkington tiles.*

ALL WOODEN FURNITURE FROM MFI STORES.

WHO'S SEXY NOW?

A sexy man will make you catch your breath, go weak at the knees, spill your drink and drop your ashes. More than a perfect physique, less than a defiant expression, sexiness is an energy transmitted through such fragile processes as a look or a thought. Some of these men could already be under your skin—some of them are about to be.

By Genevieve Cooper

Jack Galloway was the rogue who strayed in the TV series, *Mackenzie.* A Scotsman, he possesses that unfiltered sexiness unique to men of the North. After Connery, Finney, Conti—it's Galloway.

The classically sexy man—Richard Gere. Sexual awareness is in his eyes, his walk, his clothes. His attitude assumes you'll want him, his manner presumes you'll make the first move. A totally involving presence.

Sting of the group, Police. A cool hero, the type who collects adulation like rich men gather mistresses. His looks would be fashionable in any century, but his character belongs to today's laid-back liberated times. Combines gentle intellect with strong resolve; you could trust him not to exploit your adoration. In *Quadrophenia* he proved he could act as well as sing—somehow one feels that anything he attempted would be unquestionably successful.

Mick Jagger, audacious on stage and unpredictable everywhere. The preening, the prancing, the magnified mouth, the minimal hips almost parody the idea of sexiness. Now wears that expression of ennui born of excess. But still stylish. Still sexy.

Jack Nicholson: forever sexy for every reason—not least his fascinatingly flat voice and amused satanic eyebrows. Soon to be seen ravishing his co-star in the lusty *The Postman Always Rings Twice*. A vicarious thrill from Jack is better than no thrill at all.

Nick Mancuso (above left) married the heiress in TV's *Scruples* and left the rest of us bereft. A master of the penetrating, meaningful gaze that sees in past your eyes and on, down and out through your toes.

When Denis Lawson (above right) is on stage in Pal Joey*—at the Albery Theatre—you hardly notice anyone else. Commanding, charismatic and talented, Mr Lawson has power, an irresistible force.*

ROLLERMANIA

The squeals-on-wheels trend called roller disco attracts the most fanatical and famous of followers. Paula Yates is our voyeuse on the London scene and Larry Eisenberg whizzes at The Roxy in New York.

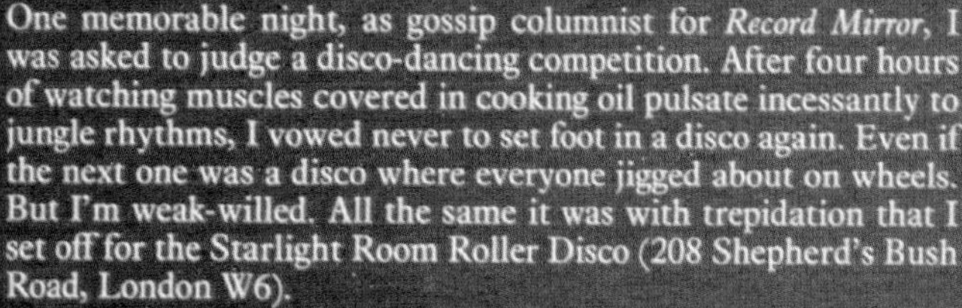

LONDON

One memorable night, as gossip columnist for *Record Mirror*, I was asked to judge a disco-dancing competition. After four hours of watching muscles covered in cooking oil pulsate incessantly to jungle rhythms, I vowed never to set foot in a disco again. Even if the next one was a disco where everyone jigged about on wheels. But I'm weak-willed. All the same it was with trepidation that I set off for the Starlight Room Roller Disco (208 Shepherd's Bush Road, London W6).

With a name like the Starlight Room I thought it would look like the penthouse flat around which Gloria Vanderbilt heaves herself in the jeans commercial. It doesn't. It's like a very large barn with a nice floor and thousands of black boys skating around agilely at seventy miles an hour—a scene from *Mandingo* meets *Rollerball*.

You can tell the beginners—they're the ones rolling uncontrollably forwards, flapping their arms and grimacing as they skid downhill towards the dance floor. Luckily there are little handrails around the walls for them to clutch on to. If they miss them, they just pray they'll hit a chair and come to a halt. Also it isn't trendy. My friend had made an effort to look disco-fied, wearing what seemed like a melted black Durex and black cowboy boots. She was more than a trifle out of place.

The ladies were very game: one of them gliding around the floor, a leg delicately poised in mid-air (I'm not sure that was deliberate). Another was being dragged by the arms by a seven-foot-tall sixteen-year-old, determined she'd get her balance come hell or high water. Meanwhile the music pounded on, blending perfectly with the scratch and swish of hurtling bodies on wheels. These places are not discos as such; you don't go to be seen, or pulled, or to drink or wear glamorous clothes or even to dance; you simply go to skate and get plenty of exercise. The atmosphere is more like the local youth club than a steaming emporium of hotter-things-to-come-if-you're-lucky.

The atmosphere is very friendly and if you want to learn, people are more than willing to help you get into the flow of

NEW YORK

The Roxy is the poshest rink in New York if not the world. Born in December 1979 in the shell of a warehouse, it is the inspiration of rock entrepreneur, Bill Graham and financial whiz, Steven Greenberg. New York always needs one place that is tough to get into and when Studio 54 collapsed, The Roxy inherited all those crowds hungry for fun and/or rejection.

The Roxy is more than a rink, it's a way of life. Outside, in cement, are footprints of famous skaters. Inside, there are lights that blink, run and jump from every angle, a New York skyline in silver, a VIP lounge, a tiny rink off to the back that insiders call "the kiddy pool", a snack bar that serves French pastries and Perrier and a maple hardwood floor that cost £50,000. It has dash, flash and style. And the jazziest patrons in the world.

"I love eet! I love eet! I love eet!" shrieks Bianca Jagger as she whizzes by, somewhat unsteadily, on the arm of Andy Warhol. On the last "eet!" she roars past a kid skating down the lane—Brooke Shields. Richard Gere, hunched over the rail in zip jacket, is watching it all.

Outside, as papparazzi blind the night, limousines the size of houses disgorge celebrities. Halston strides in majestically, laces on his skates and waves to Bianca and Andy as they zip by. "You get a similar crowd to the one that used to go to Studio 54," says Richard Newhouse, The Roxy's manager. "But you won't get all of them. Chic people don't want to do anything that makes them look foolish." On a skating rink, everybody can see immediately if you're no good.

I put on my hired skates and instantly discover ten things I like about roller skating:

1) With your skates on you're three inches taller.

2-10) When you're three inches taller, everything in life is better.

I step out, a bit unsteadily, not having skated since I was a kid. The wheels were slower then. Now they're urethane like those on a skateboard, contributing, experts say, to the popularity of the sport. Here I go in a wide sweep. Well, I didn't fall. Amazing. Now I'm coasting around and getting into the rhythm of the

MAIN PHOTOGRAPH AND TOP LEFT BY STU RESNICK (EQUIPMENT FROM ALPINE SPORTS); PHOTOGRAPH, TOP RIGHT, BY JACQUES AND DOMINIQUE SILBERSTEIN.

Main picture: heaven is a deserted rink at Picketts Lock, London. Facing page: (left) even the protective clothing looks bright and fun; (right) glamour and the New York skyline at The Roxy. This page: (top) singer Cher was one of the first stars to put roller disco on the map and she continues to shine at it; (above) Linda Blair, child star of *The Exorcist*, in a roller dancing competition.

PHOTOGRAPHS OF CHER BONO AND LINDA BLAIR FROM REX FEATURES.

LONDON

traffic. There are slow songs for beginners and then fast ones for the regulars. A boy is likely to come over and gracefully kick your boot mumbling, "Wanna skate babe?" and then if you do, he will probably take off at full speed leaving you shuffling around the well-worn edge of the rink. The next time you see him, he'll just be a flash of teeth. A few committed couples spent the evening circling each other constantly and dizzily until the young ladies drunkenly collapsed on to the boards, pretending to adjust their padding. Most people are content to whiz along, fighting the G forces. Occasionally, one of the chains of people collapses and everyone slides towards the walls at high speed. Like the Grand National, if you fall at the first fence, everyone then jumps on your head.

I spoke to two young ladies dressed up as Pocahontas and Minnehaha. According to them, "It's incredible exercise, we've all lost some weight and firmed our legs up." I mentioned that I'd been watching John Curry ice-skating that afternoon and he had quite a large behind, but they told me, "Well, that's great if you fall on it a lot!" (Having just compiled a book on *Rock Stars In Their Underpants*, Virgin £4.95, I've tuned in to bottom watching).

They thought that if you decided to come each week you'd need your own boots and also protective bands, so you didn't leave looking as if you'd been in the scrum. You can buy all that sort of thing in bright colours at any roller-skate shop. A couple of really pessimistic types even had little yellow crash helmets. I then asked a young man who had been travelling at breath-taking speed for a few tips on how a beginner can get going. "The most important part of a beginner's body is the hips. Thrust them out, back and then to the sides. Not too far or you'll fall over. If your weight is on the left skate, push your left hip out. Keep your arms fairly close to your body to start off with," he said, "and if you go with a friend and he falls, don't stop and pick him up, or you'll cause a pile-up and might get hurt." A few people do get sprains and things—I saw one young man with a roller-skate on one foot and a plaster cast on the other. I almost expected to see chair castors on that foot! The Starlight is open seven days a week from 2 p.m. until 6.30 p.m. and then from 8 p.m. until 12.30 a.m. If you'd like to take your kids, then go to the afternoon sessions. On Tuesday evenings there are teaching sessions and Wednesdays are for beginners. It costs £2.50 to get in at night and £1.00 to rent skates.

If you enjoy getting embalmed with Chanel or entrancing men with the swish of ostrich feathers, the local roller-disco isn't for you. However it *is* a great place for a casual evening of exercise to music and if you're determined, maybe you could just sew a couple of feathers on your track-suit.

NEW YORK

song. I've lost awareness of my feet. I'm floating on my own cloud. As are the skaters around me. They look as though a summons went out to all the gorgeous of the world. They are in jumpsuits and swimsuits; black ties and black eyes; red leopard leotards and cowboy hats; lots of parachute material. There's one in a Scarlett O'Hara gown, pulling the stole over her face. Show-off. And there's another one in iridescent sequins. And a man with white silk pants, lights on his skates and a T-shirt reading "Try Me". A chimpanzee—not a person in costume, but a real chimpanzee—rolls past and nobody seems fazed. Mick Jagger stares at the action then slinks out (he returns later for a lesson).

A display of flash bulbs almost erases Caroline Kennedy and boyfriend Tom Carney. After several hundred thousand pictures, Caroline's smile begins to droop. She rolls her right skate impatiently and, with a last burst of good cheer, says, "I just wanted to skate," then grabs Carney's arm and heads out on to the rink where photographers won't follow.

There's a lot of commotion now. Lee Marvin, as recognisable as Mount Rushmore, is on the floor with his wife. Lee, who hadn't skated since childhood, is amazed at how easily it's come back to him. He is laughing and shaking his head. "You know what's great about this?" he says, "Everybody looks beautiful. They're all sexy without being dirty."

People rush over to say hello, because at a skating rink talking to a film star—assuming there's one around—is as easy as asking somebody for directions on a motorway. People are shouting "How ya doin'?" to strangers. Another thing: many people are kissing. Roller-skating has revived that lost art—not that social cop-out of a peck in mid-air, but kissing and hugging, because people are glad to see each other and even gladder to be alive.

I have now been skating eighteen times. I have skated side by side with Cher. I have seen Justin Henry (the *Kramer Versus Kramer* kid), celebrate his ninth birthday on wheels with a party at the Roxy. I've observed Olympic ice-skater Eric Heiden put on his first pair of roller skates. I have watched the distinguished of New York's theatre give out awards at the Roxy, following which they all put on their skates and got rolling. I've watched the look of fear in Dustin Hoffman's eyes give way to one of confidence from skate-day one to skate-day four.

I suggest you try it. I don't know what skating will do for you, but here is what it's done for me: I've gained a control over my body that I never thought possible; I've lost nearly two stone—not from skating alone, but skating has made me more aware of how I look as compared with all the other gorgeous people doing it; and every time I feel down, I put on my skates and, in minutes, I feel as if I could pull King Kong off the Empire State.

Skates: Precision bearings, urethane wheels and leather boots are best, but, providing you go to a reputable dealer (not a small shoe shop), you will find adequate cheaper skates. Basic, £25-£40 (Beadle, Hamaco, Variflex); £45-£60, more comfortable, flashier, longer lasting (Hamaco, Axel, Surgrip, Gioca); £65 upwards, high fashion, custom-painted boots (Surgrip, Axel, Snyder). Good places to buy would be: North Side Truckin, 415 Holloway Road, N7; Alpine Sports, 158 Notting Hill Gate, W11; The Natural Shoe Store, 325 King's Road, SW3; Roll Rider, 94 New Bond Street, W1; Roxy Rollers, 42 Beaconsfield Road, Brighton. (See *The Ardent Shopper*, page 121, for more roller-wear ideas.)

Places: Roller rinks are considered to be an easy source of revenue and come and go overnight. Sports centres often have roller skating facilities so check locally. For further information, including a list of roller figure and dance clubs throughout the country, contact The National Skating Association, 117 Charterhouse Street, London EC1 (Tel: 01-253 3824).

London rinks: check opening hours and hire facilities.

- The Starlight Roller Disco, 208 Shepherd's Bush Road, W6 (Tel: 01-603 2901).
- The Cornet Roller Boogie Palace, 49 Lavender Gdns, SW11 (Tel: 01-228 3744).
- Jubilee Hall Recreation Centre, Central Market Square, Covent Garden, WC2 (Tel: 01-836 2799).
- Picketts Lock Sports Centre, Picketts Lock Lane, N9 (Tel: 01-803 4756).
- Finsbury Leisure Centre, Norman Street, EC1 (Tel: 01-253 4490).
- Greenwich Baths, Trafalgar Rd, SE10 (Tel: 01-858 0159).
- Harrow Leisure Centre, Christchurch Ave, Wealdstone, Harrow (Tel: 01-863 9580).
- The Electric Ballroom, 184 Camden High Street, NW1 (Tel: 01-485 9006).
- George Sylvester Sports Centre, Wilton Way, E8 (Tel: 01-985 2105).

Nikki Henriques

WHY THREE CLEVER GIRLS CHOSE OLYMPIA ELECTRONIC TYPEWRITERS

Josephine Kingly is a senior secretary to the head of an advertising agency, so when it comes to correspondence, appearance matters. And that's one of the main reasons why she asked her boss to buy an electronic Olympia ES typewriter for the office.

"It produces such beautifully clean copy," she says enthusiastically. "And it does everything a normal, electric typewriter does, but has such fantastic extras. For instance, it will remember the last line of characters I have typed and wipe them out automatically if I have made a mistake. That means goodbye to messy erasing fluid or rubbers. And my fingers need never leave the keys because all functions, including the tab key, are conveniently laid out at the front."

In a smart office, where people bustle in and out to discuss private business, peace and quiet is essential. And Josephine's boss is particularly pleased that the ES is so silent. Switch on and there is no motor noise; only a neon indicator lamp lets you know that the machine is working, and when you're typing, it's almost silent.

One look inside the machine and the real design advantages are blindingly clear. There are only six assemblies—which means fewer moving parts, therefore less to go wrong. And in the rare event of a break-down, it only takes fifteen minutes to reassemble. Says Josephine, "My work has never been better."

Fran Leboyer is a personal assistant in the drama department of a regional television station. Every day brings new problems and excitement. "I love the work, but I'm also glad I've got the new Olympia ES110 to make my life easier," she smiles. "It closes the gap between typewriters and text-processors. But if that sounds frightening, let me say right away—it's very simple to operate. I didn't have any special training, yet I'm able to type and store for the future up to 8,000 characters altogether, which amounts to around four pages of A4 text. You can imagine how useful that is when I'm given a report or script to type and have to hand it back to the author for corrections. He or she can then correct or delete words or paragraphs and return the manuscript to me for minimal re-typing."

The ES110, like its sister, the ES105, automatically deletes, underscores, corrects, repeats, indents, double spaces and so on. And it can type either ten, twelve or fifteen characters to the inch, and also has proportional spacing—which helps when filling in forms.

"One of the super things about the ES110," adds Fran, "is its ability to centre text and justify right-hand margins automatically. When I'm typing out stage directions and dialogue, it's important for these to be absolutely clear and identifiable. I haven't had a complaint from an actor yet!"

Lynne Low is a powerful woman. As secretary to a solicitor in the City, she has the ear of many a Top Person; financial scandals often reach her before they touch the gossip columns. But Lynne is too busy for tittle tattle. "The sheer volume of work is huge. Lengthy reports, legal documents, contracts, complex forms and records all have to be filed by me—and be quickly accessible. Fortunately my Olympia Memory Typewriter (the TP6020) takes a load off my mind.

"It has a combined display and print unit so is very compact; and it has unlimited storage because, besides its internal working memory, it stores information on mini disc, each of which can take up to 70,000 characters. You can have as many mini discs as you want, and keep them almost indefinitely. As you have probably guessed, the 6020 is also a text-processor and, besides all its typewriting functions, it has a visual display unit of twenty characters which means I can spot any errors and amend them before going ahead with printing."

Lynne is especially pleased with the automatic phrase and format capability—which means that the machine can store, say, legal precedents on disc and, at the press of a button, recall them when required for a letter or report.

Lynne's employer is an active writer, too. So when she is typing up his latest manuscript, she uses the 6020's "global search" ability. In other words, if she spells a name wrongly, she can delete then substitute the correct word throughout the manuscript.

Lynne took Olympia's free two-day training course in order to learn how to make the most of the TP 6020. "It was time very well spent," she confirms.

WHO'S AFRAID OF WORD PROCESSING?

Don't let anyone kid you that you couldn't use a word processor. If you can work an electric type-writer, you can use its big sister. A word processor is just a type-writer but large—and more capable. Here we answer some of your most frequently asked questions.

Olympia TP6020

What does a word processor do?

It will type your everyday correspondence, like letters, reports and so on—and store them for future reference. It will then, if you ask it nicely, type them out again as many times as you want, sending every person a perfect copy. You've probably already received many seemingly personal letters from large mail order houses or credit card companies. Do not be misled. You are not on their VIP list necessarily—you are just in their micro-processor!

How could it improve my work?

By speeding up the rate at which you can deal with boring, repetitive work—like organising mailing lists, or re-typing long documents for the sake of only one mistake. As a result, you are free to put your mind to more important matters—like sending a memo to your boss recommending yourself for promotion, perhaps!

What does a word processor look like?

Depending on which model you choose, you can expect to sit before a regular keyboard which has many extra functions. For example, it has special keys which you press to store or recall text, delete or insert, merge text and addresses and so on.

The greatest single achievement for the typist is that re-typing becomes a thing of the past. The ability to make alterations by deleting or inserting is taken care of by the machine and when the final copy has been achieved it will be printed out automatically.

With a sophisticated machine, you can expect to have a storage unit—a box which either sits on your desk or hangs under it, storing easily accessible magnetic media. Many thousands of characters can be stored and are instantly accessible.

The printing unit—either golf ball or type reel—will print directly from your keyboard or from the memory.

How could a word processor help my company?

In many practical ways. Take the recent case of a medium-sized company which has been in the holiday tour business for thirty years. The Managing Director ordered an Olympia Text Processor because she needed to speed up work flow, and wanted equipment that could be installed without any major adjustment to staff or office layout.

She is delighted with the results. Each customer now receives personal and original letters which are absolutely correct, grammatically and in every other way. (This is important when a client is foreign, with a very complicated name!)

Second, it has improved the company's image dramatically. Customers are now given personal travel schedules and tour information, plus a personal follow-up letter after their holiday, asking for any comments about their trip. All of which reflects the professionalism of the company, and breeds confidence all round.

Third, the Olympia machine now produces the company's booking forecasts which give the M.D. an accurate and immediate analysis of her business. In the old days this took hours—now it takes minutes.

Whether, your company is large or small, handles products or people, mailing lists or manuscripts, there's a word processor to fit the bill.

Sexist chat to avoid...

Do you operate a double standard when assessing people? Would you describe a man as "angry" and a woman as "neurotic" for similar behaviour? Here Paul Keers lists some eye-opening sexist verbal traps to sidestep.

At home

He keeps himself in good shape . . . She is a health freak.
He is a modern househusband . . .She is unliberated.
He cooked a fabulous Indian meal . . .She just cooked dinner.
He's got a healthy appetite . . .She's greedy.
He looks casual . . . She looks a mess.
He's a good conversationalist . . . She uses too many long words.
He is persistent . . . She nags.
He is hen-pecked . . . She knows her place.
He drives well . . . She drives too fast.
He is honest about others' shortcomings . . . She bitches.
He treasures mementoes . . . She hoards junk.
He is sociable . . . She flirts.
He is with-it . . . She is just a trendy.
He is in with the in-crowd . . . She is a hanger-on.
He is the life and soul of the party . . . She makes a fool of herself.

Emotional

He has old flames . . . She has ex-lovers.
He is a confirmed bachelor . . . She sleeps around.
He really has a way with women . . . She is a tart.
He has had a hard day . . . She is frigid.
He appreciates attractive women . . . She fancies other men.
He has been drinking a lot of beer . . . She has got cystitis.
He is a shoulder to cry on . . . She has hordes of whining friends.
He has concerned, intimate conversations . . . She gossips.
He is frank . . . She is unsubtle.
He has an open marriage . . . She does the dirty on him.
He lets his emotions show . . . She is crying again.
He is honest about his sex life . . . She washes her linen in public.

Financial

He is managing his finances . . . She is pennypinching.
He is bargain-hunting . . . She is wasting money at the sales.
He invests in gold . . . She buys more expensive jewellery.
He values a good tailor . . . She only buys for the label.

At work

He shows driving ambition . . . She is pushy.
He's discriminating . . . She's fussy.
He is having a bad time at work . . . She is having a breakdown.
He is under a lot of pressure . . . She can't cope.
He is outspoken . . . She swears like a lorry driver.
He is intelligent . . . She is a bighead.
He is well-groomed . . . She is tarted up to the eyeballs.
He is a personal assistant . . . She is a secretary.
He doesn't just accept things . . . She asks too many questions.

PHOTOGRAPH BY HOWARD ZAGER

Glamour at A. Price!

Antony Price (above), show-biz couturier to the stars, designs glamorous clothes for people who value their public image. Here, he talks to Paula Yates about the thinking behind his designs *plus* Cosmopolitan offers you an exclusive Antony Price dress to make.

FASHION BY JILLIE MURPHY
PHOTOGRAPHS BY NEIL KIRK
HAIR BY GREGOR AT SCHUMI

Antony Price's clothes are irresistible. Once you've tried them on and touched them you might as well resign yourself to living on carrots for the next three months. The minute you slink out of Antony's mirrored dressing room into his lilac salon at 341 King's Rd, London SW3, you know this is *it.* And slink you will, because in his clothes you've little alternative—unless you want to fall flat on your face.

Above: Jerry Hall wears a bronze lamé figure-moulded sheath dress and earrings, by Antony Price. Leather mules, £36.50, by Claudio Rocco at Ivory. Men: each man wears a black worsted suit with a 'Sixties lean cut, £250, white Italian cotton shirt, £45, and black grosgrain tie, £20, by Antony Price. Leather shoes, £99.50, by Rayne.

Right: an exclusive Antony Price dress for you to make—the star quality is in the design so you don't have to pick expensive materials. We used a silky, movable fabric: polyester crêpe de Chine; make-up price, approx £6. Brass foil earrings, £4.60, matching armlet, £9, by Corrine Edwards. Men: as above except bow-tie, £20.

For that Oscar-winning look, show off your figure in these tight-waisted, glamorous dresses that move as you do.

Honda Caren Deluxe £339
inc. Manufacturer's del. charge, special m/cycle tax, V.A.T. and 12 months unlimited mileage warranty.

Every morning's the same.

The alarm goes off like a starting gun. The rat race is on and you're behind already.

You throw back the bed clothes and pray you can do the same to a coffee. You pelt to the bus stop to miss the convoy of six by ten yards.

You catch your breath, but nothing else.

You do a Sebastian Coe to the rail station and hear that there are leaves on the line so the train's cancelled. You pile on when it decides to show up, but there are no seats, so all of a sudden, you're a sardine. Only it's a smoker so you end up a kipper. If only someone had told you about the Honda Caren sooner.

The Honda Caren is an ideal commuter bike. It's easy to ride (if you can press the electric starter button, you'll be an expert), it's spotlessly clean and you don't need a degree in Mechanical Engineering to master it (a full or provisional car licence will do).

What's more it's cheap.

Even allowing for its price, the tax and insurance, a 120 mpg* Caren works out at about 4p a mile* to run. Best of all, it frees you from the hour of hell each day. See your local Honda dealer this weekend. And, come Monday, join the human race and leave the rats to their own.

*Source: Which Bike.

Believe in freedom. Believe in HONDA

CUT-PRICE CHIC

Street Sheets!

Wake up to the new shapes for summer. Look no further than your bedroom for inspiration. Susan Spencer, a fashion student at Newcastle Polytechnic, designed these stunning, ritzy outfits for you to make from a pair of sheets. Hot tangerine is the colour, and for a really devastating effect, stick to strictly black accessories. Make the most of your sheets and stay streets ahead!

FASHION BY
JULIA FLETCHER
PHOTOGRAPHS BY
TONY McGEE
Hair, Nicky at John Frieda
Make-up, Cheryl

(as hatband), satin ribbon (as sash), John Lewis; shoes, £39.99, Pinet. See page 209 for stockists.

Left: to make the loose shirt and elasticated, ankle-length trousers with tie bottoms, all you need is one white, flat, single size, 100% cotton sheet, 70 ins wide by 100 ins long. We used a white sheet by Allander at Dickins & Jones, £10.95 per pair. The sheet was dyed with Dylon cold water dye, colour Mandarin, and Dylon Colour Fix, 59p each per tin. Necklace and earrings made from jewellery components from a selection at The Warehouse.

Above: loose shirt is the same as pictured left. To make frilly rumba skirt, use second sheet from the pair (there will be some fabric left over) and dye as before. Necklace and earrings as left.

PAULA YATES INVESTIGATES BRITAIN'S MOST GLAMOROUS STEP-GRANNY . . .

IN THE ROYAL PINK

The princess of punk weighs up the queen of romance

A feminist's nightmare, romantic novelist Barbara Cartland comes out with statements like: "Men have superior strength and, in most cases, superior intelligence . . ." Yet Paula Yates is an ardent fan.

There are several problems inherent in having afternoon tea with Barbara Cartland. If I was warned once I was warned about fifteen times by various friends who'd already lived to tell the tale. At all times you have to remember to sit up straight, not swear, speak clearly, look extraordinarily clean and not smoke. The latter rule apparently caused Lord Snowdon such distress when he went to photograph the great lady that every time she left the room, he could be found hovering in the fireplace puffing up the chimney.

As a great fan of Miss Cartland I followed all these bits of advice as if my life depended on it. When I got into her Rolls at the station, my face was so clean I felt as if I'd massaged it with Vim. The house itself looks very like Buckingham Palace, if you can stretch your imagination to encompass Buckingham Palace with bright turquoise paintwork and the occasional Tyrolean-style shutter for good measure. As I spotted Miss Cartland sweeping across several acres of drawing room, the chauffeur warned me not to touch TwiTwi the dog in case he removed my hand.

Truly it was love at first sight. She was wearing Cartland pink, of course, but only touches of it on her turquoise dress, which matched her eyeshadow, which, I later noticed, also matched the drawing-room walls.

It should be mentioned immediately that not only is Miss Cartland soon to stun us all with her choice of hat at the Royal Wedding (she's step-granny) but she's also been voted one of the Women of the Year in America. I asked if she was surprised at the incredible success of her books over there. "Of course I'm not surprised. After over 200 million sales, it's obvious everyone reads them. A recent survey showed that my books sold well in Boston which considers itself sophisticated. Pornography had begun to fade and I was the only one with 150 virgins lying around. When I came out in America I was the first person to go straight to number one in the Dalton charts. In fact, I was number one *and* two."

I then asked her what she thought of the writers who copy her, but in a more racy style? "They're disgusting. I bought a few of their novels at Inverness station, which you'd expect to be quite a respectable place, and I thought they were revolting. I've never met women who behave like that. When a woman is in love she wants to feel it's sacred, not all that filthy carry-on."

I wondered why Miss Cartland felt that men today were reluctant to marry (you have to remember that *she* had an incredible forty-eight proposals before she met Mr Right). "Well, dear, it's quite simple. Why buy a cow if you can milk it?" This shut me up sufficiently for tea to be announced. We moved into the dining room, which was about the size of Shea Stadium.

After my eyes had popped out on stalks at the sight of all the food, thoughts of diets were quickly done away with. "Why do women all want to be so thin? Because designers tell them they have to be, and of course they're all pansies and want us to look like boys. No, men like a handful. I was always fat and men were madly in love with me."

I managed, with great dexterity, to stuff my face, sit bolt upright, and ask questions clearly all the time, and we moved on to the topic of careers. "I was keen on politics and after my brother died I was offered two safe political seats. But I had a husband and children. What you have to remember is no English husband will dine alone, they hate it. So they go off with a go-go dancer. And children need you, especially at night when they are going to bed, saying their prayers. Parliament is from three in the afternoon to goodness knows what hour. So when people ask me, 'What's the most famous and successful thing you've done?' I tell them, 'Being a wife and mother.' I was lucky to have a job I could continue in my own time. When my husband came home at five I stopped working. Otherwise women have got to choose between a career and a family.

"Today I feel men are afraid to be romantic because women slap them down. But, in fact, girls really only want to hear I love you, I love you, I love you. Man is the natural hunter. In nature, male chases female, and the male is always rather cocky. You must remember that a man must desire a woman, but a woman can oblige." I was a trifle taken aback at that one.

"If you want a man to love you you must tell him you love him, not go on about rights. *What rights?* You don't sit around accepting him, you coax him into doing what you want. Why do women want to change it all for some miserable creature in a plastic apron doing the washing-up?

"It's so much easier to get power from the pillow. No one had more power than mistresses. There have been two queens and three female prime ministers who've been successful, but in romantic and spiritual matters . . . there's never been a greater woman painter than Poussin, Rubens or Turner. In most things, men are superior."

Her final comments on a woman's role in today's society: "In olden times, women were worshipped as goddesses because they could conceive. This is what they should return to—not conceiving all the time, but being worshipped. Men have superior strength and, in most cases, superior intelligence. A woman is good at guiding and inspiring a man. Many famous men have said they owe their success to their wives. *That* is a woman's job."

Miss Cartland's record of romantic love songs, which she recorded a while ago with the Royal Philharmonic Orchestra, is now available on a much cheaper record or cassette (in Cartland Pink, of course). She's designed a range of wonderful curtains and bedding called "Decorating With Love" which is being sold through Macy's in New York, has a monthly romantic magazine out over there, and has written some romantic travelogues for British Airways to go with various destinations. All this, plus a scent named after her, *and* the Royal Wedding . . .

Paula Yates is a gossip columnist, and author of the book Rock Stars In Their Underpants *(Virgin Books, £4.95).*

MAIN PHOTOGRAPH BY NORMAN PARKINSON/CAMERA PRESS; PAULA YATES BY BRIAN ARIS

"Women will be free the moment they stop caring what men think about them"

By Quentin Crisp

A baby is like a cake. It scores you higher marks if you made it yourself.

I can't think who invented these kinds of rules; they are quite unfair and, worse, they are anachronistic. The new science is ecology and its message is that the world would be a wonderful place to live in if we could just get rid of the people. Nevertheless, women seem reluctant to tidy up the universe by using the existing children; they regard ready-made babies as a last resort. So, until science fiction comes to their aid, the females of our species will depend on the males—even if only for a few unpleasant moments. Their view of the world is conditioned by this fact.

The theory that the rearing of children prevents a woman from being a first-class man is obsolete. The wealth and sophistication of today's women means they need not see too much of their offspring. The bother of giving birth is not a worry any more; the real problem is the search for a suitable man to father the offspring.

Men are not in the same leaky boat. They regard a family as misfortune incurred by accident and bravely borne. Looking back over his life, a man can be heard saying, "I always wanted to go to Africa but the children came along so we stayed in Carshalton." Even schoolgirls know that children don't just come along. I am aware of this because I once sat on a bus behind two members of this dangerous species. One of them announced shrilly that when she grew up she intended to have children, to which her friend replied that if you got married they happened automatically. For this remark she received an abrupt reproof. "Oh no they don't. You have to make special arrangements."

A man ransacks the environment for a girl, but not with the same thoroughness as a woman searches for a man. He is only looking for a playmate, not for a mother to his unborn progeny. The woman's task is made even more desperate by her having to find what she wants within a limited time—somewhere between the ages of fifteen and thirty-five.

This desire for motherhood wrecks a woman's life; it imposes on her the necessity of appearing desirable and trustworthy at the same time—frankly an almost impossible feat. It makes being a woman a career in itself to which all other professions are secondary. This situation becomes even more obvious when you consider that there are about three magazines for men in the British Isles and that none of these tries to teach its customers how to become likely candidates for fatherhood. Nay, they explain how to escape the contingency. All the other journals that a man might allow himself to be seen reading are technical: they concern fishing, gardening or keeping a car in working order—never maintaining a wife in a similar state.

In contrast with this dearth, there are hundreds of magazines dealing with how to increase the likelihood of becoming a mother—how to use make-up, how to dress attractively and so on and, since left to herself a woman's idea of lunch is a glass of whisky and a cheese biscuit, even the exotic recipes must be considered obliquely sexy.

The superficial differences between past and present-day society which seem to have made the business of being a woman easier, have in reality done no such thing. They all spring from the same cause. The very moment the first Beatle twanged the first note on his first guitar, the young became rich and inevitably with their wealth came power. When I was young, there appeared to be no teenagers. After a female child stopped being a dear little girl, a hurt and angry silence reigned until her parents deemed her ready for matrimony. Now adolescents have life on their own terms. Promiscuity runs through the world like fire in stubble. It's great fun but it robs women of the only weapon that enabled them to keep their quarry in sight for long enough to determine whether he would make a suitable husband and potential father. They have thrown away their remoteness. Now, every time a film from the 'Thirties or early 'Forties is warmed up for television we are made aware of how important unattainability always used to be. When Mr Novarro reminded Miss Garbo that yesterday she told him that she loved him, with a Garbovine smile she replies, "That was yesterday." When Mr Atwill cried out in anguish to Miss Dietrich that she was driving him mad, her response was, "Sit down, Pasqualito; I will give you a kiss in a minute." Mlle Bardot, being a more recent sex object, had nothing to offer but her infinite availability. Indeed, she did not even have time to comb her hair between one man and the next.

The delaying tactics of the old-time sirens were imitated so universally that there came to be what the newspapers, when they had nothing better to write about, called The Woman Problem. Girls were said to be capricious, moody and perpetually misunderstood.

In this country the inscrutability gambit only worked fifty years ago because then sex was so hard to find. A man couldn't see any alternative to a protracted courtship which left him so exhausted that he was almost glad to flop into marriage. Now sex grows on trees and the word "wooing" is used only of the behaviour of manufacturers trying to interest foreign markets. In these circumstances remoteness is a dangerous ploy. One equivocal answer, one sphinx-like smile and he's off to the girl next door.

The entire situation is made more complicated by the present fad for liberation. Women will never throw off their chains by winning equal chances to become plumbers with wages the same as those of men. They will be free the moment they stop caring what men think about them. What then will become of the home-made baby? Mr Huxley's brave new world must come; test-tube babies will eventually populate the earth. When this happens, *Cosmopolitan* will be a much thinner magazine than it is now. It will contain far fewer cosmetic advertisements, no fashion pages and no exotic recipes.

Until then, there will still be a Woman Problem . . .

Quentin Crisp's new book Doing It With Style *(co-authored with Donald Carroll) is to be published by Eyre Methuen Ltd on 22nd October at £5.95.*

PHOTOGRAPH BY BRIAN MOODY SCOPE FEATURES

DEAR COSMOPOLITAN

"MONEYBAGS" MEN—WHO NEEDS THEM?

With regard to *Talkabout* "It surprises me that women who earn as much as I do expect to be paid for" (October), I suggest David Thomas comes to live in Liverpool along with all the other Moneybags. We've got them all: the Lemon and Lime Fitness Freak who's on G and T when it's your round. The Clean Guy who wallows, chin-deep, in oodles of your hot water while you boil kettles all week. The Won't Go Homer you have to pay a taxi to take away. The Weekender who's been too busy to get to the bank, but whose appetite will eat you out of house, home and purse well before Monday morning. The Concertgoer who phones, says, "I'll meet you there", then arrives so late you're bound to have got the tickets. The Self-styled Gourmet who chooses all the most expensive dishes then with a generous flourish divides the bill in two.

I could go on, the list is endless. David Thomas could probably retire if he plays his cards right and comes to Liverpool. But he needn't call on me: once bitten, twice shy, this worm is about to turn.

Jacqueline Lewis, Liverpool

CONTRIBUTING TO THE COMMUNITY

I was so pleased to see, in *Cosmopolitan*, an article on local councillors *(Women with the power to change things*, October). It took me ten years to gain a seat on our town council but now, after two years spent learning the ropes, I am so glad that I am beginning to be of use, and I do enjoy the variety of work involved.

Everyone ought, at some time in their lives, to contribute something to their communities, on a par with jury service. We all tend to take social services for granted, yet someone has to spend time sorting out the running problems of bus services, etc. Therefore I hope your article will inspire more women to have a go, and perhaps we can achieve more practical and down-to-earth schemes as opposed to the idealistic, often less practical male-inspired ideas.

Being a town councillor means I play a large part in contributing to my community which I find richly satisfying, and the feed-back from personal endeavours makes me feel a better person and, I hope, more interesting.

Thelma Paines, Thetford, Norfolk

STAY-AT-HOME LUXURY

Rarely do I write, but this time you have provoked me, enraged me, made me see red. In your questionnaire *Are you being served? Tell us what your firm is doing for you* (October), how *could* you print, "I do full-time UNPAID work as homemaker and/or parent"? This is rubbish. Just think of the benefits these stay-at-home women get—all tax-free, and financed by their husbands:

Average weekly repayments on £20,000 mortgage, say £40. Average weekly fuel bill, say £15. Rates, water, insurance, say £10 a week. Weekly food, household expenses, at least £25. Clothes, say £10 a week. There's £100 per week tax-free for a start. Not bad is it? Then add £4.75 per week child benefit for each child they so conveniently produce—on the national health of course—to stop them going back to work for another five years.

No, housewives/mothers are *not* to be pitied. They are *not* the downtrodden masses. No nine to five-thirty for them, no boss to answer to, no hurried shopping in the lunch hour, no midnight washing and ironing sessions, no worry over the gas bill. This is the privileged élite, the ladies of leisure cushioned from all responsibility.

Yes they *are* being served—by people who *do* work—their husbands, you and me. And what's more, with the current divorce laws still so strongly weighted in their favour, these cosseted stay-at-home ladies have just about the most secure jobs of the 'Eighties.

Margret Prior, Reading

PORN DEGRADES MEN!

In response to Eileen Fairweather's contention (*Women in a violent age*, November) that pornography serves only to encourage the male's shallow and degrading view of the female, may I express my sympathy that Ms Fairweather has apparently never met a man who is not totally obsessed with rape fantasies.

While *Cosmo et al* continue to publish material which divides the sexes—be it sexual instincts, emotions, intellect or whatever—then these divides are emphasised, *not* reduced, and both women and men (Paul Keers "Why I feel I'm being discriminated against", *Talkabout*, same issue) will feel uneasy about the business of getting along together. And that *is* what we're all aiming for, isn't it?

To balance the views expressed in Ms Fairweather's article, it could be purported that pornography actually degrades *men* in that while women have a choice as to their participation (and payment), men are effectively being conned into buying a fantasy world. Male violence against women is not the problem. What matters is one human being having disregard for another—be it the sado-masochist addict with his porn mag or the "actress" earning herself some quick money by posing for the pictures he wants.

Wise up *Cosmo*, you can't be humanist, feminist, escapist and political at the same time —inconsistency is an insult to your readers.

L M Wild, West Yorkshire

PERFORMING PAIN

I was so glad to see John May's article *Stop the circus, I want to get off* (October). I recently attended a local charity show, where a dramatic hold-up by Red Indians on horseback was staged. In the interval I went to look at the two horses. I noticed that they both had an identically shaped scar on the the right-hand side of their backs, just behind the saddle. One of the scars was raw.

On attending a meeting soon afterwards at the House of Lords, convened by a peer to inquire into the treatment of performing animals, I asked the speaker (an expert in this field) what these marks denoted. He said that metal is introduced under the skin and left, like shrapnel from a war injury. The rider then has only to touch the horse ever so lightly in order to cause enough pain to make the creature prance prettily.

I reported this matter to the RSPCA who passed it on to the police. But I don't know if it was ever followed up. May I ask all *Cosmo* readers who are animal-lovers to look out for this sort of thing and ensure it is followed up next time?

Ruth Plant, The Catholic Study Circle for Animal Welfare, London

WHY NOT ADVERTISE?

If the extract from *Futurewoman* (*Where the men are*, October) is anything to go by, Shirley Conran should have stuck to housework rather than advising women about finding a mate. First, she offers absolutely nothing new, and second, she ignores the fact that many of the services mentioned—marriage bureaux, etc—are used by professional people who are too busy to use more conventional means of meeting partners. It's absolute rubbish to suggest that "happy people rarely advertise", and that advertisers "generally have problems".

The biggest problem is where to meet men when you are over twenty-five/busy at work and at home/have friends who are already paired off so you have no one to go "hunting" with! This is hardly the same as having a personality problem. Why should lonely hearts advertisers be any different in that way from those who use computer dating services? Except, perhaps, that they are more individualistic!

Elaine Malcolm, London

DATELINE'S DEFENCE

Dateline Computer Dating would like to point out that contrary to the impression given in Ms Shirley Conran's article *Where the men are* (October), Dateline provides a very acceptable, popular and viable way for people to meet.

We welcome clients to our offices, and are always happy to give assistance and advice, either personally or by telephone. Also, provided that our comprehensive questionnaire is completed with the recommended care, it is impossible for anyone to be given an introduction to someone in an age group or area which they have not requested. We would also dispute that Dateline is expensive. By comparison with marriage bureaux and for the quality of service provided through a year's membership, we feel that the amount a girl would spend on a new coat is not a vast amount to pay for at the very least a year's social life, and at the most, love and a marriage partner.

The basis of the Dateline system is that we can match people physically, psychologically and sociologically. We have 47,000 members on our files, fifty-two percent men and forty-eight percent women, and in the fifteen years since our establishment there have been more than 14,000 marriages as a result of Dateline introductions. Surely to be recommended!

Pamela Audouin, Dateline Computer Dating

COSMOPOLITAN is published monthly by the National Magazine Co. Ltd. 72 Broadwick Street, London W1V 2BP (tel: 01-439 7144). Typeset by Technical Editing Services and Southwark Studios Ltd, both of London, England. Printed photo rotary gravure by Burda Druck GmbH and bound by Burda Druck GmbH, 61 Darmstadt, Schöfferstrasse 8, Germany. Conditions of sale and supply: COSMOPOLITAN shall not without the written consent of the publishers first given be lent, resold, hired out or otherwise disposed of by way of trade except at the full retail price of 60p, and shall not be lent, hired out, or otherwise disposed of in a mutilated condition or in any unauthorised cover by way of trade: or affixed to or as part of any publication or advertising, literary or pictorial matter whatsoever. MSS and illustrations are accepted on the understanding that no liability is incurred for safe custody, but COSMOPOLITAN cannot consider unsolicited material for publication. All characters in any story are purely imaginary and no reference or allusion is intended to apply to any living person or persons. COSMOPOLITAN is fully protected by copyright and nothing may be printed wholly or in part without permission. Annual subscription to COSMOPOLITAN costs £13.00 (12 issues) post paid inland and £16.00 overseas and may be booked through all newsagents and bookstalls or from COSMOPOLITAN Subscription Servicing, Oakfield House, Perrymount Road, Haywards Heath, Sussex RH16 3DH (tel: Haywards Heath 59188), who deal with all subscription enquiries. COSMOPOLITAN is distributed by Condé Nast & National Magazine Distributors Limited (COMAG), Tavistock Road, West Drayton, Middlesex UB7 7QE (tel: West Drayton 44055); Telex: 8813787 COMAG G). Managing Dir. Phil Harris.

"The '80s man is more inclined to grab a box of tissues than a wooden club"

By Colin Brown

When the social history of the 1980s is written, it will be seen as the decade which buried the Machismo Male. There will be pockets of resistance, such as Glasgow, where men will continue to regard sex as a poor substitute for masturbation (or sex with someone you love, as Woody Allen describes it). Tom Jones will go on baring a chest which resembles a doormat transplant. And Italians in Rome will still pinch anything including bottoms. But in the sophisticated Perrier-sniffing circles of the South of England, Macho Man is already doomed.

The next ten years will see the blossoming of the Truly Caring Male. The TCM will make the sexists of the 'Sixties and the punk masochists of the 'Seventies look like Neanderthals. The 'Eighties man is more inclined to grab a box of tissues than a wooden club when deserted by his mate. And as he is likely to be left literally holding the baby, the 1980s could see a flourishing industry in new court cases as he sues the mother for maintenance.

The "tug of love" sob story is now so common place that newspapers refuse to devote space to such cases although they made the headlines not very long ago.

Hollywood has kissed a long goodbye to the old style Macho star with the stiff, if slightly sneering, upper lip. The symbol of the 'Eighties male film star is definitely the quivering bottom lip. If they shot a remake of *"Alfie"* today, it would be Michael Caine who would be accused of getting "mumsie" by his bird.

The collapse of penis power has been an inevitable consequence of women's struggle for equality, but the Truly Caring Male is in danger of over-doing his readjustment. I discovered this at a typically English barbeque party. It was raining. The men were huddled under a parasol after a cloudburst. A few years ago, the talk would have been about cars with poke and rear seats wide enough to prove it in. Today, the conversation was all about Farley's Rusks and breach births (which I'd always imagined to be like firing a gun) led by a fully paid-up card carrying new recruit to the TCM movement. A burly military police officer.

We were heavily into father recognition by less than one-month-old infants, when suddenly there was a distant cry, barely audible to someone like me (who has yet to have his paternalistic instinct aroused), but which had the effect of an alarm call to the military police officer. "I'll go," he shouted to his wife who was engrossed in plans for a hen party. A few minutes later he came back blissfully reassurred and said, "Wind."

The conversation went on to diet and the cause and effect of flatulance among infants. His advice was to steer clear of fig and prune surprise unless you want to clear up a human Torrey Canyon disaster. "I know quite a bit about child birth, don't I, Tina?" he called across to his wife, who had decided on a weekend with the girls in Paris. "I've been going to a clinic for expectant fathers."

This information had hardly sunk in when there was another cry, this time audible even to me. I was fast becoming attuned. "I'll go," he said. "She'll probably need changing." His wife was discussing sex the French way with her friends, when he came back looking downcast. "She wants feeding."

Breast feeding was the only area where he felt completely inadequate. The clinic omitted to teach him how to cope with feeling unfulfilled as a perfect parent. And if there are many more TCMs like him, I can warn doctors to expect a queue of males suffering from postnatal depression. Help will not exactly be at hand. "I've tried bottle feeding, doctor, but it's just not the same. There must be something you can do. A hormone injection with a squirt of Carnation milk perhaps?" High Streets will sprout Fathercare shops offering Gucci leather gasmasks for squeamish nappy changers and, for those who hanker after the old days, perambulators with extra-wide alloy racing wheels.

There was a poster which depicted a pregnant man in a controversial advertisement for contraceptives. The headline was intended to prick the conscience: "How would you feel?" More and more men are asking the same question, but for very different reasons. Some of them really want to know! One of the first must have been James Joyce whose central character, Leopold Bloom, has a vision in *Ulysses* of giving birth and becoming the first motherly man.

The change of roles has been going on for some time in many countries as a result either of revolution in Russia or war in the West, but even in Russia it is the male who is still very much the master of the household.

Not until this moment has Western man attempted to adopt the role of mother as well. In the animal kingdom, this is quite rare. Lions want nothing to do with their young, and although most birds share the nesting and even the incubating, few males cope with all the ante natal care on their own.

I have a friend who has completely reversed roles with his wife. While *she* goes out to work, *he* has given up his full-time office job and stays at home. His intention was to write plays, but he finds that so much time is spent entertaining the kids, cooking and doing housework, he has not much energy left for writing. His conversation revolves around how bad Geraldine was in the butcher's, while his wife talks about winning promotion over somebody else's husband. And with rising male unemployment, more men could be following in his house slippers.

Battered by circumstances beyond his control and criticised by his mate, the new emotional male may seek security in his old sexist aggression, but there appears to be no sign yet of a backlash of that old male self-assurance.

Already we have in Margaret Thatcher a PM who is said to be the only Macho man in her Cabinet of wets. Men already accept that women are bound to rise to more posts of pre-eminence in society. When they make the next charge on banks, the civil service, industry and perhaps even the church, they will find the door already ajar and leaning open. This time, instead of countering with his Machismo, the male is learning to take it like a woman—lying down. Pass me the tissues, I think I'm going to cry.

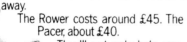

COSMOPOLITEN

By Marcelle d'Argy Smith

The *Cosmo* girl's a paradox,
ms Worldly Wise ms Punk Pink Sox.
She smiles a lot through lip-glossed lips,
she's dazzling to her fingertips.
She thinks, she feels, she's "there", involved,
and *Cosmo* gets her problems solved.

The kid has style, she's chic, exclusive,
her age—well that's a bit elusive.
She's flip fifteen, she's thirty-five,
she feels it's great to be alive.
And if life didn't work as planned
then *Cosmo* calmly took her hand . . .

And helped her when her man turned gay,
and when her husband went away.
And guided her and helped her grow,
delivered news of the "Big O".
Made her aware of sensual treats,
these days she sleeps on satin sheets!

She lives alone, she lives with him,
she's Pizzey plump, Dance Centre slim.
There's independence, a career,
she reaped the best of Germaine Greer.
Of course she's had her fingers burned,
but most importantly, she's *learned.*

Men it seems cannot resist
this sexy healthy feminist.
She's soft, she's strong, she likes to flirt,
her brain's amazingly alert.
Her head's held high, she walks erect,
a *Cosmo* girl commands respect.

And *Cosmo* baby you've grown too,
it's funny now to look at you
and think back to ten years ago.
Your British birth was painful, slow,
that first bright issue, pages crammed,
when you thought "Publish and be damned"!

"The modern woman's silent shrink,
that stretches her and makes her think."
These past ten years you've taught her plenty.
God, what'll you be like at twenty!
You are sensational at ten,
McSharryied *Cosmopolitan.*

The *Cosmo* Lady thinks you're great
and she'd like to congratulate
you on your grown-up tenth birthday
and breathlessly she'd like to say
your written words are loved and needed,
Cosmo baby, you've succeeded.

PHOTOGRAPH BY LORENZ ZATECKY

We know you listen to what we say—but how much do you remember from our dazzling decade? Do this quiz and see how we've kept you in touch since 1972! By Paul Keers

How well do you

1 Only one of the women pictured above has not appeared on the cover of *Cosmopolitan*—which one?
a Raquel Welch c Bo Derek
b Elizabeth Taylor d Marie Helvin

2 Which woman stated in *Cosmo* that: "Women's liberation . . . is a movement that mounts an attack on practically everything that women value today . . . their sentiments are certainly offensive and need to be exploded . . ."?

3 The first *Metropolitan* in November 1976 gave you hot news on the Zanzibar Club, *Ritz* magazine, and tipped punk as "the breakthrough of the decade"—but who wrote it?
a Janet Street-Porter c Peter York
b Compton Miller d Nigel Dempster

4 Who told us, "I like a girl who can understand and tolerate me and, above all, she must have good knockers"?
a Phil Lynott c John Conteh
b Oliver Reed d George Best

5 *Cosmo* printed extracts or abridgements from all of these novels except one—which one?
a *The Exorcist* d *The Great Gatsby*
b *Fear of Flying* e *Richard's Things*
c *The World According to Garp* f *Jaws*

6 Which of the famous wits pictured above invited you into their kitchen in February 1980 and offered this recipe for pork chop with basil and rosemary: "Fry the pork chop, then ask Basil and

know Cosmo?

Rosemary to come round for dinner"?
a Rowan Atkinson c Jilly Cooper
b John Cleese d Penelope Keith

7 The first issue of *Cosmopolitan* cost:
a 35p b 30p c 20p

8 *Cosmopolitan* is the largest-selling magazine for young women in this country—but what is its circulation?
a Around 160,000 copies.
b Around 260,000 copies.
c Around 460,000 copies.

9 What, according to our first issue, is "the most beautiful thing a man can do for a woman"?
a Give her a baby.
b Give her an orgasm.
c Have a vasectomy.

10 What did we say that Dudley Moore, Edward Fox, Felicity Kendal, Twiggy, Lady Antonia Fraser and David Hockney all possess?
a Individual style c Charm
b Englishness d Generosity

MOORE/SCOPE FEATURES: GRAHAM HARRISON: STEVE SANDON: ROGER STOWELL

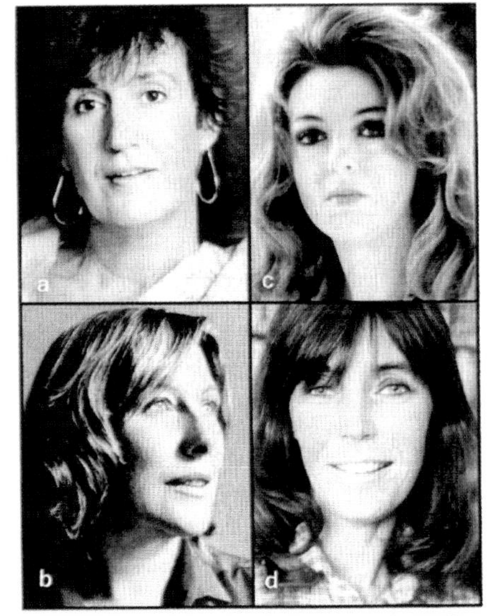

11 Which of the four famous writers who are pictured above is the odd one out and why?
a Jill Tweedie c Catherine Stott
b Fay Weldon d Penny Vincenzi

ANSWERS
1 c Bo Derek. Marie Helvin was on the cover in Feb 1976; Elizabeth Taylor in Dec 1976; and Raquel Welch in Feb 1978.
2 Arianna Stassinopoulos, in an extract from her controversial book, *The Female Woman* (Nov 1973).
3 c Peter York.
4 b Oliver Reed, who told us *What I Want in a Wife* (April 1972).
5 c *The World According to Garp.*
6 b John Cleese in an article, *Cleese on Toast* (Feb 1980).
7 c 20p. At the time 20p would have bought you five Mars bars.
8 c Around 460,000 copies—with about four people reading each copy!
9 c Have a vasectomy. Michael Parkinson was the man on the end of the kindest cut of all.
10 c Charm. They were all in our list of Great British charmers in *What is This Thing Called Charm?* (April 1980).
11 b Fay Weldon. She is the only one who has never written *Cosmo's* book reviews.

SCORING
(One point for each correct answer)
8-11: You must have a stack of carefully-kept *Cosmos* as your adviser and friend.
4-7: *Cosmo* is so full of up-to-the minute information that it drives everything else out of your head.
Under 4: You must be one of our latest acquisitions. Keep reading!

Enjoying a rare moment of respite from their tornado tour of gay Paree, Paula (centre) and Martin (left) take a breather over a **café au lait** *and a mineral water, respectively.*

In an attempt to "do Paris properly", diminutive blonde bombshell Paula Yates, accompanied by Steve Strange and Martin Kemp, paints the city *rouge* on *rouge*, ending up face down in a plate of snails. Here she reveals all . . .

Shocking the

"Oh yes we'll be doing Paris properly," I gloated at *Cosmo's* Genevieve. "Maxim's by candlelight, Versailles by moonlight, Thierry Mugler in a tent."

Little did I know that the whole weekend was going to disintegrate into madness. My first big mistake was to embark on the venture with two boys far prettier than me. They say that one night in Paris is like a year in any other town, and after spending it with Steve Strange and Martin Kemp from Spandau Ballet I'd be inclined to agree. As far as Martin's concerned, the whole hotel could have blown up and he'd have been straight back in there to save his hairspray.

Due to the chaotic nature of Paris during the week of the October fashion collections, the lobby of our first hotel was filled with toffee-coloured people sitting forlornly on their suitcases. From the looks of the cases most of the crocodile population of South America had been turned into luggage for the trip. Not that this was helping the visitors to get rooms. It turned out that all of us were booked into the same suite: the photographer had been booked into my bed (literally), and it looked as if Martin was going to end up with a very suspect Louis XIV chaise-longue that could have been imported from the local brothel specially for him.

In the street, the limousine spread itself across fourteen parking spaces and the little driver was preparing himself for an SAS type endurance test. "Which limo is yours?" I asked Steve. "The biggest," he replied simply.

The first night stretched on for ten hours, going from club to club. I saw more clubs than Toulouse Lautrec; no wonder the poor bloke walked around on his knees. I was doing likewise by the time dawn was cracking across the Eiffel Tower. "Looks like a pylon, doesn't it?" remarked Martin, adding his Islington-style touch of romance to the proceedings.

At about two in the morning we were having dinner in one of the best clubs in Paris. By about 4.30 a.m. the bill had entered the outer stratosphere. When it arrived, I thought it was an A-level economics paper. I spotted the bit that appeared to say £700 and Martin decided to carry me upstairs to the limo. OOOOH, I thought, this is really the high life; here I am clad from head to foot in gold lamé, having stuffed my face with scrambled eggs at £16 a mouthful, and now this incredibly handsome person is carrying me upstairs amidst cries of *"Superbe"* and *"Encore"* from the excitable frogs.

Later, in another little club, Steve Strange gave a spirited demonstration of northern soul dances. "I used to do these at the Wigan Casino," were his exact words as he flung himself into a double-turned back flip. He then sashayed impressively down the street to the limo, and flung himself onto the floor of the car. "Open the window!" he shrieked. Sadly, it was one of those cars with enough buttons to re-equip mission control so by the time I'd opened the window I'd also made the back seat into a double bed, re-connected the fridge, made a movie screen shoot up out of the front window and turned on the stereo.

Day two: Saturday

The hotel manager was seeing his whole career vanishing in a crimson-haired haze

PHOTOGRAPHS BY ANDY EARL

down the nearest plug-hole. Here he was with ex-President Richard Nixon in full make-up (in case of photographers) surrounded by male models with berets and three days' growth all waiting for rooms, while upstairs, slumbering like babies in his best suite, were Steve in silk jammies and Martin in nothing.

In the end, we gave up our room to the American contingent, but Martin left the brown boots that went with his brown dress up in the suite. We all immediately had visions of Dicky posing in the boots in front of the mirror. Finally Martin rang up to get them back. "Hey I wouldn't want you guys to go to the show in your socks," said the deep American voice—unmistakably Nixon himself—at the other end of the line.

Steve had a good chance of upstaging the whole world at the fashion show that afternoon. Mainly because he was wearing an overcoat made of anaconda skins with a twenty-foot anaconda wrapped around his head and its tail drifting down his back. I had given up. Martin was in his frock and boots, showing acres of muscular rippling thigh. What can a girl do?, I wondered, resigning myself to walking three paces behind the two of them, like a tiny blonde version of the Duke of Edinburgh.

"You have to look totally over the top in Paris because at the collections you'll actually see money walking," they said. I wondered whether I should put my Sainsbury bag over my head.

Outside the show, women were sobbing and offering their all for a ticket to see Mugler's models flouncing around in glamorous chambermaids' outfits and dinky nurses' uniforms . . . I grew exhausted from the strain of hissing jealously at the girls and attempting to spit on their feet. I also had a stomach ache from wanting all the clothes so much. All the girls had fourteen inches of eye make-up making them look as if they'd been bitten by a tse-tse fly before going down the cat walk. The strain of keeping their eyelashes aloft and their tits inside their aprons was worth every penny they were getting.

Day three: Sunday

Had a photo session for Paris *Vogue* with the bloke who directed *Emmanuelle.* He was blessed with the confusing name Just Jaeckin, or Just Joking as Steve claimed, or Just Jacket as Martin claimed. So there we all were, steaming away in front of the hot lights in Just's studio, which is actually his basement, while he shrieked things at us from his perch up a ladder about two feet away from our faces. It was all in French: the more we smouldered, the more Just shrieked and the more Martin and Steve found it impossible not to collapse giggling from the horror of it all. When we got the Polaroid pic, I looked as if I were auditioning for a biblical epic, Martin looked as if he'd just left the Nuremberg rally for a quick hot-dog and Steve as if he'd just removed a very tight crash helmet. We wandered out into the street and stood there for an hour. The limousine driver had fallen asleep further on up the road.

That night we all had very glamorous rooms in very glamorous hotels, so we decided to go and eat at La Coupole. We must have been doing something right because as we walked in everyone stood up and applauded. Then again, maybe we all looked so tired they thought we deserved a medal for making it across the room. I was in the middle of my eighth snail when my head started its descent towards the bread. Martin was polishing off the remainders when the Man from the *Daily Mail* came over and, staring at the back of my neck and the remains of snail sauce on my thigh, said "Oh, you must be Paula Yates."

At the airport, on the way home, the French police were unable to contain themselves. They took Martin to one side and searched him. A couple of minutes later they emerged shaking their heads in a disappointed fashion. All they could find was his lip gloss.

French

Above: Paula (she's the one in taffeta) and Martin (he's the other one) pause before the most looked-at "pylon" in existence. Left: the tireless trio in lamé, frock and make-up set off on a wild foray into Paris nightlife.

HEAVY PETTING

Men's pets provide paws for thought. As acceptable objects of male affection, they allow his emotions to show through the masks of masculinity and machismo. So what do a man's animals reveal to you about his anima? **Paul Keers** investigates . . .

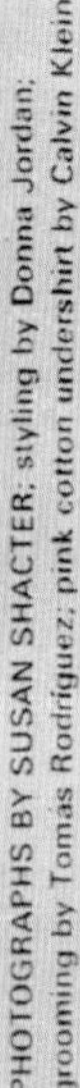

PHOTOGRAPHS BY SUSAN SHACTER; styling by Donna Jordan;
grooming by Tomas Rodriguez; pink cotton undershirt by Calvin Klein

A man with a pet is a caring, sharing man. He's allowed love into his life, and opened both his heart and his home to another. Show him kindness and he'll be touched and affected, and he'll show his affection by touching—animals can provide a soothing way for a hard-working executive to have a stroke.

To live in peace with a prospective partner's pet, see it as a mirror of the man and not a rival for his love. According to animal psychologist Konrad Lorenz, dogs are a combination of chum and child to a man—so they won't take the place of a partner. Their character echoes his own, their lifestyle reflects aspects of his own attitudes and desires towards women. Perhaps that's why Jim Allcock, of the British Veterinary Association, says that, "All vets have

Michael with friends: Noodle, the [illegible] collie...

HEAVY PETTING

had cases when a woman arranges t
have an embarrassingly over-sexed do
castrated—and her husband cancel
the appointment. Men have a ten
dency to see their dogs as reflections o
their own masculinity."

A load of . . . ? Well, if a ma
yearns for a private life, away fror
home for days on end (and nights o
tiles) he might not choose a dog at al
A cat, whose return to a house mean
it's happy there and not that it's
dependent prisoner, is a much bette
reflection of the bachelor stereotype.

Whether a man's pet is a dependen
dog or an independent cat coul
indicate the type of partner he'
prefer. But, if his pet fills one of thos
relationship requirements, he ma
want *you* to fill the other. So just tr
asking if he'd prefer a bird instead.

. . . Tiffany, the miniature Yorkie . . .

At least there's one problem she doesn't have.

No one makes a tampon quite like we do.

And we don't think anything else can give you much comfort. Or as much peace of mind.

In the first place, our applicator helps you position e tampon effectively. Then as it expands, it fits ugly into every contour of your body.

Because unlike other tampons, ours expand in length and breadth as well as width. This gives you more protection.

And means whatever problems you come up against, your Tampax tampon will never be one of them.

TAMPAX. tampons 10 Regular

istered Trademark.

MADE ONLY BY TAMPAX LIMITED, HAVANT, HAMPSHIRE.

FUTUR

WHEN OFFICE AND

If they all laughed when Edison created sound, then New Technology should really slay them. And what about The Industrial Revolution Part 2 for real rib-cracking entertainment? That may sound like a Monty Python film title, but it's actually *our* future we're talking about, a future where an industrial revolution, a social revolution, a medical revolution, a time revolution and a *revolution* revolution is about to happen. Only eighteen years away, the twenty-first century is when you get the key to the word-processors and computers that will free your life. If you thought you'd come a long way already, baby, the best is yet to come—especially for women. Here's the low-down on the high-life of the future. By Genevieve Cooper.

Work

Instead of trundling off on the 8.33 every morning and spending hours commuting to a desk in the City, you will be getting out of bed and working the word-processor or two-way video screen which is installed in your home. A network of computer links will make these as simple and cheap to use as a telephone, so just about everyone will own or have access to one. You will not have to go *out* to discuss business matters with colleagues because you will be able to confront them face to face on your two-way video. You will only visit the office—if there is one—for *social* reasons (which may not be news to some people). Life will be more *discriminating* since we'll all be spending a far greater proportion of our time with the people we want to see, and less with those we currently simply *tolerate* (if we're unlucky) for work reasons. Office hours, of course, will be flexible, although the really conscientious will be able to carry around portable word-processors. Oh yes, and you'll be able to speak to Japan as easily as if it were Croydon because we have already invented a simultaneous translation technique, which means that her/his Japanese speech will come out your end as English. Quite an advance on the crossed-line service now found on British Telecom.

Your work should be far more interesting by then because machines and robots will have taken over the more repetitive, boring stuff. It's estimated that by the turn of this century, 4.4 million workers will be replaced by robots (mostly in the manufacturing area, particularly the car industry). But the work of creating the robots will make for millions more jobs. Women will gain here because brawn will no longer be so necessary in industry. The robot business will be one of the largest new manufacturing booms, along with telecommunications, but domestic robots will remain a cartoon joke, as they'll be too inflexible and costly for just a spot of dusting and putting the cat out.

By the year 2000, if the experts are right, you'll be working a twenty-five hour week. That leaves 143 hours to play, learn a lot and sleep a bit. Inevitably, you will be spending a lot more time with the family—so you'd better learn to like them.

So by the year 2000, if the experts are right, you can expect to be working a twenty-five-hour-week—which sounds to me rather like civilisation re-discovered.

Family Life

With this twenty-five-hour working week you'll be left with 143 hours to play around, learn a lot, sleep a bit . . . and clean your cupboards. (If you're lucky, they will be self-cleaning: a woman in America has just invented a cupboard that dry-cleans the clothes when you shut the door—a fantastic proposition for us domestic inadequates.) Most of all, you will inevitably be spending more time with the family, so you'd better learn to like them. Shirley Williams said recently that considering all the leisure time we'll be spending with one another in the future, lessons in social skills and survival techniques to cope with long periods of unemployment should become part of the school curriculum—and some of us could do with them right now.

Because of job-sharing, fathers will take over more of the responsibility for the children, although children will probably only be at school part-time because they can easily pick up lessons on their two-way videos at home. Technological and academic studies will be given equal importance in schools, as they are in France already. More than half of all secondary schools in this country now have micro-computers and perhaps this new early appreciation of technology will make for a less divisive, more classless society in the future.

Following a trend that started in the 'Seventies, more women will be initiating divorce, but since we'll all be living longer (see Medicine section), divorce will be a more frequent and accepted part of life. In fact, experts are saying that we will no longer regard a first marriage as the *only* marriage, but that we will have three mates through life: the first for romance and excitement, the second for having children, the third for companionship.

And *at last* there will be a birth control pill for men, as well as the improved

PHOTOGRAPH BY RICHARD ROCKWOOD

WORKS

HOME MERGE AND THERE'LL REALLY BE TIME TO LIVE

morning-after pill for us ("your turn to take the pill, dear . . ."). That's if we aren't using the side-effect-free method now being tested—a device that, on insertion, measures your vaginal temperature by lighting up red for fertile and green for infertile. A supposedly extra-reliable method of contraception, it also paves the way for thrilling bouts of neon-lit intercourse. And it's been said that more women will be initiating sex. About time, too. Take *Cosmopolitan's* assertiveness training course and be prepared . . .

Money

Millionaires will be even more elusive than they are now because tax reforms will mean that we'll all be earning a similar amount. The richest people will be entertainers and athletes who will be piling in the loot from television appearance payments. Clearly, if you're a guitar-playing athlete, you'll be laughing. All our financial dealings will be done on the word-processors at home, so at a press of a button—or, more likely, your voice-print—you will discover the hideous truth of the state of your bank account, pay bills directly, and even order up shopping from the local supermarket (a service that's already in use in parts of London).

Another development, from a company called EyeDentifier Inc, is withdrawal of money from your bank account by eye print. A machine takes an electronic picture of the retina and feeds it to a micro-computer which subsequently identifies your unique eye print every time you gaze at the machine and so releases your money to you. The machine is being installed soon at a bank in Oregon, so if you should happen to be there you'll know what those meaningful stares around the Oregon banking district mean . . . A cashless, chequeless society where coins will become quaint *objets d'art* does seem to be on the horizon. Maybe then, there will only be one all-round credit card to lose rather than a wallet-full.

Transport

Amazingly, of all the advances being made, transport seems to be the slowest to benefit. As long as economies are run on oil, it seems cars will, too. Engines have been developed that run on water, but the oil companies, protective of their interests, have bought out such schemes. There are trains in existence in Japan that run on a magnetic repulsion system. Perhaps these will eventually emerge in Britain, too, but at the moment it's hard to tell from week to week, let alone a century ahead, whether we will have trains at all. More advanced aeroplanes such as Concorde have proved not to be economically viable; perhaps a cheaper form of nuclear-powered flight will be developed for the future.

The richest people in the next century will be athletes and entertainers, who'll be piling in the loot from television payments. Clearly, if you're a guitar-playing athlete, you'll be laughing. As for coins, they'll just be quaint* objets d'art *from the past.

Meanwhile, back with the cars . . . they will be twice as expensive as they are now because they'll be made entirely of durable plastic, and you won't *drive* them so much as *talk* to them. Your voiceprint will transfer the instructions. For example, you'll say, "I want to go to Scotland," and your car's in-built computerised map will set itself to take you there. Your car will also talk back to you, telling you when it's dynamo needs replacing, when it needs a service, etc. A fairly meaningful relationship could develop between you and your speaking car if you're not careful. Will we need to learn social skills for that, too?

Medicine

Oh joy . . . finally the medical profession will have perfected mood modifiers: pills that can elevate or calm our spirits without side-effects. Even better news for some of us will be the nasal sprays that improve concentration—but please, no squirting during dinner.

Another study shows that a protein present in the hormone that helps to tan the skin also heightens your powers of concentration. Doctors now think that people with particularly good memories also produce an excess of this hormone, and they are working on condensing the ingredients into pill form. If they succeed, they could also prevent senility. Which is just as well, since with life-extending drugs, it seems that we will all be living to around 120 years, and it would be nice to remember how many children you've had. These pills, though, will be laced with sterility compounds, otherwise we wouldn't be able to find a standing space, let alone a parking spot.

Operations will be bloodless thanks to laser surgery which will remove unwanted growths as easily as cutting out coupons. For *wanted* growths, like hair and height, there will be drugs available, while the medical profession is already developing a nut-like snack to keep teeth cavity-free.

And the last laugh on the joggers: doctors are saying that one of the most common complaints in the future will be arthritis. All that running may have given us sturdy hearts and lungs, but our joints will be shot to pieces. No doubt by then, though, they will have found a cure for that, too.

THE HOME IS WHERE THE WORK IS, WITH SPACE FOR PLAY

ILLUSTRATION BY RICHARD ROCKWOOD

Compare the *Cosmopolitan* office of today, pictured on page 142, with the office of the future as conceived by Peter Laurie, editor of *Practical Computing*, and illustrated above right. The desks have all gone because the routine work is done at home (above). The office will be more like a club or fashionable salon than anything we know today. Meanwhile, the not-so-weary editor will be able to lounge at home with her pocket-sized computer and run the magazine from there.

HOME

A The woman in the background enjoys a keep-fit class that meets by TV—the instructor lives in Corfu.

B The craft area with a computer that acts as a drawing-board on which you sketch an object, paint it, change it and shape it. The computer then produces engineering drawings of the various parts. You could make animated films, call up plans from computerised libraries overseas, etc.

C School in the sitting-room: the child joins in classes with her teacher via the video screen. Course material is pre-recorded and the pupil is taken through it by the computer and teacher combined.

D Kitchen area with video for reading

Plugging into the future

THE OFFICE IS WHERE PEOPLE MEET AND SWOP IDEAS

and storing menus, and for placing general shopping orders.

E The home work-centre, where the *Cosmopolitan* art director designs layouts and checks copy on the large screen; smaller screens tap into the office (see J) or other rooms in the house.

F The coloured lines represent glass fibre links that send information as pulses of light, enabling you to use the same computer both for work and home tasks.

WORK

G Video screen for long-distance link-ups and for keeping in contact with *Cosmopolitan* offices worldwide.

H Book library—it's in the office because we'll have more time to read there.

I The video mag reference resource screens, which tap through to various issues of *Cosmopolitan* past and present.

Some would say that electronics, by pouring its bounty on us in the form of colour TV and wristwatch calculators, has destroyed civilisation as our grandparents knew it. Now chips and hair-thin glass fibres look like destroying the city as we know it—and in the process, enriching our lives.

Every day, millions of office workers leave the suburbs by train and Tube and head for their city centre offices. Here, they work on documents which are only streams of electronic pulses in the word-processor and which could have come to them at home at the speed of light, 186,000 miles per second, rather than lugging their body to them at about eight miles per hour.

Why shift masses of bodies using slow, expensive and unreliable railways and roads when you can take their work to them? Why live in suburbs around city centres if you don't need to go anywhere to work? And if you don't have to accommodate millions of office workers in city centres, then you don't need office blocks. In fact, you don't need city centres in anything like the form we have them now.

How, you may ask, will you be able to communicate with colleagues if you stay at home? The answer lies in glass fibres and their capacity for TV pictures. People will have TV cameras built into their work stations, and they'll be able to have two-way picture and sound conversations with each other as easily as we now talk on the phone.

This will make possible all sorts of new activities. For example, when you "go to the office" you'll go more for a social occasion, to meet colleagues, discuss new ideas, refresh and stimulate your mind. The computerised network will make possible new social arrangements: people might have network parties with their friends—you couldn't do much in the groping line, but it would be better than a phone call.

Improvements in computers will produce a new art form in which the audience or viewer is also part of the action and the author. You might, for instance, re-cast *Gone with the Wind:* Rod Stewart as Rhett and yourself as Scarlett O'Hara. The computer will redraw each frame of the film with the new likenesses and remake the soundtrack with your voices. Who'll need real life when you can have this sort of fantasy? **Peter Laurie**

WORK OUT WITH MOI!

Can you work out without creasing your clothes? Will you retain a fabulous figure when your frog insists on taking you to smart restaurants? Will you feel like a wet noodle after your aerobics session? These are the questions which America's most talented and glamorous superstar (*her* description) seeks to answer on *Miss Piggy's Aerobique Exercise Workout Album.* As an exercise in style it is unsurpassed, and style—as we have come to learn over the years—is the *sine qua non* of all Miss Piggy's actions. Hence her unique fitness programme that avoids "getting out of breath" and "boring calistheniques", and promises to show you how to "keep fit and stay slimme and trimme with a few minutes of daily dance movements so simple you can actually do some of them in your sleep."

At the time of going to Press, Miss Piggy was rumoured to have a fractured femur—the result of an over-strenuous workout with her beloved Kermie, we believe—and was unavailable for interview. But a sneak preview of her album, not yet scheduled for release in this country, enables us to reproduce some of her thoughts on diet and exercise. Says Miss Piggy:

- Sadly, many people believe that to be effective, exercise must "hurt". Phooez! That is like saying that you are not enjoying your ice cream unless you get an ice cream headache.
- Always dress stylishly when you work out. Remembeur, the most difficult exercise is the exercise of good taste.
- *Moi* does not thinque that people should stand on their ears or twist themselves into pretzels. It will just make you dizzy, and could give you posture like the Lunchbox of *Notre Dame.*

Thank you, Miss Piggy. And now for the workout. If in any doubt—about anything whatsoever—please consult Miss Piggy's gynaecologist. You have nothing to lose but your bacon . . . **LK**

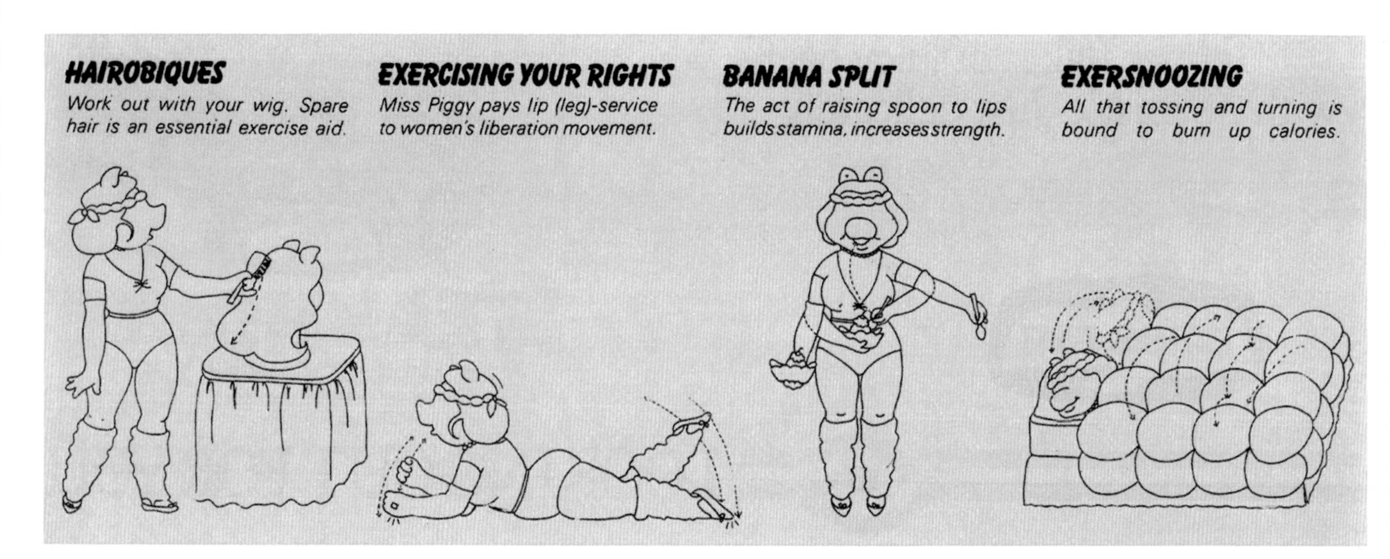

HAIROBIQUES
Work out with your wig. Spare hair is an essential exercise aid.

EXERCISING YOUR RIGHTS
Miss Piggy pays lip (leg)-service to women's liberation movement.

BANANA SPLIT
The act of raising spoon to lips builds stamina, increases strength.

EXERSNOOZING
All that tossing and turning is bound to burn up calories.

Style

WHEN TO WAIT . . . WHEN TO POUNCE . . .

Sexual Manners

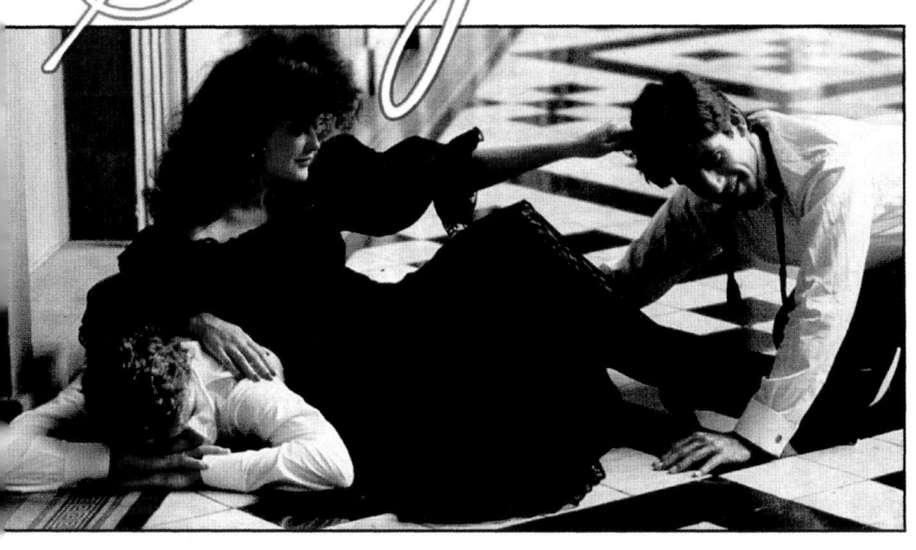

If he can't have an erection . . . don't point, stare, groan, or suggest he was stuffing socks down his trousers. It's just bad manners! And never say, "He was richer/funnier than you." By Marcelle d'Argy Smith.

Despite enormous strides made by Herpes, Aids, Syphilis, Fear of Rejection and Terror of Commitment, there *are* are few reported cases of couples in 1983 enjoying good sex lives. Of course, there is always an element of luck in such matters, but even in today's bewildering atmosphere of complete sexual and personal freedom, there are rules. Sex textbooks explain graphically what to do when you are in bed but omit vital data on *how* to get in, out, and back again. Or why, if, with whom and why not. The new sexual etiquette demands that you know what to say, when to say it, what not to say and how to treat a telephone. It also requires you to be quite ruthlessly honest with yourself while considering deceiving your partner. Etiquette in the socio-sexual arena has little to do with good manners (Heaven forbid) and a great deal to do with appearing relaxed and confident while you're wondering if he's the right man for the job.

When to say "No"

Unless you feel an overwhelming physical urge to jump on someone—say no. Also refuse unhappily married men and men who claim to be happily married, unless it is to you. Avoid mercy-fucking—he'll probably come back for more. *Never* feel obliged. Sex is no way to say "goodnight" or "thanks". Say no to lovers and husbands of friends or relatives. It's rarely worth it.

When to say "Yes"

Your inner sense will tell you when the time is right. It could be the first night, or the fifth date. It is worth waiting until you feel deliciously ripe and excited.

Is it best to wait for sex?

It's up to you. If you wait, there is the thrill of unleashing the sexual tension which builds up after a few dates with someone. Plus there is the special pleasure of exploring the body when you are familiar with the mind. However, many people find it easier to sleep with someone they don't know well. "Sex is a hurdle over which you have to somersault in order to get to know someone"—quote from an exhausted ex-stud, circa 1982.

Can I see someone just for sex?

People play squash together. Why not meet for sex? It's much more relaxing!

When is it best to start an affair?

Friday night or anytime Saturday. Lazy sex over a weekend is the best start.

Should I fake an orgasm?

Perish the thought.

Can I proposition a man?

It's fine by many men, provided you're warmly good-humoured. But never press a reluctant man. He may have a headache.

Does he have a disease?

If you meet him through the Personal Columns, it is a risk. If you meet him on your usual social circuit, chances are that any bad news will have circulated. By all means mention the subject. It's no worse than asking to see his driving licence. Ask *before* you go to bed.

His place or mine?

Men are normally very relaxed on their own territory. Provided you can stand scrutiny in last night's clothes and can face the morning without your Carmen rollers it is often a good idea to play away. Also you can leave when it suits you. But if you're happier at home, by all means seduce him in the familiarity of your own kitchen or bedroom.

If he can't have an erection . . .

You don't point, stare, groan, or suggest he was stuffing socks down his trousers. Sometimes enormous anticipation coupled with fear of performance will cause a man to go limp. You could stroke him everywhere, kiss him gently, masturbate slowly while gazing into his eyes or suggest toasted cheese and tomato sandwiches. Do not refer to "it". If he does, tell him you are happy to wait until next time. Tell him it's reassuring that even *he* can have off-nights. Be affectionate if you like him.

Can't face breakfast?

If you're at his place leave *before* the next morning. Say you have to meet someone at the airport. If he's at your place wake him at seven with black coffee and tell him he has to leave immediately and you'll explain everything later.

What does he like in bed?

Enthusiasm is always appealing. Most men like most things. Remember to be active rather than passive and don't *bite!* Be affectionate as well as seriously horny. It's essential to remember the right name at peak moments.

If he leaves in the night . . .

Ask him to shut the front door properly.

What if you really like him?

You're in big trouble. Stay calm—act as if liking someone with whom you have spent the night was an everyday occurrence. Flash your best post-coital grin, whip up a superbly simple breakfast and then, hiding your feelings, appear to be going purposefully about your day.

How do you say "Goodbye"?

Give him an impulsive warm hug, say he was wonderful and you loved having him.

Will he really "be in touch"?

If he says, "I'll be in touch," it means that he may or may not contact you. Sometimes an enthusiast will suggest a date there and then. But often men prefer to go away and think about it.

Shouldn't he call me?

In ancient Japan it was mandatory for the lover to write a love poem to his lady and deliver it to her before she woke. But today even a 'phone call isn't obligatory after a night together. However, it does indicate the level of involvement you can expect. If you sensed that he was friendly, you could call him. Keep it light and brief. Do *not* let him think that the call was just

CONTINUED

PHOTOGRAPH BY MONTY COLES

Sexual Manners

CONTINUED

an excuse to make contact to force him into asking to see you again. As a general rule, when in doubt—don't.

Things never to say to a man

What are you thinking? Why didn't you call me? Where have you been? Where are you going? Where is our relationship going? Why don't we plan a holiday? Why don't we plan anything? All I want is a reasonable discussion. He was bigger/better/richer/funnier than you. I've lost the keys.

Who should pay?

Pay for yourself if you are with a fellow student or worker. But if a man *invites* you for dinner, do *not* offer to pay for yourself unless he makes it very clear from the outset that that is what he expects. If in doubt, ask beforehand. With men *friends* it is an arbitrary arrangement. Treat *them* if you can afford it sometimes. But drop the man with a company car, a good salary and an expense account who asks you to dine and then demands your share of the bill. He'd be mean in bed as well, so why waste your valuable time?

Can I give him a present?

A nice idea but you can overdo it. Don't be too lavish. He may think you're trying to buy him, and he could feel smothered. Try to keep the relationship on an equal footing. If he isn't spontaneously generous then curb your tendencies. Presents can be guilt-inducing and that is often the subconscious motive behind an apparently thoughtful gesture. Flowers and books are easy low-key gifts. Eternity rings are not!

What if he hasn't called?

If you want to see him, call him with a *definite* invitation—you have theatre tickets, or you're giving a dinner party, or you have been invited to Sunday lunch with friends and would he like to come? If at first you don't succeed, try again. And then give up because it's not only foolish to chase a man who is obviously not interested in you. It can also be extremely humiliating.

Should you discuss ex-lovers?

It is a fairly normal topic of conversation. But be vague and not over-enthusiastic about previous encounters of any kind. Don't name drop even if you and a Sex-Pistol, an MP or an Olympic Gold Medallist were a hot item at one time.

Should you always be available when he calls?

No.

If he's unfair, can reason work?

You're asking *me?* A man I know was heard to say recently, "It's not that I don't think you are fair and probably right. It just doesn't happen to suit me." In short, you cannot reason with an unreasonable person. After all, contemporary socio-sexual behaviour for the male is all about how much he can get away with.

What should I hide from him?

Depression, fears for the future, broken veins, cellulite, a previous abortion, ex-lovers, dirty laundry, your bank account, your mother, that you could be in love with him.

What should you tell him?

You adore going to bed with him, he is wonderful, you love being with him, you love his body, he makes you laugh, it feels good, it's so soft, nobody does it better.

What if you suspect he's bisexual?

As long as he pleases you, accept it. Keep him away from good-looking men friends. If you feel shocked, forget it!

What happens if you're bisexual?

Quite a lot, one hopes.

Shouldn't love come into sex?

We are a repressed society. The Victorians had love without sex and we have sex without love. So much for progress. Sex is a powerful adhesive that glues people together. Of course it's better to be glued to someone you love. But sex is also a terrific sport. It's healthy, relaxing and frankly it beats aerobics any day.

"This could be the end of something small"

Waking thoughts on one of those mornings after the night before . . . By Marcelle d'Argy Smith.

What am I doing here? How much wine did I drink? Do I have any codeine? Did last night really happen? Isn't the back of his neck vulnerable? Aren't his shoulders nice and masculine? What do I mean nice? Is he sleeping as deeply as it sounds? Did we say anything embarrassing to each other? Is he moving? Will he wake up? Shouldn't I creep to the bathroom? What do I look like? Why wasn't I more prepared? Doesn't my mouth taste awful? Can I slide out of this bed without waking him? Will he open an eye and see me? Why aren't I more confident of my body? Will I wobble as I walk? Why was I so anti-exercise? Why didn't I go on a diet? Does it really matter at this point? Why didn't I sleep on the side near my clothes? What are my suede trousers doing on the window-sill? Why don't I go to the bathroom now? Did he stir? Which door is it? Why wasn't that door marked "Cupboard"? Who designed this room? Did he hear the door click? Can he hear me? Do I flush the lavatory and wake him up unromantically or do I act like a charming slut? Does he like sluts? Whose toothbrushes are these? Does he have guest toothbrushes? What is that bottle of Chanel 19 doing there? Does he still see her? Is she good in bed? Is she good out of bed? What am I thinking about? Why isn't the hot water working? Where's the Nivea? How do you regulate these damned taps? What do you put on a scald? Shall I wash everywhere? Did I imagine he'd have a bidet? Isn't baby powder a nice touch of innocence? What's he doing with it? Don't I look rather good, considering? Don't my eyes have a certain shine? Shall I use his razor? Aren't my legs a little rough? Will he be mad if I use his razor? Will he notice if I've used it? Isn't it a relief I had my hair washed yesterday? Does he like tits? Can I get back into bed without him noticing? Shall I douse myself with Chloé or is that too terribly obvious? How high is this room? Why does he keep that photograph of his ex-wife and baby on the walnut chest? Is she a natural red-head? Isn't that baby about 12 years old now? Does my stomach look flatter when I'm lying on my back? What'll we do when he wakes up? Will I get to like him? Does he have plans for any part of this weekend? Will this ruin a friendship? Do I need a lover? Can I cope with one? Will he rush out of bed to play tennis at nine o'clock? Will he drive me home, leave the engine running and say "I'll be in touch"? Why don't I go now and leave a note saying "This could be the end of something small"?

Does he always sleep this soundly? Is he really turning over and smiling with his eyes closed? Will the men delivering my new sofa be livid I'm not in my flat? Isn't it good to have this arm thrown gently over me? Isn't it wonderful it's starting to rain? What else can he find to do in this weather? Do I care about Chanel 19? Or where my boots are? Or if I'm slightly overweight? Shall I wake him? Or is he going to sleep till lunchtime because *he* can't face the morning after?

IT'S FUNNY-
ALL I CAN REMEMBER ABOUT HIM WAS THAT HE SEEMED IN ONE HELLUVA HURRY TO GET ME BACK HERE AFTER THE MEAL.
DICKS

PHOTOGRAPH BY RICHARD ROCKWOOD; CARTOON BY IAN DICKS

So you think you're independent?

Many of us fondly believe we're equal to anything. But we may find we don't practise what we preach . . .

You may think you're truly liberated, but independence doesn't come easily to everyone. And it's not just men whom we rely on: some of us can't make a decision without consulting our network of friends or our parents. Does this include you?

We've concocted a list of things which we believe will sort out the real independents among you. Whatever you may have thought, you're not really independent if you:

- Haven't yet tried a holiday alone—just once.
- Wouldn't dream of going to the cinema or a party unescorted.
- Haven't a clue what your annual income really amounts to, and have certainly never filled in a tax return form.
- Swear blind you'd never, ever, ring any man unless he left a "ring me back" message while you were out.
- Don't know how the electrical wiring system works in your flat—if a fuse blows, someone else always fixes it.
- Hate the thought of spending an occasional relaxed evening at home with just a good book or the television for company.
- Always insist on your friends telling you what they think of your latest man.
- Look blank when the man in your life tells you the brakes on your jointly owned car aren't working because you omitted to fill it up with brake fluid during your recent 600-mile round trip.
- Always deliberately turn up 10 minutes late if you've arranged to meet someone in a public place, in case people think you've been stood up or are just hanging around waiting for a casual pick-up.
- Wouldn't dream of climbing a ladder to the roof to adjust the aerial or unblock the gutter.
- Shy away from lunching or dining alone in case people might think you had nobody to take you out.
- Never go to the bar in a pub to buy a round of drinks, preferring to give a man the money, so he will go and do it for you.

PHOTOGRAPH BY BENSIMON/TRANSWORLD

- Wait to be asked out—whether by prospective lovers or girlfriends—rather than take the initiative.
- Don't have you own bank account.
- Never make the first move in bed.
- Don't make long car journeys or journeys to strange places on your own, doing your own navigating.
- Say "We're going to knock this wall down/strip the doors/build an extension" when what you really mean is *he* will do all that and you'll collect the credit.
- Never see your friends without taking your man along, too.
- Let him arrange the mortgage/survey/solicitor on the new house you're buying together.
- Give dinner parties for eight or ten people but ask the male guests to open the wine.
- Never invest money without consulting half a dozen experts.
- Can't make *any* decisions without consulting someone else.
- Never invite a man out to dinner and calmly foot the bill.
- Don't make any social arrangements without consulting your partner first.
- Insist on dragging someone along when you shop for a special outfit and refuse to make a purchase until your companion shows full approval.
- Don't have ideas about how the country should be run.
- Rely on the good old family handout when you've overspent or when the bank manager is starting to sound threatening.
- Won't budge from your convenient flat-sharing set-up to buy your own place, even though your fellow flatmates bore you to tears/have nothing in common with you/are perpetually rude to your friends.
- Wait for him to organise the weekend's entertainment.
- Move in on him possessively when a slinky blonde corners him at a party.
- Have never taken your bank manager out to lunch.
- Think that *any* man is better than no man at all.

A body like Victoria Principal's for only 25p?

GET INTO SHAPE – FEEL AND LOOK GREAT!

The Body Principal is THE exercise book for the health and beauty conscious woman of today – and costs only 25p if you join the Fitness & Health Book Society now.

From the stunningly beautiful star of Dallas comes a revolutionary and easy workout that you can do anywhere. Exercise for as little as 15 minutes a day and take a few tips from Victoria Principal's very own lifestyle diet and you could be fitter than you've ever been before.

It's a simple, effective – and fast working – programme, and lots of fun to do. But it's only the beginning ... If you're concerned about being healthy, vital and beautiful there are many more books in the Fitness & Health Book Society that will help you to realise your full potential. Books on natural beauty, slimming, exercise, wholesome cooking *– all at vastly reduced prices* (usually 25% off publishers prices). And you only have to buy four during your first year of membership. Join now by filling in the coupon below and we'll send you The Body Principal – your first step towards positive, healthy living.

- **A fast effective way to retone your body.**
- **A revolutionary – yet easy – programme of isometric exercises.**
- **Focus on *your* problem areas – resculpt your body with the minimum of time and effort.**
- **Exercises to do almost anywhere, anytime.**

***Plus* For those who wish to progress further – an extensive programme using exercise machines.**

Published at £8.95 – **Yours for only 25p** plus p&p when you join.

THE BODY PRINCIPAL

The Exercise Programme For Life

Includes a safe and effective 30-day diet plan

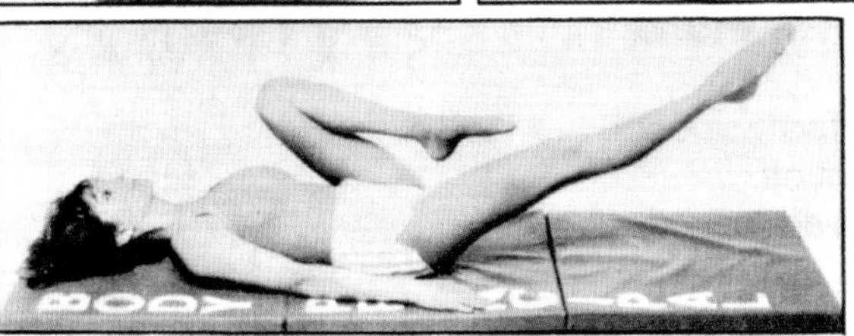

ESTABLISHED 1937

Readers Union, Brunel House, Newton Abbot, Devon Reg. in England No. 843946

YOU NEED SEND NO MONEY NOW – POST TODAY

CB 31 84 N6

To: Fitness & Health Book Society, Readers Union Ltd., PO Box 6, Newton Abbot, Devon TQ12 2DW

Please enrol me as a member of the Fitness & Health Book Society and send me *The Body Principal* at the special price of just 25p *(plus *45p total towards post and packing)* for which you will invoice me later.

If not delighted I will return the book within 10 days and owe nothing. My membership will then be cancelled.

As a member I agree to buy at least one title from each quarterly magazine for a minimum of one year. I may resign at any time thereafter on a month's notice. I will pay upon receipt for any book I choose.

1

Mr/Mrs/Miss ____ Initials ____ Surname ____ PLEASE PRINT CLEARLY

Address ____

Town ____ County ____

Postcode ____

Signature ____ (must be signed by an adult) ONE MEMBERSHIP PER HOUSEHOLD

FITNESS & HEALTH

Stab in

Stop right there! Don't do anything, say anything . . . don't even
Disregard all other information and watch this space every month

in	out
Dandies	Pansies
Jermaine Jackson	Michael Jackson
Laser 558	Capital 194
Speech	Memos
Hard news	Bingo
Anything but . . .	SDP
Shy looks (Princess Di)	Aloof pouts (Phoebe Cases)
Word processors	Typewriters
Long lunches	Exercise classes

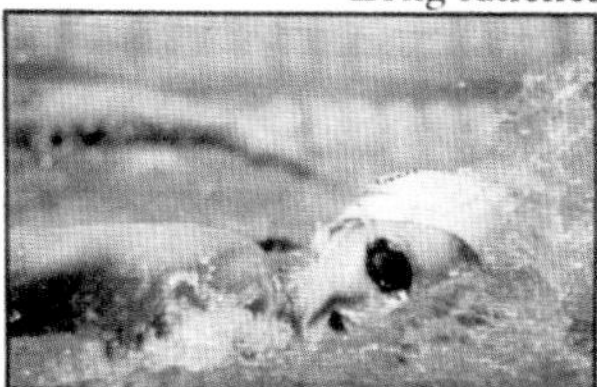

in	out
Swimming	Aerobics
Freelancing	Regular work
Individuals	Clones

in	out
Board Games	Video Games
Acoustic sound	Synthesisers

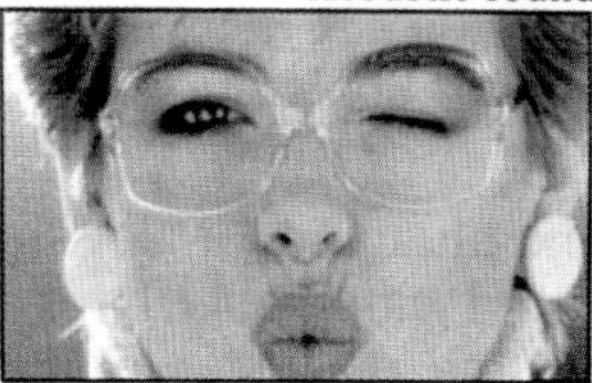

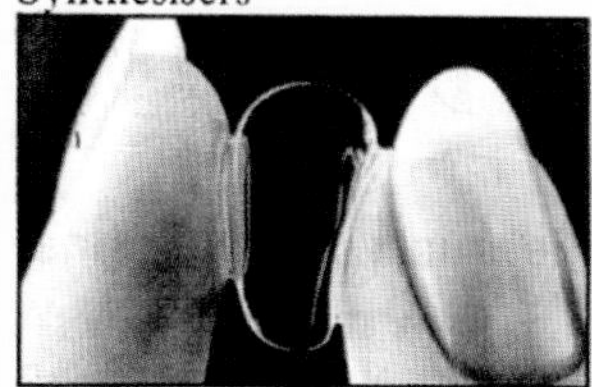

in	out
Spectacles	Contact lenses
Glamour	Depression wear
Wallpaper	Paint
Viennese secession	Memphis
Older men	Toy boys

in	out
Hill Street Blues	Dallas

in	out
Plate cameras	Polaroids
Anywhere but . . .	Spain
Babies	Dogs/cats
Cuba	Sri Lanka
Pearls	Diamanté
Builders	DIY
Jungles	Landscape gardens

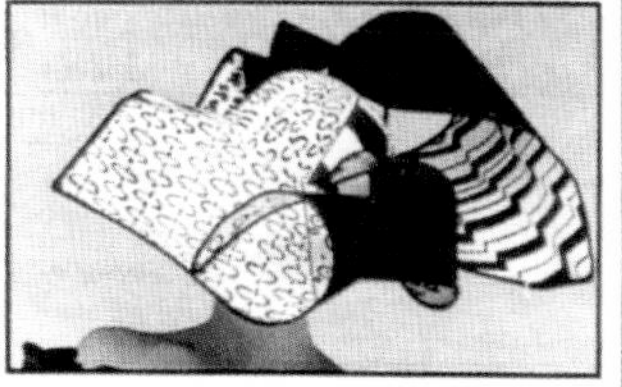

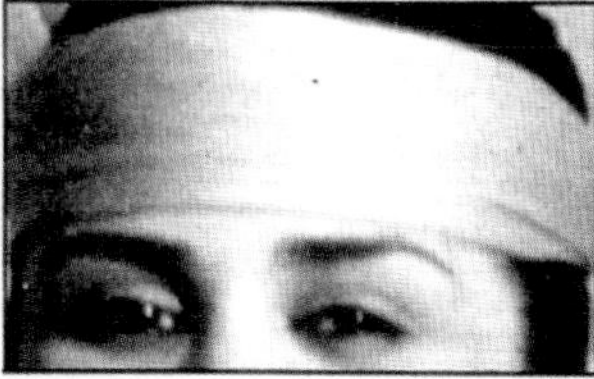

in	out
Hats	Headbands
Decathlon	Marathon
Trash Camp	Culture

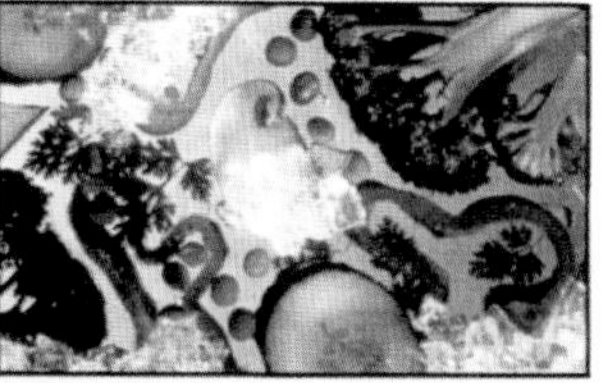

in	out
Comfort food	Nouvelle cuisine
Trompe l'oeil	Marbling/ragging
Brookside	Coronation Street
BBC 2	Channel 4

in	out
Jaguars	Morris Minors
Pyjamas	Lingerie
Princess Anne	Prince Andrew

in	out
Wapping	Hampstead
Charles Dance	Robert Redford
Heteros	Androgyny

the back

breathe until you've read this: *Cosmo's* definitive guide to what is, and what is not, IN for 1985! for more piercing stabs of humour, outrage, sex, gossip and topical tittle-tattle. By Paul Kerton.

in	out
Farce	Tragedy

in	out
Jackie Collins	Joan Collins
Condoms	The pill
Escort XR3	VW Golf GTi
Tufty	Roland Rat
Combi Pens	Ball Pentels
Anything European	Everything American
1st Class	Any compromise
Women	Girls
Styling mousse	Chocolate mousse
Thermal underwear	Legwarmers

in	out
Cafés/brasseries	Wine bars
Chocolate chip	Water biscuits
Cinema	TV

in	out
Croquet	Tennis
GLC	Ken Livingstone
Radio Times	The Face
Expense accounts	Charity
Combat jackets	Barbaur jackets
Books	Video

in	out
Cowboy boots	High-heeled boots
Lira	Dollar

in	out
Glynn Boyd Harte	Hockney

in	out
Brutes	Non-sexist men
China	India
Aesthetician	Beauty therapist
Tofu	Kung Fu
YAPS	Sloanes
Collapse	Relax

in	out
Cyndi Lauper	Sindy Doll
Terry Wogan	Michael Parkinson
Cash	American Express
Musician's briefcase	Photographer's metal case
Broiled food	Boiled food
Resigning	Job loyalty
Ties	Bow ties

in	out
Tassle jackets	Denim jackets
Slides	Hairdresser's clips
Flirting	Dating
Optimism	Cynicism

BUT RAYBANS ARE FOREVER AND EVER AND EVER

Male

What's a male orgasm? Just one lonely release, and then exhaustion? No more! Using Taoist techniques, men can teach themselves how to have multiple orgasms—and come back for more. By Julia Stonehouse.

Female orgasm used to be just an "orgasm". In 1966, Masters and Johnson wrote: "Are clitoral and vaginal orgasms truly separate anatomic entities? From a biological point of view, the answer to this question is an unequivocal 'No'." Today, however, mystery is accepted, diversity allowed, and a large vocabulary required to help map out the complex landscape. Experts speak of orgasms that are "clitoral" or "vulval", "vaginal", "blended", "G-spot", "ejaculatory", "uterine", or part of a "multiple group"! A male orgasm, however, remains "an orgasm".

But what is a male orgasm? Dr Bernie Zilbergeld, sex therapist: "Ejaculation is the physical process involved in propelling semen through the penis. Orgasm refers to what you feel. Generally the two go together and you ejaculate and feel very pleasurable feelings. But one can occur without the other. You can have orgasms without ejaculating. Some men have trained themselves to do this, and according to their reports, have been able to have multiple orgasms, like women. And some men, who have trained themselves carefully to tune into their sensations during sex, say that they sometimes notice very high peaks of feeling, long before ejaculation.

"Were they not so indoctrinated in the idea that orgasm occurs only with pelvic contractions and ejaculation, they would be inclined to call these peaks orgasm. The reverse situation is more common, where the man ejaculates—there's the white stuff to prove it—but feels very little."

Could men make love for longer?

So, if these "very high peaks of feeling" occur independently of ejaculation, and ejaculation can occur with "very little feeling" it seems that despite what is "normal" in most men's experience, male orgasm and ejaculation aren't the same. This is important because it's ejaculation which causes loss of erection and "refraction" (he's exhausted and falls asleep). Being able to have orgasms without ejaculating means men can enjoy prolonged lovemaking without feeling they're holding back or being left out for the sake of the woman. They could have more fun.

In sexology, distinctions are made between capacity (what someone is capable of), performance (what they usually do), and drive (what they want to do). Culturally there is great variation in what men *want* to do, and this is determined to a degree by what's considered "good" or "normal". The man who grows up in the Chinese Taoist tradition is taught that the absorption of female sexual juices through the membrane of his penis is good; that he should therefore endeavour to stimulate the woman to many orgasms (so that her juices flow); while maintaining his erection so it's still in contact with the vagina, and its juices. But the Chinese recognised the man might become bored with this prolonged lovemaking if he weren't to experience orgasm himself and so Taoist technique teaches the man to separate orgasm from ejaculation, bringing performance into harmony with drive.

But while the Chinese tradition emphasised male and female pleasure—without ejaculation, the Judeo-Christian tradition has emphasised the opposite—the suppression of pleasure and encouragement of legitimate procreative sex. Which, in male terms, *is* ejaculation. It may seem contradictory to say that the Judeo-Christian culture has repressed pleasure if, at the same time, ejaculation feels exquisite. But it's difficult for a man to deliver his sperm *without* feeling pleasure. A woman's orgasm is easily repressed, however, with guilt and ignorance, while in no way affecting her capacity to conceive the next generation; and the rush to ejaculate and get the whole sinful business over with clearly brings everybody's pleasure to a speedy halt.

So what's going on?

The text books tell us that the male experience is broken into two components: *emission* and *expulsion*. *Emission* feels like "I'm starting to come", and is the contractions of the internal reproductive organs, the prostate gland, *vas deferens*, seminal vesicles, and the internal part of the urethra. There's a time gap (usually seconds, but which some men can extend), and then *expulsion*—contractions of the external pelvic muscles which force the semen out of the urethra—ejaculation.

Ejaculation is easy to identify in the lab (with the muscles at the base of the penis contracting involuntarily three to seven times at 0.8 second intervals). But measuring the activity of the internal organs and deducing what they are actually up to is more complex. It is, for example, only "speculated" that the function of emission is to deliver the various components of the ejaculate to the bulbar urethra—at the base of the penis. Text books are full of words like "presumably" and "probably", along with expressions like "recent evidence indicates". We just don't know what happens between "It's starting" and those ejaculatory spurts. Emission is controlled by the pelvic nerves, operating in the inner portion of the complex pelvic muscle (the pubococcogeus muscle—PC for short). Ejaculation is controlled by another nerve root (the pudendal) in another portion of the

orgasm
It's good news

same muscle. So there's a physical basis for making a distinction between the processes that accompany "I'm starting to come" and those that go with ejaculation. Usually, whatever sensations occur with "I'm coming" are drowned out by the contractions of ejaculation, happening simultaneously, and the two processes get confused. But that doesn't mean they *have* to get confused.

Jolan Chang, a Taoist, doesn't like them confused, and explains why, "... ejaculation is a release of tension in an explosive way. Like a shout of rage or a burst of laughter ... If that is true, then I can say that sex without ejaculation is also a release of tension but without the explosion. It is a pleasure of peace, not of violence, a sensuous and lastingly satisfying melting into something larger and more transcendent than oneself. It is a feeling of wholeness, not of separation; a merging and a sharing, not an exclusive, private and lonely spasm. Beyond that, it eludes words." *(The Tao of Loving, 1977.)*

How to have a multiple orgasm

It takes skill for a man to separate the two phases and here sex author Michael Morgernstern gives his multiple orgasm technique: "When a man is about to come, the muscles in the pelvis and legs are generally in a state of high tension. If you consciously relax the muscles—let the tension go—the sensations become very intense. You can allow yourself to feel a deep throbbing that approaches orgasm. In fact, it *is* orgasm without ejaculation." I would add to this that the man should consciously relax his jaw and mouth muscles as these are, for some reason, related to the pelvic muscles. Whether the "deep throbbing" described by non-ejaculatory men is caused by contractions of the prostate gland or by contractions of a particular portion of the PC muscle surrounding the internal organs, remains a mystery.

Biofeedback techniques and the discovery of the body's natural opiates, endorphins, have convinced the medical community that many "involuntary" physical processes are, in fact under voluntary control. "Mind over matter" has arrived in the West, millennia after it arrived in the East.

The prostate gland is sexually sensitive and partly explains the attraction of passive homosexual love. The chestnut-sized prostate can be felt through the wall of the rectum, directly under the bladder. The urethral tube runs right through it, picking up its contribution to the seminal fluid at the "emission" phase of male response, before it's spurted out of the penis during the expulsion phase of ejaculation. Stimulation of the prostate is, apparently, very sexy, and the orgasm produced this way "different". One respondent in the *Spada Report on Male Homosexuality* (USA, 1979) described it thus: "to say that it feels different is putting it mildly. It's like comparing a little Cessna to a Boeing 747." A quote like this can make a heterosexual woman feel somewhat inadequate but if our men want to experience this, it can be tried—with the fingers.

The Spada report makes interesting reading because it shows just how diverse male orgasms can be. James Spada asked over 1,000 men: "When you are anally penetrated, does your orgasm feel different? How?" This is his summary of the replies: "Men in these responses spoke not only of heightened penile orgasm created by the rubbing of their partner's penis against their prostate gland, but also of anal orgasm, of general orgasm impossible to fix at any one location, continual orgasm which lasts throughout the sexual act, and of penile orgasm achieved without any contact being made with the penis either by themselves or by their partners." One man said, "I experience multiple orgasms—feelings from my head to my toes"; another, "The pleasure is so great and builds steadily until I think I've come—but I haven't, at least not through my penis ..." And one said, "I seem to orgasm internally, if that's possible ..." And it is.

Good muscle tone is known to reduce post-coital exhaustion, and to be a factor in ejaculation control as well as multiple orgasm technique. But in this culture, strength and control of the male sexual muscles is a subject as undeveloped as the muscles themselves. This isn't surprising because, traditionally, sexual "control" has meant "to suppress". In the East, however, sexual control means "to manoeuvre"; they've learned what men can do.

New nerve route found in the penis

Muscle action is triggered by chemicals, which are released on the arrival of nerve impulses. In 1981 Dr Julia Polak and her associates at Hammersmith Hospital identified a nerve system in the penis "of a newly recognised class". The chemical found in these "peptidergic" nerves is also a new discovery—it's called VIP for short, and controls the erection. It also regulates blood-flow, secretion and muscle tone, and affects the contractions of emission to an unknown extent. The positive properties of VIP (or, for biologists, vasoactive intestinal polypeptide) are extensive, as at least one pharmaceutical company has realised, and it won't be long before we see advertisements saying: "Become a real VIP—overnight!".

But an erection guarantees orgasm less than the appearance of "the white stuff", so how can we measure ecstasy? When we find the answer it'll probably have something to do with the hypothalamus—that sophisticated balancer of sympathetic and parasympathetic nerves; controller of glands and secretions. Deep in the brain, it receives messages and sends orders to every moving part of our body. It is a Pandora's Box, regulating the chemicals of ecstasy through nerve routes and blood stream into the furthest recesses of our whole being. Indeed, we would be closer to truth if we thought of ecstasy as a chemical phenomenon, rather than as a mechanical one. But the system works as a whole, of course. The brain decides which of its chemical tricks it's going to play and that's determined by the psychological state of a person as well as the physical stimulation they are receiving. The nerves are important, and their health depends partly on the tone of the muscles. Make a fist, or flex your biceps, and you'll see that muscle action is regulated by the brain. Mind over matter—what we think, what we feel, and the choices we make will determine how we develop our sexuality. And in the future, men will be faced with a new choice—will they take the new "erection pill", or learn to be our *natural* VIPs?

Irma Kurtz's AGONY COLUMN

Q I have been involved for two years with a man I met 13 years ago. We went out for 18 months, then broke up and didn't see each other again for eight years. He says he wants to marry me but not for a long time because he is very ambitious. He has everything a man of 36 years could want—including his own established business. He stays with me every night but goes home at 4.30 a.m. as he lives with his parents and doesn't want them to know that he is sleeping with me. I love him and so does my 14-year-old son but waiting for him to decide is killing me.

A A 36-year-old man who lives with his parents and does not want them to know he's sleeping with his girlfriend, has certainly not got everything a man of his age could have. In fact, it sounds as if he hasn't got anything much *except* his own business. Where is his freedom? Where is his maturity? Where is his joy in life? Where is his home? Where are his children? Where are the lazy Sundays in bed with the woman he loves? Stop waiting for him to decide. He's probably not able to make his own decisions. Expect nothing from him beyond what he is able to give you. Get on with your own life. See other people, men too. It's up to him to solve his own problems and up to you to make sure they don't become your problems too.

Q I'm 20 years old and my problem is that I'm hopelessly in love with Michael Jackson. I know I'm probably too old to have crushes but I can't seem to shake this off. My parents are worried because he's black, plus they think he occupies too much of my time. I've tried to forget him. I realise I'll never meet him but I can't help wondering what he's really like. He makes me happy and I just wish there was some way I could help him. I know I must sound like a real lunatic. I know many girls are caught up in Michael-mania, but he's more to me than a superstar, he's someone I'd really like to sit and talk with and help him overcome his hang-ups.

A You are not alone. Admittedly, most of the letters of this sort I receive are from considerably younger girls who will probably have outgrown their little mania by the time they are your age. Mind you, I also have one similar letter from an infatuated 40-year-old so perhaps age is not so telling in such matters as maturity and satisfaction with life in hand. I do not for the life of me see how you imagine you can help Mr Jackson beyond being his fan (where would he be without them?) as the problems of a superstar's life are way beyond your ken—as they are mine. Somewhere inside that pretty young man there is doubtless a real person who is entitled to his privacy and who is none of our business. It won't do you any good to hear from me what you already know: it is a flight from reality to fall hopelessly in love with a voice and a picture. It's not your flight into fantasy that is the problem but whatever it is about your real life that makes you prefer Cloud-cuckoo-land. Love Jackson if you must, but concentrate on organising a good job, further education perhaps, and a place of your own in the world. As your own existence becomes satisfying, you will need your dreamlife less and less. Tell your parents not to worry that Michael Jackson is black, or blue, or green. It isn't likely he'll be coming home to dinner.

Q My husband is often away on business trips. He says he wants to be faithful to me and that I am the only person he loves. We have discussed the sexual frustration he faces on these long trips and he has told me that he masturbates. Now he has asked me to have my picture taken wearing lingerie. It doesn't bother me that he wants my pictures but recently I found some nude pictures of his first wife. I don't think of myself as a cheap centrefold type. And as he has kept his first wife's photos I feel as though he might also keep mine, (should something happen to break up our marriage) and other people might see them. I don't mind the thought of him using the pictures for his own personal needs but I am worried that they might some day be used against me. Why do I feel so guilty about doing something that would be for my own good?

A Like a lot of men, your husband is turned on by an image. It's convenient that he likes the image to be of you, but remember photos are all only paper-thin, even those of his first wife, and they don't do much more than save him the price of a girlie magazine when he's on a working trip. I cannot imagine how you could ever be compromised by such photographs. There is no law against your having them taken. A lot of men carry similar snapshots of wives and girlfriends which they keep as secret, personal things—"talis-women", in a way. If you are really worried about future blackmail, why not ask him playfully to give you a few centrefold photos of himself? Pose him with a rose between his teeth. That way he'll have a lot more to lose than you, should it ever come to a showdown!

Q I'm in love with a bachelor at work, but he seems reluctant to ask me out because I'm the boss's daughter. My father makes fun of him because he wants me to stay single (I'm in my thirties), not have any children and some day rule the family empire. I live with my parents, and my father says this helps their shaky marriage. My father pays me a pittance so I can't move out and see this man in private. I treasure every moment I spend with him and people are starting to notice us together. What can we do?

A If you are strong enough to rule the family empire, then you are strong enough to leave it. If you are smart enough to be considered as heir to your father's business, you're smart enough to be employed elsewhere at a fair salary. It is time for a revolution in daddy's little kingdom, and ▶

◀ you're the one who had better pull it off right away because your head is on the block. Your father uses you not just as slave help but also as a cover to his unsuccessful marriage. These are the tactics of a tyrant and if you put up with them you are not helping your mother, yourself, or even in the long run your father. Get a job somewhere else and move into a flat of your own. You must put your building blocks down now or on what will you ever found your own empire? You are still young and you should have the energy and courage to start taking charge of your own life. As for the bachelor, please move cautiously. I suspect your heart has not become a mature organ under your father's jurisdiction, and you need experience before you commit it to a great love. You may not be seeing the facts, only dreaming like the sleeping princess. Start establishing your own province. Make it big enough for two or even more, but don't pin all your hopes on the bachelor joining you. If children do owe their parents a debt, you have certainly paid yours. To be honest, it has always seemed to me that it is parents who owe their children everything.

Q I am 26 years old and have known that I am a lesbian since I left school at 18 but I have never had a lover, male or female. I am reasonably good-looking and I get on well with people. I can easily attract men but I've never been interested in carrying that further. I have recently moved and for the first time in my life, I am able to go to gay clubs and mix with other lesbians on a regular basis but I feel very unsure about my ability to attract women. I've made friends with a few couples but no single woman has approached me and I feel too shy to approach anyone myself. I'm so terrified of rejection.

A Shyness around desirable people affects everybody and the fact that you are a lesbian doesn't change that. Keep seeing the people you like, male and female, and mixing with those whose company you enjoy. Look on every new person of either sex as a potential friend and sooner or later one of them will emerge, perhaps even to your surprise, as a lover.

Q I have a beautiful son who lights up my life and my husband's. However, we've decided not to have any more children. We've looked at it objectively and emotionally and decided we don't want any more. What is worrying us is the fact that our son might be lonely. Our families have said we're being cruel and that our son will resent the fact he has no sister or brother. There are playgroups in the town, but I do worry that this might not be enough, and that he will miss the companionship of a sister or brother. However, I don't think it would be right to have another child simply to be a "companion" to our son.

A We don't live in tight family units anymore. Your son's friends will soon be tramping through the kitchen and staying overnight. Loneliness is something within, not lack of company, and if you help him build his resources there is no reason why solitude should then be anything but his own choice. If your families think nurturing, loving and protecting can be cruel under any circumstances, then they are prejudiced and haven't thought things out. You and your husband should continue to do what you both know is the correct decision for you and your son.

Irma Kurtz's Cosmopolitan *book* Crises: a guide to your emotions, *is available from Vandek Mailing Ltd, 8 Holyrood Street, London SE1 2EL, price £2.95 (Republic of Ireland, £3.75) inc p&p. Please make cheques payable to* Cosmopolitan.

If you have a problem, write to Irma Kurtz's Agony Column, Cosmopolitan, *National Magazine House, 72 Broadwick Street, London W1V 2BP. Irma regrets that she is unable to answer your letters personally.*

Sex on the job

You don't want sexual harassment, but that doesn't mean you don't want sex! What *are* the rules about office liaisons? By Ros Miles.

You all know the rule about drinking alcohol on aeroplanes—it looks good and tastes good but makes you feel bad and you finish up more hairy than airy. Yet look around you on any long flight. From the moment of take-off the hooch will be glugging down every throat including yours as if prohibition had just been re-invented in the world outside.

It's the same with sex at work. You know the theory. The truly dedicated professional has her mind on her work. Business and pleasure don't mix, so the cool cookie keeps them in separate compartments. In the words of the Canadian film critic Maurice Yacowar (he swears it's a Russian proverb), "You don't eat in the toilet, why crap in the kitchen?" But life has a habit of refusing to stay in watertight compartments. Work and love frequently get inextricably confused, for one very good reason.

Quite simply, work is often a place where you meet a lot of men. Now don't let's knock badminton clubs, evening classes or countryside reclamation programmes as a way of winkling out some good-quality males. But the workplace is still the prime area for making social/sexual contacts, especially for a newcomer to a city. "I meet men all the time," says Lynette, who is a secretary in a Birmingham Chambers. "Everything from arch-villains to top barristers. It was great to have someone to go out with when I arrived—it helped me to get settled in."

If your relations with your colleagues are confined to a lunchtime game of basketball and a glass of plonk at Christmas, or if you are deeply into an old-fashioned courtship with the altar beckoning, you have little to worry about. But what about the tricky situation that faces many working women, an attraction for a boss or colleague who you will not expect to marry. What then?

Let's be clear that we are *not* talking about sexual harassment. This is a major problem for large numbers of women in the work force. Just how many is not yet certain. A NALGO survey found that 36 per cent of the women who responded had experienced SH; a Manchester University study of British female managers put the figure at 52 per cent; and a recent study, undertaken by the Inland Revenue Staff Association, produced the staggering result of 75 per cent. But by its agreed definition SH means "repeated and *unwanted* sexual advances". And just because you don't want sexual harassment doesn't mean you don't want sex! So on the assumption that your daily stamping ground is also your hunting ground, what do you do?

Rule number one is that at work, work must be seen to come first. Don't let your employer get the feeling that she/he is subsidising your sex life in the form of late arrivals, early departures and extended lunch hours, after which you're no good for any thing anyway. They do expect you to squeeze your carnal blisses into the *other* 133 hours of the week. They get shirty at the prospect of continuing to pay you at your normal rate while you moon openly over Joe Bedworthy, spend hours on the phone to him, or drool onto scented notepaper everything you forgot to tell him last night in bed.

More serious than the loss of their time may be the loss of your credibility. At work, you only gain respect by how well you do your work. Many bosses are already convinced that all that "girls" think about is their love life. Confirming this old myth lays you wide open to criticism.

"I really rated Jane," said one manager to me of a trainee. "Then she fell in love and really blew it. She was never there, never any use when she was there, and once she came rushing back from lunch with her jumper on inside out. Well, there's no future in that!"

Credibility is like virginity. You can only lose it once. And you could lose more than this. A wild affair at work can even cost you your job. Two lovebirds in a London manufacturing company were sacked for canoodling in the workplace. They then lost an appeal against dismissal at the Industrial Tribunal, on the grounds that they had brought it on themselves.

But this is a rare occurrence. Recognise that even in today's climate of opinion, *you* are far more likely to have to leave than *he* is, if love goes wrong. "The girl is expected to go under these circumstances," explained a prominent industrialist. "The bloke is usually the one we want, after all."

In the nature of things, women rarely fall for their equal at work. We're conditioned to look for men who are older, richer and more successful than we are. Men also tend to crack on with career advancement and get further sooner than we do. The chances are, then, that your lover may have a more important position than yours—he'll be a boss or manager, or on the sales force, say, while you're in admin. That means your lover will tend to hold the cards in your affair. You'll be working to his schedule rather than the other way around—and when the chips are down it'll be his hide they'll try to protect, not yours, because he's more valuable to the organisation.

OK, enough of the awful warnings and cautionary tales. Love and work are a volatile combination, and any explosion produced by their mingling may be violent. But thousands of people mingle delightfully and avoid the fallout. How do you get it right? As follows!

PHOTOGRAPH BY GIANNI SPINAZZOLA

1 Be positive. Decide what you want. Women on the move, women moving upwards, often deliberately choose short-term relationships. If that's for you, be honest with yourself. Don't play the sentimental hypocrite, convincing yourself that you're an innocent victim of this irresistible passion, when in your heart you know he was a dead duck from the moment you eyeballed him as the newest hunk to hit Accounts. Self-knowledge gives self-control. And control is the secret. So:

2 Be selective. Don't pick the men with whom you'll be out of control. Choose your working lover with care. What this means, at the risk of sounding like your granny, is beware of the boss and miss out on married men. Both of them have too much going on in their lives, both for them and against them, that you don't know about and can't allow for. Julia thought it was wonderful when her boss in the firm where she worked as a data processor became interested in her. The imbalance of power and status between them never troubled her. They had a happy affair over a period of years which ended without trauma. But later she found out that he had systematically blocked her promotion during that time, just to keep her with him.

As to husbands, remember Iris Murdoch's warning: "A married couple is a dangerous machine." Sue accepted John's assurances that his wife didn't know/wouldn't care about their involvement at the college where they both worked as lecturers. He was as horrified as she was when the wife found out, and took to haunting the college till they became a local scandal. When the college principal issued a "one of you has to go" ultimatum, well, John was a married man, wasn't he? He couldn't move because he had a house, children at the local schools, and his wife's job to worry about. So Sue had to go. That's the unacknowledged reality of it all.

3 And finally, **be ready to call the tune.** If you don't, you risk finding yourself cast as an extra in your own psychodrama, constantly revolving round the central character—him! Positive action for lovergirls means being able to say:

○ No, I'll call *you*—possibly Wednesday of next week when this big push at work is over. *Subtext:* I'm sick of hanging around the phone waiting for you to give me a ring.

○ We need a weekend away together to unwind—can you manage one next month if I book somewhere? *Subtext:* I'm getting dissatisfied with snatched lunchtimes and abortive get-togethers in the graveyard hour after work.

○ Can we find a new pub for a change? *Subtext:* I'm up to here with being polite to your goofy gang of local oiks when it's you I want to be with.

All this is important because to succeed, affairs at work really do call for constant and careful management. At your peril do you either let them take you over, or else hope they'll wither away as you can afford to do with an off-duty relationship. Work is a public arena, there are a lot of unspoken pressures on everyone in it, and if you are just blundering along you can risk electrocuting yourself on crossed wires. So go carefully. You can enjoy love in your work life without finishing up all over the floor. And at the end of the day, the situation provides you with the perfect formula for bringing things to a conclusion when you want to—you simply tell him that he will always be very precious to you, but work comes first!

"New Men are worth waiting for."

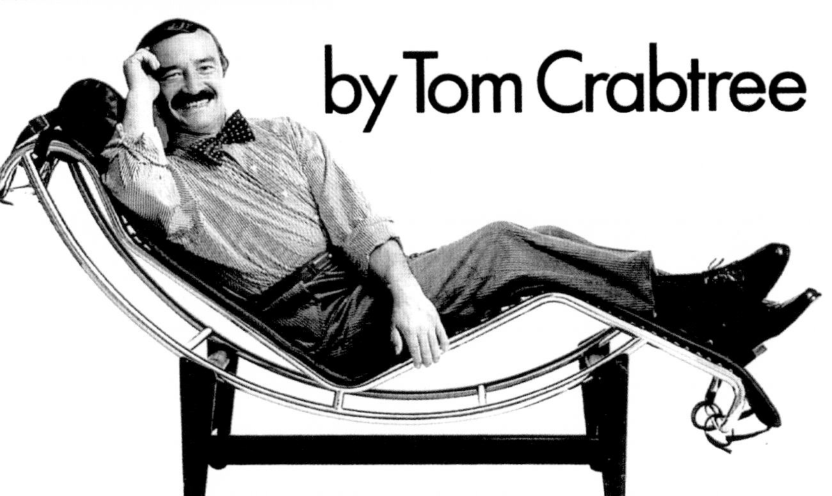

by Tom Crabtree

Q **I am a 32-year-old divorcee with two children. My problem is not finding boyfriends but keeping the ones I like. In the past two years since I have been divorced, I have had numerous relationships, the longest of which has lasted about three months.**

I am intelligent, have a good figure and am reasonably attractive, with (as my friends tell me) a good sense of humour. My divorced friends all have steady relationships—so where am I going wrong? I don't even want to get married again; it would just be nice to have someone special in my life.

I've tried being cool, totally honest, sleeping with them, not sleeping with them, being myself and not being myself. They seem keen enough to begin with but it always finishes with them not telephoning, starting to see someone else or generally treating me badly.

I am a fairly assertive person. Do you think I am frightening them off or have I just been unlucky? *S.*

A Dear S. You aren't the only one who has experienced this problem: and I think the truth is that you *could* be frightening them off just a little.

It's natural that now single, with two children, you should want to find a partner—a man who can be a good friend to you (and the children) with whom you can feel a woman and be happy. Fine. The lump in the custard is anxiety: rushing at things, forcing the pace, wanting to be at stage P (permanence) when you're still really at E (exploration). The approach should be to play it cool, enjoy the company of the men you go out with, relax. The relationship will grow if you take it easy. It's surprising how over-anxiety transmits itself to men. You don't have to do the candy-floss lady bit or pretend in any way. It's just that no man I know wants to feel, on a first meeting, that he's being weighed up as a suitable permanent partner. You should, at this stage, be looking for one or two good male friends; you can turn your mind to long-term commitments later—when you've learned to relax, be you and have a little fun together.

Try not to be too tense and to understand that men like to think that they are the hunters. Don't expect a man to talk about love, trust and intimacy on the very first evening: they're probably more concerned at how great a dent the evening is likely to make in their wallets.

Men feel threatened by touch, by real contact, by intimacy. That's why some men talk of women in terms of "scores" or "birds" they can "knock off". Men are obsessed with performance. Don't expect too much from them on the first date: imagine you are teaching an elephant to ice-skate and be very patient.

Build up your support network of friendly men and women. Centre upon yourself for a while: work out who you are, what you need and want. Don't go from the frying pan of an unsatisfactory marriage into the fire of some passing man who will fragment you and lead you up some emotional dead-end. Enjoy your freedom and don't settle for second rate. Be reasonably assertive but not over-aggressive. I don't think you should lower your standards of what you want. There is a shortage of tender, intelligent men, but the New Man is coming. Like the typewriter, it's one thing to think up the idea, another to get it into mass production. The New Man is on his way, though: the ideas of old style men don't work any more.

Stick out for a New Man (one who talks to you and knows that affection is vital to human beings) and for a relationship that *works.* It won't work if you force it: success depends on you sticking to what you believe in.

Teach men about love, life and sharing. That's what they need to know. You will have to stay cool if you want to be a woman who shares, rather than commands or obeys.

Whether you sleep with them or not is irrelevant. Find somebody you like, whose company you enjoy: if you take the performing seal approach to men, you're really colluding with the Tarzan-Jane model of partnership. Tarzan swinging through trees, Jane bored out of her mind.

If men get their way because women are desperate for "someone special" in their lives, those New Men will never arrive and life will be nasty, brutish and long. Men will change once they learn that co-operation is as vital as competition. Women must teach them. Shall we have womanly times or live out our lives in an emotional desert? It's as simple as that. With women, men must learn that tattoos and biceps don't count, that bossiness doesn't pay and that women are entitled to be assertive from time to time.

Through friendship with women, men can learn to modify their innate aggression, their competitiveness. Look for a man who has something valid to say, something valid to share. Don't be in a hurry. New Men are worth waiting for.

What is life without tenderness and love? What is life without affection and caring? Women's values are vital to us all.

Relax, S. Enjoy your freedom. Enjoy your children. Teach those men, younger or older, by example. Show them that you can be alive, have lots of fun, laugh, feel good about yourself. They'll get the idea and feel that way when they're with you. Be you. Do what you want to do for you, and for the future of your children. Find a man who deserves you.

Remember that every time you jump through a hoop, instead of building up genuine networks of friendships from which a lasting partnership can emerge, you are letting yourself down. You are a woman. There will be womanly times, I promise.

Write to Tom Crabtree, Cosmopolitan, *National Magazine House, 72 Broadwick Street, London W1V 2BP. (For specific crucial problems please continue to write to our Agony Aunt, Irma Kurtz.)*

Cheers for th

CAPITALIST

Why can't a woman reach the top, earn big money, dress to kill and still be loved by the sisterhood?

by Dr Leah Hertz

Why do so many independent and career-minded women disassociate themselves from feminism? Why do they shudder at the suggestion that they might be feminists? What have feminists done to feminism so that it has alienated so many women who strive for equality? As I understand it, feminism is simply a matter of equality: women's financial and social equality with men. Who could argue with such a basic and logical assumption? But something must have gone wrong, for this simple message has not come through.

What has gone wrong is the hijacking of the women's movement by the left, whose interpretation of feminism is in terms of the rejection of capitalism and with it women's traditional roles, the family structure and the economic rat race. The rationale behind their rejection of capitalism was that, as women were underprivileged, and as capitalism was the oppressor of the underprivileged, women who wanted equality had to reject capitalism. What utter nonsense! The route to women's equality is *through* capitalism, through economic and political power. To win, women have to beat capitalism at its own game; to master it and demand their equal share in the world's wealth.

Instead of inspiring women to go for it, to emulate the economic and institutional achievements of men, these so-called feminists offered women a softer but inferior option: the creation of a new order without the strain of capitalistic achievements, and without the rewards of the capitalist system; a new society where they would not have to compete with men. The idea was alluring and appealed to those whose efforts for equality were thwarted and crushed by a male establishment. But women were expected to pay a high price for this reprieve from the rat race. For this ideal order—where women were freed from bourgeois concepts of self-adornment, pride in sparkling homes and demure children—lacked the economic base that has made our society into the most advanced social order in history.

It is this mistaken interpretation of feminism that has alienated the go-getting women, the high achievers, those women who could be the role models; whose achievements of equality could inspire a new generation. While the millions of underprivileged working women joined forces to become the new female proletariat under the flag of feminism, those who were already halfway up the ladder and needed just a little push to reach the top were left in isolation without the support of their underprivileged sisters or their privileged brothers. They fitted nowhere. They looked like well-groomed suburban housewives, acted like tough entrepreneurs and felt lonely. It was not only the feminists who rejected them; the home makers, too, would have nothing to do with them. For them such women were androgynous, with female looks and a male spirit.

But is this really so? Is it necessary to characterise assertiveness, ambition and success as non-feminine attributes? Can't a woman be a high achiever as well as good-looking and in harmony with other women? Of course she can.

It is time to bring in from the cold all the female high-flyers who have been alienated by the women's movement, the extreme left, and the GLC Women's Committee. Women who have had the strength and stamina to fight it out in a man's world deserve a redefinition of feminism.

The time has come to set the record straight by introducing the new species of feminists: the Capitalist Feminists. A woman who sees herself as equal to man, believes that women deserve an ec share in the economic and political stru ture and sets out to get it, can consi herself a Capitalist Feminist.

The best thing about the Capita Feminists is that their achievements tangible. A better-paid job, a higher po ical appointment, a bigger bank accou are all easily measurable achievements.

Because they, as well as their achie ments, are individually identifiable, Capitalist Feminists are a more formida force than the old-fashioned femini Margaret Thatcher is a typical Capita Feminist—as is Joan Collins, or Jenn D'Abo who presides over the Ryr shops. All set out to get their equal sh of the economy or politics, and got Capitalist Feminists constitute a m dangerous species than the classical t because they combine many qualit They have learned the secret of succ they borrow from all and adapt fr everything. They recognise the time to feminine and the time to be masculi Dressed according to the fashion, coiffu by top crimpers, they manage to smug themselves along the corridors of po without disclosing that the competition arrived. And with the true tenacity women they stay put, consolidate th achievements, stake their claim and cre a precedent for other women to follow

As the Capitalist Feminists do not c form to the established patterns of mas inity, femininity or mass feminism, sc men find it difficult to know how to har them. On one hand they are good looki softly spoken and alluring, and on the ot they are capable and assertive, know w they want and how to get it; a fundamen deviation from both classical femini and old-fashioned femininism, definitel new breed of women. For men this n species might be a problem. But then w do we have to concern ourselves w men's problems? They don't bother the selves with ours!

Dr Leah Hertz's new book, The Busin Amazons, *will be published in May André Deutsch, £8.95.*

FEMINIST!

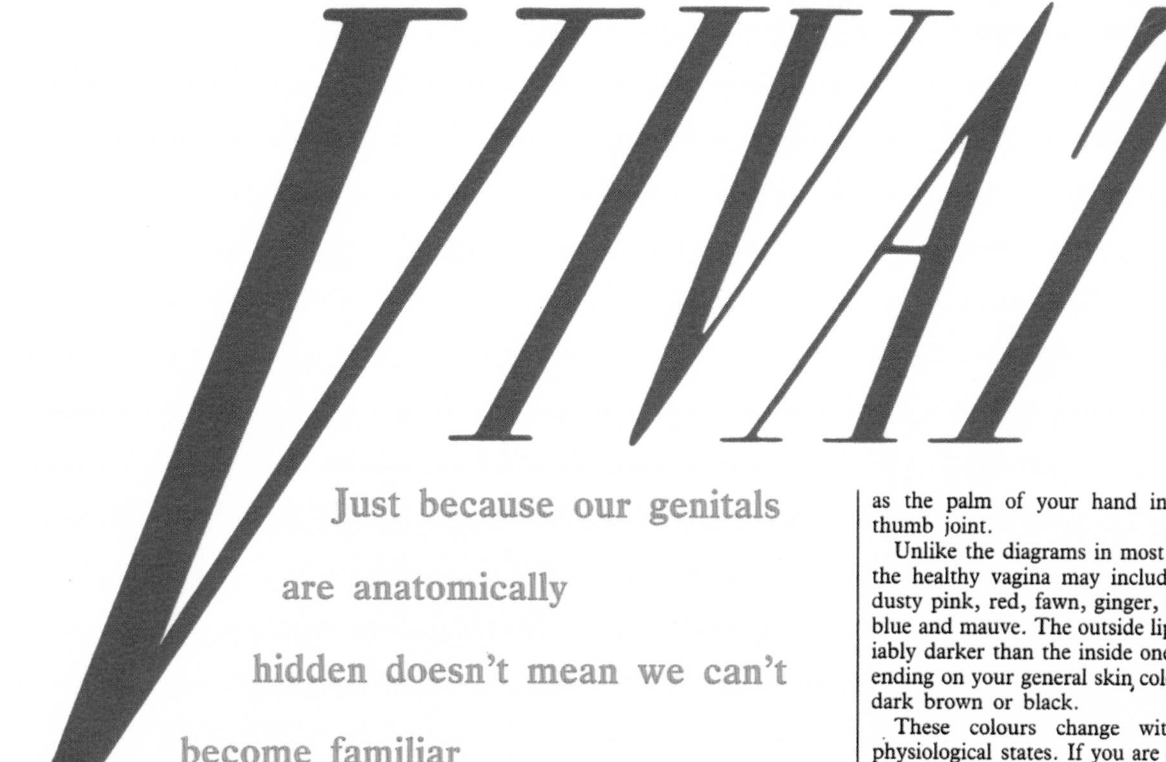

Just because our genitals are anatomically hidden doesn't mean we can't become familiar with them. Every woman owes it to herself to be on good terms with her vagina. By Sheila Kitzinger.

A woman knows her face pretty well. It is part of her public self, which she presents socially to show the kind of person she is. The vagina is just as much part of a woman—yet she may know very little about it. Even if she decides to have a session in front of a mirror to discover what it looks like, she may not realise how it changes at various phases of her menstrual cycle and at different times in her life—and may have no idea how to tell whether or not it is healthy.

It seems odd that women should have handed over their vaginas to doctors to prod and poke and examine, and to male lovers for penetration, without having themselves got to know about this important area of their bodies. The truth is that for many women the vagina is in the territorial possession of strangers—and sometimes of outright enemies.

Part of the problem is, of course, that it is difficult to examine yourself. But it is more than that. Many women feel faintly ridiculous looking at these parts of their bodies. Some even feel ashamed. It is almost as if because women's genitals are anatomically hidden, they ought to remain unknown to the woman herself. A man can get to know his penis well. As a boy he compares his with other boys. He has a familiarity—almost a friendship—with it. Compared with this, a woman's relationship with her vagina can be said to be one of total ignorance.

Oh yes, there are the anatomical diagrams, the drawings in sex books, the demonstration equipment at the birth control clinic—but the real vagina bears only a vague resemblance to those neat little drawings which show a tidy slit with even-shaped lips on either side of a little dimple and a pretty frill inside. Have a look at your vagina, using a mirror in a strong light, and you will notice that the outside lips are irregular and lop-sided. There is a second pair of silky, smoother lips tucked inside, which often protrude between the outer lips so that the shape is a fleshy version of the conch shell. The tissues fold over each other to close the vagina. The soft, stretchy, damp tissue that lines the vagina is corrugated. It fans out and opens up the vagina during sexual arousal so that the outer third swells and plumps up to form a thick cushion, while the inner two thirds spring apart to form a tent-shape. In childbirth it can unfold until it is as wide as the palm of your hand including the thumb joint.

Unlike the diagrams in most books, too, the healthy vagina may include shades of dusty pink, red, fawn, ginger, coffee, dark blue and mauve. The outside lips are invariably darker than the inside ones and, depending on your general skin colour, may be dark brown or black.

These colours change with different physiological states. If you are pregnant an increased blood supply to this area makes the colours more dramatic. The red may change from crimson to scarlet. In the post-natal weeks there is much blue and violet. After the menopause the colours change to gentle pinks and greys.

Just as noses are different, the size and shape of the clitoris may vary. Some clitorises are large and stick out between the upper fold of lips. Others are hidden. When a women is sexually aroused and the lips swell, the clitoris tends to slip under them and be hidden. Some of the phrases men use about the clitoris, included by Shere Hite in her *Study of Male Sexuality*, are vivid and tender: "a pearly little head", "a baby clam", "a red pea coming out of its shell."

The sensitive area of the clitoris extends beyond the part that can be seen. The root of the clitoris branches round the vagina and is responsive to pressure. When you slip a finger inside you can feel this sexually responsive area in the upper part of the vagina, and if you then press it gently and rhythmically, keeping your vaginal lips parted, the area of the clitoris you can see will swell in response to this stimulation.

Further inside still there is a pad of spongy tissue at the front which lies between your vagina and the pubic bone forming the front of your pelvis. This has been called the "urethral sponge" because it is close to the urethra. If you press down towards the anus you will discover another thick, spongy pad, the "perineal sponge". Pressure against both these tissue pads can be sexually exciting.

A figure eight of pelvic floor muscles coils round the vagina and anus so that you can squeeze your vagina and can tighten

VAGINA!

your anus. As you contract the muscles you can feel your anal sphincter shut and muscles higher up inside your vagina being pulled toward your pubic bone at the front. If you rest your hand over the base of your abdomen you will feel the muscles there drawn in and hard, and there may be pressure against your bladder.

These muscles are important in lovemaking, in controlling the bladder and bowels, and supporting all the organs in your pelvis. The health and vitality of this whole area depends on them being strong and well-toned. And muscles work well only if used regularly. So pelvic floor exercises—alternately tightening the muscles, relaxing and then tightening them again—are a vital part of health care. This is especially so after having a baby—once a woman is over 40, and for anyone who does lifting or who is on her feet for much of the day.

The walls of the vagina constantly release moisture so that the surface is damp. During sexual arousal this moisture pours out. It is not merely lubrication—the name usually given it—as if the only point of having a vagina were to provide a lubricated container for the penis. Nor is it an unhealthy "discharge". It is a natural secretion from healthy tissue.

Just before a period starts, and during pregnancy, this secretion gets thicker and more copious. It is also more plentiful during ovulation, the time when a fresh, ripe ovum breaks out of the ovary and makes its way into the fallopian tube, bouncing along towards the uterus. This is usually about 16 days before your next period is due.

You can tell if your vagina is healthy by checking for any itching or tenderness and that secretions are normal. If secretions are yellow or green or smell bad, this is an obvious sign of irritation—from an allergy to nylon, spermicidal cream or rubber, for example—or an infection which may be higher up in the pelvis. The infection may be in the bladder, the cervix (the opening from the uterus) or a more generalised pelvic inflammation. Infections of the cervix produce inflammation in and around the small cushion-like mouth of the uterus which projects into the vagina. You can see it best if you use a plastic speculum, obtainable from a Woman's health centre, but even without one you can do so fairly well by squatting over a mirror and shining a bright light on it. An inflamed cervix is red and sore and there may be a lot of discharge. Chlamydia is one of these infections of the cervix and, like pelvic inflammatory disease, is more common in women on the pill.

Non-specific vaginitis is a term doctors use to cover all the bacterial infections which can occur in the vagina itself. They, too, often produce a yellow or green discharge which smells unpleasant.

Yeast is present in the healthy vagina, but if it grows too thickly—which often happens in women who are on the pill—it can lead to itching, stinging as urine passes over tender tissues, and a thick discharge like cottage cheese. This is thrush, and can often be treated by avoiding soaking in hot baths, washing daily in plain water, wearing cotton pants and using a simple remedy, live natural yogurt—from a health food store—which you suck up from a bendy straw and then release into your vagina. If the yeast curds have not cleared up after a week of this treatment, go to your doctor.

Trichomonas is a sexually transmitted disease caused by a minute animal, one symptom of which is an itching yellow discharge. It can be cured by antibiotics, but *both* partners must take them.

Genital herpes is usually transmitted by sexual intercourse, too. It takes the form of red bumps which turn into blisters and start to weep or bleed after a few days. By the end of a week they begin to form crusts, and then heal. The whole vaginal area may burn or ache.

Although there are treatments which can relieve the pain of herpes, there is no complete cure at present. Keep your vagina clean with salt baths or by soaking in water in which you have dissolved bicarbonate of soda—one teaspoon to half a pint. Wash your hands carefully after touching the sore. Do not have sexual intercourse while you have an open sore. Fortunately, most people who have herpes only have one attack.

Genital warts are painless hard bumps which usually appear at the base or on the lips of the vagina. It is important to avoid rubbing or pulling on them. They can be removed surgically or by cauterisation, or may often disappear suddenly without any treatment at all.

There are two small glands shaped like haricot beans on either side of the lower vagina—Bartholin's glands. Occasionally they become infected and swell, and this can usually be cured by antibiotics.

Getting to know how your vagina looks, its natural changes, and early signs of any infection or other problems should be an important part of your general health care. You then have an early-warning system, and can treat some conditions by simple home remedies. Some women find they can cure recurrent vaginal infections by cutting out all sugar, junk food and alcohol from their diets.

When self-help is not enough, though, it is important to get medical treatment and not keep on putting up with the discomfort. A hospital clinic for sexually transmitted diseases will usually give the most expert help and you can attend one without going through your GP.

Any untreated vaginal infection can ascend through the cervix into the uterus, and from there through the fallopian tubes which branch out at either side, into the ovaries which lie at the end of each. The result is not only pain and an infection which may be difficult to clear up, but often infertility or, if a woman does conceive, an ectopic (tubal) pregnancy.

One reason why this happens is that the fallopian tube is blocked by scarring from infection so that the ovum cannot move along the tube into the uterus. If it is fertilised it grows in the tube itself until it is so big that the tube bursts.

A woman's vagina doesn't have to be uncharted physical territory which only her lover and her doctor ever see. Every woman owes it to herself to get on good terms with her vagina.

Step into a mini for maximum impact.
Right: Bottle green top, £99, Joseph Bis. Maroon poodle knit jacket, £115; matching *mini skirt*, £37.95: WilliWear. Purple and green crystal necklace, £225; matching earrings, £60: Eric Beamon. Green suede *button front shoes*, £89.50, Xavier Danaud. Natural tights, £2.50, Wolford.

BY CAROL WILSON

“Fatness is not a problem – other people's attitudes are”

I am a large lady. Rubenesque is the graceful way of putting it—some people just call it fat. I have no particular quarrel with my size and shape. It's other people who seem unable to come to terms with my weight and especially my attitude to it.

I wasn't always so relaxed. From the age of 19 I've fluctuated between large and extra large. For years I was miserable and obsessed by my size. I felt guilty, gluttonous and fatally flawed. There must be something very wrong with me if I'd been greedy enough to eat my way to that size. I must be lacking in moral fibre if I couldn't F-Plan my way back to a size 12. Diets, doomed from the start, only served to increase my self-loathing at each new failure.

I neglected my hair and make-up—what was the point, when I was so fat no one would want to look at me anyway? I tried to squeeze myself into small sizes in a vain effort to convince myself I wasn't really that big. I moved awkwardly and sat hunched up, hiding the spare tyres with my arms. I was always tense, wondering where I might be showing a bulge. My self image was so low it was right out of sight.

Suddenly, a few years ago, something exploded inside me. First I became angry, then exultant. I wasn't going to feel inferior and unhappy any more. Why should I? I was going to accept myself as I was—big—and learn to love it. Of course, it didn't happen overnight. There were some shaky steps, self doubts and near relapses. First I threw away the scales, tape measure and calorie counters. I started going regularly to a good hairdresser. I learned how to use make-up. I exchanged the embarrassment and frustration of tight-fitting clothes for the unadulterated joy of clothes in large sizes—*huge* sizes even! I discovered the sheer fun of putting together outfits and accessories I felt good in. More importantly, my confidence developed generally. I started going on courses and getting involved in politics. I felt I was growing again after a long period of stagnation. I was enchanted with the new me who had managed to crawl out from under the weight of society's expectations. I felt liberated, happy—I couldn't wait to spread the good news. It was received, however, with all the enthusiasm accorded to a cockroach discovered in a delicatessen:

Me: “Listen, I've stopped dieting, I'm not worrying about it and I feel terrific!”

Friend or Relative: “Oh! Yes, well it's not good to diet all the time—best to have a break sometimes, eh?”

Me: “It's not just a break. I've stopped doing it.”

F or R: Winter isn't a good time to diet, really. Wait till summer comes and lettuce is in season again—you'll feel better then.”

Me: “But I feel really wonderful now . . .”

At first, friends and family were sure the phase would pass. When it didn't, they changed their approach. On meeting me, they would gush brightly, “I'm sure you've lost weight—you do look thinner.” What they mean is, “You haven't lost an ounce, but you certainly ought to—when will you start trying?” They look incredulous when I say I don't actually know if I've lost weight because I never weigh myself.

When that tactic failed, they tried the health approach: “Excess weight gives you heart attacks and high blood pressure. Shouldn't you take steps before it's too late?” Yes, I am aware of the risks. However, I also know what being unhappy was doing to my mental health. Nor is it encouraging to know that 98 per cent of weight lost through dieting is likely to be regained, so even if I did put myself through purgatory, long-term results are not guaranteed. Others urged me to practise more self-control. A common fallacy, which is both irritating and amusing, is that fat people spend their lives gorging, while thin people eat modestly at all times. I have to hide my smile when this little gem of a theory is expounded by a slender person delicately wiping traces of her second Mars bar from her mouth.

More dispiriting is the assumption that fat people, purely by reason of their size, are somehow sick. Fatness is unassailably wrong; fat people can never obtain a state of social grace. No matter what their other attributes, first and foremost they are seen as fat, and many people never look beyond that. At times I describe to someone my latest achievement. They smile pityingly, not hearing a word. The only thing that's registered is that I'm no thinner. For some people, nothing can compete with the fascinating topic of my weight, and how to persuade me to reduce it.

There are other provocations. The friends whose new clothes have been produced for my admiration for years, but who are now struck down with *ennui* at the mention of mine. The doctors who, because I am “overweight” (over whose weight?), consider it unnecessary to look further for the cause of any symptoms I might have. On many occasions, I've chosen an outfit with care and pleasure only to be told it would be more slimming in a darker colour, plainer pattern, or without the belt. It's as if, because I transgress by being big, I should efface myself as much as possible by wearing unobtrusive clothes.

Racism, sexism and ageism are all well-known areas of prejudice. “Sizeism” is so much a part of our culture that we're scarcely aware of it unless we happen to be on the receiving end, when we are likely to feel personal guilt instead of anger. Being fat is not a big problem—people's attitudes can well be.

SMART GIRLS CARRY CONDOMS

The condom may not be ideal contraception but in the battle against AIDS and other sexually transmitted diseases, it's the best protection we have. By Denise Winn.

"There is no such thing as safe sex, only safer sex," said Dr Connie Wofsy, co-director of an AIDS project for women in San Francisco, at a recent conference. The message has to be blunt. For it is only slowly starting to sink in for women that casual sex is now a very risky business.

In parts of Africa where AIDS is rife, equal numbers of women and men are affected. And a now much quoted recent study of military recruits in New York found that eight in 1,000 men and six women in a 1,000 between the ages of 19 and 25 are carrying the HIV virus (Human Immuno-deficiency). A recent report from America shows that it is increasing there at a greater rate in heterosexuals than homosexuals. By the end of last year, a small number of women had already died from the disease in this country.

Estimates of the number of carriers in Britain vary wildly from the Department of Health's 30,000 to more than 300,000. It is more likely to be somewhere near 100,000. Most are still gay men and intravenous drug users, but experts are convinced that it will spread through the general population soon, as a sexually transmitted disease, unless we take steps to stop it. Many gay men are bisexual and drug users do have sex too.

FURTHER COMPLICATIONS

Carriers have a 10 to 30 per cent risk of developing the killer disease within the first five years but ultimately 70 per cent or more may succumb. Even if they don't get the actual disease, many will suffer neurological problems and face premature senile dementia.

Women carriers have to be advised not to become pregnant, as not only is there a 50 per cent risk of giving AIDS to the baby but also a greatly increased chance of developing it themselves while their immune systems are depressed during pregnancy.

The facts are alarming. Yet, despite the panic (The Terrence Higgins Trust, a charity which informs and advises on AIDS, receives nearly 60 per cent of its calls from worried women), there hasn't yet been a great deal of positive action. Perhaps the main reason is that for women who are not in monogamous relationships, the single most protective measure against AIDS, apart from celibacy, is the cruelly condemned condom. "According to the most recent information, condom use is going down," says Kaye Wellings, research officer at the Family Planning Association.

Condoms are not exactly conducive to the carefree sexual activity which, post-pill, we seem to assume is our right. Yet in the current climate, it has its definite pluses for any who engage in casual sex or who aren't sure of their partners' sexual activities elsewhere. It also protects against other sexually transmitted diseases which hit women hardest, like genital warts which are linked with an increased incidence of very aggressive cervical cancer.

The diaphragm is by no means in the same league and the Pill and the IUD are not in it at all. None of these can protect against AIDS. "Friction during sex causes minute abrasions so if you cover those with semen, there is considerable danger, says Dr William Harris, consultant in genito-urinary medicine at St Mary's Hospital in London. The AIDS virus is passed through blood, semen and vaginal secretions, with anal sex an extremely high risk.

So why have we still made no measurable move to welcome back the condom? According to several experts, it seems that it is men rather than women who are really resistant to reinstating the rubber. Janet Green, organiser of the women's campaign against AIDS for the Terrence Higgins Trust, says, "Many women say that their boyfriends won't use condoms, so they fear they will be rejected if they suggest it."

SHEATHS ARE SAFER

This picture is also reflected at genito-urinary clinics in London where high numbers of people attend for HIV testing or advice. Dr Tom McManus, consultant in genito-urinary medicine at Kings College Hospital says, "Our biggest problem is that heterosexual men won't use the sheath and so women don't bother asking them. We can have a sensible mature discussion about safer sex with women and with gay men, but heterosexual men laugh at us. They still say things like contraception is the woman's responsibility or that the condom reduces sensitivity. They have got out of the habit of expecting to use one."

Dr William Harris of St Mary's, puts it very directly, "I believe the use of condoms is to a large extent in the control of the female. At present, it isn't socially acceptable to suggest a condom. But women only have to start to insist and it will become acceptable."

To be effective, both as a contraceptive and as a protection against disease, the condom must be rolled on only when the penis is erect, not before. Any air must be pressed out in the process and then it must be pulled down fully. After sex, the man must withdraw quickly and hold on to the condom to prevent any leakage. Fine condoms are as protective against disease as

thicker ones. However, a new condom that is self-sealing at the base should be available at the beginning of the year. Spermicides, particularly those with five per cent or more of Nonoxynol-9 as the active ingredient, are a sensible optional extra. Not only do they zap undesirable alien organisms as well as sperm but they add lubrication which stops the condom tearing. (Vaginal lubricant is an alternative when the woman is dry but never use anything oil-based, as that rots the rubber.)

Condoms are 85-98 per cent safe as contraceptives when used correctly but they can also be used as additional protection when necessary. As for the complaints about loss of sensitivity, it is interestingly the non-users who most protest and not those who are accustomed to using them. Spontaneous, condoms are not—but we can t have everything, or so it seems.

More important even than that, perhaps, as an explanation for our resistance, is the feelings about sex that condoms bring out into the open. The woman who starts carrying condoms in her bag is having to admit to herself that she may be in the market for casual sex. Whereas the encounter that occurs when she is unprepared, can be passed off as unprecedented passion. A woman who is in a steady relationship, but one where monogamy is only given lip-service or less, may feel that suggesting a condom is tantamount to admitting or accusing one or other partner of having sex with someone else.

"These are difficult issues but in the end they need to be confronted," says Dr Helen Ward of St Mary's who, with social anthropologist Sophie Day, is studying the success of health education for women. It is, perhaps, all part of taking a deeper look at what our sexual relationships are really about. For even condoms cannot offer 100 per cent protection against disease. So-called "safe sex" means no penetration at all, but touching, stroking and mutual masturbation—not the currently accepted content of sexual encounters.

REDEFINING RELATIONSHIPS

Someone who has already had to reassess what sexual relationships are about for himself is Jonathan Grimshaw, one of the founders of Body Positive, which started as a support group for gay men who were carrying the AIDS virus.

"I was one of the first ones to have the test and I was devastated," he says. "This was at a time when even gays thought AIDS was a rare risk, much as heterosexuals do now. We thought it was only those who had loads of sex and used lots of drugs who could get it. It was very easy and tempting to distance yourself from the threat in this way, because it was not a nice message that AIDS is around and that you might have to change your lifestyle.

"It took me a long time to adjust to not having penetrative sex any more. But I thought about what I used sex for. It isn't just about gratification, it's about self-esteem, making relationships, social life and, in fact, those things don't actually require sex. I realised that why I thought penetrative sex was the be-all and end-all had a lot to do with what I thought was expected of me. There is this macho thing in the gay world, too.

"I began to see safe sex not as a limitation but as an opportunity to be close in other ways and to put more emphasis on communication, kissing, touching, talking. I am not saying it is always easy. But I do feel I am showing respect for my own life and other people's. There are considerable rewards in that."

Many women are also now rethinking what sex means to them. "I am very aware of AIDS and everything else now," says Shelagh, a 26-year-old teacher. "I really have to be attracted to someone very strongly as a person before I will consider having sex with them. I have realised it can be so empty otherwise and it just isn't worth the risk. When I want closeness, it isn't from casual sex that I'd ever get it. If there is no one important in my life, who I can get to know first, I'd rather have cuddles with a friend."

"I think we need to look at what we as women want from sex," affirms Sophie Day. "Penetration can often be good for the man rather than the woman because it is not necessarily about real closeness. The scare of sexually transmitted diseases can be a real ally in getting sexual activity right for the woman, too. We don't have to take risks with our bodies to suit someone else. It is up to us to act on that."

Bachelor boys (from left to right): Paul Kerton, Victor Levy, Jonathan Ross, Gordon Shaw.

Are you what the lads are looking for?

FOUR SINGLE MEN AIR THEIR VIEWS ON LOVE, LIFE, SEX AND MARRIAGE. BY SHARON MAXWELL.

The buzz word at the moment is "couples". Commentators say that with the coming of AIDS everyone is rushing to be part of a monogamous, steady relationship. But is this trend reflected in reality? We decided to find out how four single, successful men—eligible bachelors by anyone's standards—viewed women and relationships in the socially volatile 'Eighties.

Victor Levy, 36, is a partner in Arthur Andersen & Co, one of Britain's most successful accountancy firms. Dedicated to his job, he is also intelligent, wealthy and cultured. He leads an international lifestyle, jetting between countries on business. **Jonathan Ross,** 26, is the sparkling chat show host of *The Last Resort* on Channel 4, where his cocky charm has attracted a cult following. Witty, honest and intelligent, he is set for a starry TV career. **Gordon Shaw,** 27, is a successful dentist with his own flourishing practice. Confident and assertive, he has worked extremely hard to set himself up in business and is now enjoying the fruits of his labours—and playing the field. **Paul Kerton,** 32, journalist on the *Telegraph Sunday Magazine* and ex-*Cosmo* staffer has worked in virtually every area of journalism, and written songs and a book. Kind, sensitive and easy-going, he is at ease with virtually everyone and always good, fun company.

We asked them some important questions—and they came up with some surprising answers.

● **What are you looking for in a woman when you first meet her?**

Victor: "It's attraction to start with, chemistry. On Saturday night I met a good-looking girl in a wine bar for the first time in ages and she said, "Why are you talking to me?" I thought about it ▶

PHOTOGRAPH BY DAVID GEE

◀ and when I was honest, the real reason was that she was a good-looking girl—I didn't know what she was like at all. Once you get to know someone, though, respect for them becomes very important."

Jonathan: "It's often just who you meet. But one of the really exciting things is when you meet someone and you have a set image of them—this woman loves books, or this woman likes to party till four in the morning—then, when you know them, you discover all sorts of different things and that's great."

Paul: "Men are looking for something different at different times of their lives. For me, it's basically the twinkle in the eye. Then if I get some sort of response from the woman I move towards her. I think these days women are good at marketing themselves. They've got their own image, their own look, off pat. There are women to have a good time with, women to take home to mum, women to stay in with..."

Gordon: "For me, it's whether I'm attracted to someone. I don't ask a woman what she does when I meet her and by the time I get round to it I know whether I like her or not. But I think you do need to have a basic respect for what that person does. If a woman was involved in the same sphere as me and absolutely terrible at it, it would matter."

● **How do you like a relationship to start?**

Victor: "When I meet someone I really like, I want to rush into it, go to Paris with her for the weekend, spend all day in bed, but women won't do that sort of thing. They are much more cautious."

Jonathan: "I like it to be deep, passionate and stupid. I like to do silly things like book a hotel room and wonder if she will turn up. You play games with each other. Then ideally the relationship develops into something more, but you keep that spark of passion."

Paul: "Depends on the person. Sometimes you meet someone and you just want to run around after her. You completely forget everything else and see her all the time, then if you get through that, you both begin seeing your friends again and it develops."

Gordon: "It's the thrill of the chase. If I get to the finishing line too quickly then it's boring."

● **What puts you off a relationship?**

Victor: "I wouldn't want a relationship where you only see each other once in a while. If you are both working 15 hours a day and have separate social lives it's not a relationship."

Jonathan: "Hassles. But when you first start going out the hassles are fun. I like picking her up from the airport or doing nice things for her. It's only when the relationship is starting to go wrong that those things *become* a hassle."

Paul: "A lot of women put you through unnecessary hoops. They're always testing your love for them, making you prove that you love them, and after a while it becomes irritating."

Gordon: "Half the problem of a relationship is when she becomes jealous and possessive. You're not allowed to do what you want, she starts to give you a lot of aggravation because you want to see your friends."

● **How important is good sex in a relationship?**

Victor: "Very. Sometimes you meet the 'right' person and the sex isn't good to start with but everything else is right, so you work on it. Sometimes it gets better, often it doesn't."▶

Are you what the lads are looking for?

◀ *Jonathan:* "I think men are looking for good sex, intimacy, companionship. If the sex wasn't working out, I'd talk about it early on. I wouldn't wait. But the first few times are always a nightmare—having to get intimate with a stranger."

Paul: "Sex is very important. I think that if it doesn't work after a certain length of time then it's not going to."

Gordon: "There are times when you go out with a girl and the sex is OK, then it just gets better and better. Other times, it doesn't matter what you do, it isn't going to work. But sometimes, for some reason—chemistry—it can be magic and there's no explanation for it at all. I think practice helps."

● **Would you want to live with/marry someone?**

Victor: "Yes. I think if the relationship is right then I want to leap into it. I am very romantic and I don't mind that with marriage there is an accepted way to behave because I think you get everything else out of your system earlier on."

Jonathan: "It can get too easy for people to start living with someone. I lived with a girl at university and it was a good experience for me and I hope it was good for her, too, but we didn't think about it enough. We just drifted into living together. Your life has to change massively."

Paul: "There are different thresholds when you *can* make a commitment—after school, university, when your career is sorted out. It is too easy to get tied up in the tradition and find yourself engaged, then whack—marriage. People who live together often have longer relationships than many marriages."

Gordon: "If I love someone and want to spend time with them I don't feel I have to get married. With marriage you start building walls around you which you can't peek over in case the grass is greener. If you live together you get on with living."

● **Have you been hurt?**

Victor: "Yes. When that happens you have to have a safety mechanism, something to help you cut it out and not think about it, at least at first."

Jonathan: "I think hurt is the wrong word. You feel upset and in turmoil but not hurt. A few months ago I was seeing a woman I liked and she said, 'It's over'. I thought, it's a shame but if that's the way it's going to be . . ."

Paul: "I don't think you get hurt because even if it was a bad experience you learn something from it and even if it didn't last long you enjoyed it while it lasted."

Gordon: "I've been very hurt because I had to hurt someone else. She was a really lovely girl but it just wasn't working out and I felt terrible that I had to hurt her."

● **Will AIDS change your sexual behaviour?**

Victor: "I think it means that you have to use your judgement more, but then it's always a question of judgement."

Jonathan: "There have always been things you can catch from sex. But death is pretty final. I use a condom."

Paul: "AIDS won't change sexual behaviour—I think by rights it should but after a few drinks I don't think it will. I think people have great intentions about wearing a condom but once you're in that sort of mood, it doesn't make a difference."

Gordon: "If a girl wanted to go to bed on the first date you would certainly think twice about it, but the virus incubates for a long time so you may get to know her and she could still have it. It doesn't change your values . . . not unless you decide to go to the doctor with her and get blood tests." ☒

"A jerk is a jerk, no matter what continent"

Having spent the last 12 years straddling both continents, who better to define the difference between British and American men than me? OK, I'll come clean, I haven't had them all. But, the ones I have had the pleasure of probing, have made me come to the conclusion that a jerk is a jerk, no matter what global chunk he's perched on.

The main difference between the two is that your average American male is much, much larger than anything over here. Force-fed on burgers, hot dogs and milk shakes, he can grow to such a huge mass of meat that often his brain doesn't know what his appendages are doing. I have seen one of these mammoths put someone in traction from a friendly slap on the back. He is deeply rooted in the "Ride 'em cowboy" mentality. Even though he doesn't have to lasso the old buffalo anymore, the American male still insists on whooping out expressions like, "How's it hangin'!", "Go for it douche-bag!" and "Yo, buddy, break me open a brewsky!". The legs are permanently spread to make room for the massive equipment and arms held ape-like at the sides ready to spin out those pistols. This man is built to "kick ass". He is computed to compete, win, conquer. Sensitivity does not have a home in this cube of 100 per cent firm-flanked *filet mignon*.

PHOTOGRAPH BY DAVID GEE

Now your English male side of beef doesn't have as much blood running through his veins, which makes him look either reptilian or like a frozen halibut. The body is elongated and noodle-like, almost caved-in, and his teeth don't all grow facing the same direction. The absence of "oomph" in the English male reminds me of trying to start a car after leaving the lights on for the last 10 years. (On a date once, the conversation ground to such a halt I thought of using jump cables to kick life into that particular stiff.) But, because the cells aren't under such pressure to form the perfect bronzed bod, they are free to develop grey matter. The Englishman has evolved an articulate, though often boring, communication facility.

Since the American male doesn't have to carry the burden of tradition or culture, he's capable of change—fast change. In the States, the male has adjusted much more to the working woman. He wouldn't dare expect the little woman to whip up a little cheese dip for the guys' poker night. The American male has accepted the "You want clean socks? Marry a washing machine" philosophy. (Except in LA where the average male is only interested in pre-pubescent bimbettes with a degree in pouting.)

The Englishman can't make these adjustments. No matter how much he tries to convince himself he's interested in an independent woman, he is still looking for a replacement for Mummy. His life is a constant hunt for another gravy-making slave to keep churning out that yellow steaming pud with a dollop of clotted jam. Also, the more educated an Englishman is, the quicker you can reduce him to a guffawing mound of jelly by mentioning any part of the body used for going to the lavatory. No matter how well-formed those vowels or how much he knows about the wines of the Loire valley, underneath he is back in school letting off stink bombs or debagging Bloggs minor.

With an American, what you see is what there is. There are no dark crevices of hidden depth. Absolutely no Heathcliffe in there. Because of this lack of mystery, for me, the arousal level is zilch. I always feel I've known him all my life . . . I know what's coming before the mouth moves. My only urge is to pinch him on those cheeks (facial) and send him home with a cookie.

The Englishman has layers of repression. You can go at them with a pick-axe and chisel for years and all you might get at the end of it is, "Jolly nice weather we're having". I find this either intriguing or boring depending on the physical quality of the merchandise. I'm sorry, I'm more shallow than both of them. Next time, ask an expert.

by Ruby Wax

morphy richards

a girl's best friend

HIS TURN TO STAY HOME

David Gerrie is bustling around in the kitchen, whipping up some meltingly light lemon pies and fennel flans with pea sauce à la Roger Verge. His wife Anthea comes home from a hard day at the office and complains that the place is a mess.

"I know I can sound like the archetypal male chauvinist pig," Anthea confesses, having the grace to see the humour of the situation. They can both joke about it, but the laughs are slightly hollow from the strain of keeping to their curious bargain.

"We've both earned walloping great salaries in our time, but not together," David reflects, putting the finishing touches to his prize ratatouille and uncorking the wine. "The one time we did—when we were in America—we decided to chuck it all in because we felt we'd sacrificed the quality of life!"

So they came back to England, after eight years Stateside, with their American-born son Ashley, now six, and set about considering how to earn a living again in a strange land.

Anthea, now 40, and David 35, met while they were both working together on a provincial newspaper. "I had a husband and a lover to ditch before we could get together," Anthea states bluntly. They sold Anthea's house and David's MGB, and gambled all the proceeds on a trip to Los Angeles on a pure whim!

"Anthea had a green card because her mother had been born there, and our dream was to renounce journalism and find industry, fame and fortune and get discovered," David recalls somewhat wistfully.

Since there was no "sin in being a secretary there", they used their shorthand/typing skills to get established—Anthea at Vidal Sassoon, David at Rogers & Cowan, one of the largest show-business public relations agencies.

Then, Anthea was quickly catapulted into the high powered world of cosmetics marketing, while David became Zsa Zsa Gabor's personal secretary.

"For a while I earned more than David," Anthea says. "Then the axe fell at Sassoon and I was one of the casualties. But luckily I got a job with a pharmaceutical company, which then wanted me to move to a different city . . ."

"By this time Anthea was pregnant," interrupts David, "and under US law that's a valid reason not to move, so she got a decent pay-off and a good excuse to work at home for a year."

When Ashley was a bit older, Anthea went back to work in cosmetics marketing, stipulating the hours of 10 a.m. to 4 p.m. without a lunch break so that she could always be free to pick him up every day—first from a childminder, later from his nursery school.

"David was always too busy," she says with a teasing smile.

After eight years of Californian life they got homesick and, since David's company had a London office, they decided to effect a transfer.

"I thought I'd come back and be a great marketing mogul," says Anthea, "but in Britain I was too old and nobody really wanted me or my American marketing techniques."

But Trevor Sorbie, the hairdresser, took her on as his marketing director, and she wrote an article for *Working Woman* magazine which gave her enough confidence to go into freelance writing.

"I was going through a huge identity crisis," she remembers, "while David was working with Stacey Keach, Sylvester Stallone, Paul Newman, Robert Redford, Dudley Moore . . . All of Fleet Street was wining and dining him and I was on my own, here. I felt totally isolated."

"Here," is Anthea and David's charming, five-bedroomed rectory in East Sussex.

But life turned upside down—with Anthea landing on the top—when David lost his job with Rogers & Cowan a year-and-a-half ago. So they decided to pool their editorial and PR talents and work together. Anthea became the hustler and a meeting at a party led to her being asked to freelance for the *Daily Mail*.

Now she has a lucrative freelance contract with them which involves her working four long days a week and being prepared to jet off to Paris or New York or Iceland at a moment's notice. David is left holding the baby—and the fort.

"He encouraged me to go," Anthea recalls, "the first time I was asked to go abroad. I was so nervous and said I couldn't possibly, I needed more notice, I wasn't prepared—but David made me."

Now she's delighted she listened to him and David says he is, too—although there are hints of envy that are only natural under the circumstances.

Anthea handles the washing and ironing but, by and large, David now does everything else around the house—assisted by the cleaning lady. He takes Ashley to school every day and collects him, and wonders what sort of perception the other villagers have of him, "since I'm apparently unemployed yet drive a Jaguar XJ6 and live in a big house". You can imagine that he rather enjoys keeping the rest of the village guessing.

David now does freelance work for trade journals and has worked up quite a respectable business based from home.

"But I'm not sure it's healthy for him to be at home most of the time and responsible for Ashley," worries Anthea. "I think perhaps we should get a nanny to free David a bit from the childcare. You can tell it gets a bit much sometimes, even though he does enjoy it."

David volunteers, "But I actually don't mind too much staying at home and there was a time when I wouldn't have wanted Anthea to come home to a house that was less than perfect."

David Gerrie is not complaining, and seems commendably thrilled with his wife's success. He is not a man for sulking or sour grapes, and doesn't feel his masculinity is threatened by the fact that she is momentarily the major breadwinner.

"But I do miss the office gossip and going out for drinks with the guys," he reveals in a rare flash of self-pity. "So when Ashley comes home from school I don't treat him like a baby any more—he's a little mate."

Ashley, a pleasant, precocious child, seems to be thriving on the arrangement.

FEELING FANTASTIC WITH THE MUCH YOUNGER MAN

Joey is wearing her "fat dress"—a wild, Mondrian-style print sack stopping just short of an enviable pair of knees. It's been one long celebration since the wedding, she sighs, and her body is finding it a strain to live up to its youthful new image—a big switch from her earlier, "eleganza" days.

Joey is 40, a divorcee with two daughters, aged 19 and 17. Mark, her husband of a few months, is 28.

He is a dealer for a bank, making "serious money"—although he insists that the sums we see bandied about are all exaggerated. She has been an interior designer and restaurateuse.

Now they are planning to pack up everything and move to a ski resort in the American Rockies to run a bar and revel in each other's company. "I want to be with Joey; I don't want to have to get up every morning and go to work at 7 o'clock without her and come home at 6 p.m., feeling grumpy," says blond, moustached Mark, smiling adoringly at the bride who is only 12 years younger than his mother.

"And I've always wanted to be a ski bum," laughs Joey, running predatory fingernails through her short hair, which has been white since she was 17.

People just don't know, they agree, why they're together. "But that's for us to know and them to find out," says Joey teasingly. "Most of my women friends are green with envy!"

"And my friends are dead jealous. They think it's quite a coup carrying off such a sophisticated lady," says Mark.

Mark has always gone for older women. The first was 29 when he was 18. "But it's not a mother complex," he stresses. "Absolutely nothing like that!"

"Younger men have simply been brought up with the attitudes women of my generation have been fighting for," Joey chimes in. "A younger man treats you like a human being! My ex-husband was Teutonic, and dead against me working. I was married for 16 years to a man who didn't—and still doesn't—know why I left him; because he never listened."

"I'm certainly not a 'toy boy'," Mark counters, playfully. "I'm too old for that—aren't I?"

Lively discussion ensues on what makes a toy boy and it is decided that even at 67 a man might be considered the toy boy if he was going out with an 80-year-old woman.

Mark and Joey got together after a drunken evening at a Russian restaurant in St John's Wood. It involved a lot of vodka, a good deal of caviar and more ▶

◀ than a few bottles of Dom Perignon champagne. Joey was wearing a black leather dress and it was lust at first sight. As soon as they could, they started to live together, and now sport "caviar" wedding rings to remind them of that night.

Joey comes from a wealthy family and her parents live in Monaco. They are stalwarts of Monaco society, and members of Prince Rainier's set.

They were aghast at her decision to marry a young man they regarded as a gold-digging "bank clerk", Joey snorts. But when Mark signed a pre-nuptial agreement, waiving all rights to Joey's money and property, they turned up, smiling stiffly, to the wedding.

"Joey's elder daughter took it hard, too," says Mark.

"She was going through her A-levels and never quite forgave us. I think both the girls hoped I'd get back with their father," Joey explains. "And I think all children like to have a mother in a pinny in the kitchen; I've never been that, although I can cook! I really feel sorry for my daughters, having a mother like me. It hasn't been easy for them!"

"My mother says she could never accept Joey as a daughter-in-law," Mark says, "but she can see her as a sister!"

Mark proposed to her, Joey joyfully remembers, on the bathroom floor. "It was wet! I told her that I did love her and it didn't matter to me if she didn't," Mark recollects.

"Mark promised that he'd push me in my wheelchair with rocket boosters and diamonds encrusted all around it," she jokes, a trifle nervously.

Does she fear approaching age, and the old adage everybody quotes at them, "When he's 38, you'll be 50 . . . ?"

"Joey does worry about that," Mark says, "but I've told her that if we've got five good years that's long enough."

She looks slightly perturbed, but agrees, "Yes, you're much better off being pessimistic and pleasantly surprised." Mark likes the fact, he says, that older women are more experienced, more confident, less conformist and much better company than the women he meets of his own age.

"Hey," she suddenly says, "you haven't really asked us about our sex life!"

"How is it?" I oblige. "Yummy!" they chorus—I leave them to it. ●

N E W A G E
RELATIONSHIPS

THE BIMBO

WOMEN OF '88

HEADLINE HOGGERS BOTH. BUT HAVE EITHER ENHANCED WOMEN'S REPUTATIONS? **BY BRENDA POLAN.**

The images which society expects men to live up to are pretty limited and fairly consistent: virile, masterful, economically successful, practical and unemotional. That's not hard to fake in the pub. New Man, who is all of that and caring, demonstrative and gentle too, is a fantasy indulged in by a minority of women who have a perverse appetite for disappointment and a castration impulse. Men who try to live up to that fantasy are wimps, gender-traitors who actually, if the truth be told, can't cut the mustard, hold 16 pints and a vindaloo or pull a bird any other way.

Yes, it's the tabloid world view I'm talking about. But it's not to be dismissed out of hand since it reflects and reinforces the attitudes of tabloid readers—the majority. And while the tabloid view of what a chap should be like is oppressive enough, it is in creating distorted images of women that the tabloids are more fecund.

Essentially, the old-fashioned chaps who run newspapers subscribe to that very simple-minded dichotomy familiar to everyone: women are good (virgins, wives, mothers, nurturing, self-denying support personnel) or they are bad (whores, temptresses, seductresses, mistresses, exciting, sexual beings). That one woman could be both is something they simply cannot get their heads around.

The poor dears have been deeply confused by the last two decades, by women who insist that the dichotomy is a false one; that women can contain within themselves, without conflict, all the elements of both virgin/mother and whore and a lot else besides—a sense of identity that has nothing to do with biology and everything to do with intelligence, talent, autonomy and ambition. So frightening were these ideas that those who subscribed to them had to be destroyed and the most effective tool of destruction is ridicule. So Women's Libbers and bra-burners (that's good and silly to start with, isn't it?) were mocked as poor, pathetic uglies who, incapable of attracting men, tried to save face by saying they didn't want one and attempted general revenge by contaminating proper, pretty women with their perverted philosophy.

It could not, of course, rest there. In a war of words, new chapters are always needed and 1988 has seen the emergence of two new tabloid stereotypes. Step forward Post Feminist Woman and the Bimbo. Of one, the tabloids wholeheartedly approve (she is, in fact, largely their creation, after all); the other terrifies them so much that they are often hard put to find enough scorn and ridicule to pour on the poor girl.

Hence that contemptuous label; bimbo is a corruption of the Italian for baby, bambino, and, in its current revival (it was once 'Twenties slang for baby, as in girlfriend) it was first used to define someone, usually female, of youth and beauty and limited intelligence but well developed self-interest, who exploited her attractiveness to keep company with the rich, powerful and not nearly so pretty.

It was a tad disapproving. After all, it's a puritanical society we live in. The label only entered the columns of the tabloids, however, in one particular context. Bimbos had sexual secrets to keep, the sexual secrets of the rich, powerful and not nearly so pretty. That also meant that bimbos had sexual revelations to make—at a price. So bimbos shopped to the tabloids

PHOTOGRAPHS BY, LEFT, REX FEATURES; RIGHT, JACQUES MALIGNON.

AND THE POST FEMINIST

philanderers and adulterers who indulged themselves with the idea that, while they were passionlessly using the bimbo for sexual and ego gratification, the bimbo was theirs devotedly and loyally for the price of her accommodation, a few dinners and a wardrobe of frocks.

Of course, telling the world who you have slept with and how many special little moments per night he managed is not a nice way to get rich or famous and it must make for strained relations with one's mum. But if the philanderer in question is a hypocrite standing for political office on the basis of a squeaky clean moral record, then it's certainly a service to the rest of the community.

In those terms, although the bimbo lifestyle is a remnant from the past (that age-old exchange of sexual favours for financial security) which the majority of women find repellent, the women who kiss and tell could be regarded as the suicidal shock troops for equal sexual accountability.

On balance, then, the bimbo has her uses. We are, however, against Post Feminist Woman who is the creation of the advertising industry, some magazine publishers and the subtler tabloids. Post Feminist Woman has it all—education, the career, the mortgage, the company car, the designer wardrobe, the good haircut, the great legs, the respect and admiration of all her peers of every gender, the lover (or series of) and, when she's ready but not yet, the children, the sharing, caring partner and the nanny.

Post Feminist Woman clinches the deals and cooks cordon bleu. She flies first class and builds her own bookshelves. She pays the restaurant bill with her gold Amex card and she knits up Kaffe Fassett sweaters for her lover. She is hell in the office and heaven in bed. She doesn't exist.

Women still only earn 73 per cent of men's earnings. A tiny minority have made it through to the ranks of management; the majority work as inadequately paid "support personnel". Of the women who work (63 per cent) most do it because they must, because there's no one else to bring home the bacon, or the other breadwinner's salary is not enough to provide adequately for the family. Most have children and most are torn between the need to work and the longing to be at home; most are exhausted and many are defeated by the insane balancing act they attempt daily; and most are just demanding far too much of themselves.

These are the real problems of women's lives which feminism, having spent a decade and a half analysing women's oppression, is only just beginning to address. Most of the media, including many women's magazines which are mostly staffed and run by women making just those excessive demands upon themselves, know that Post Feminist Woman is useful as an ideal to strive towards. To be complacent that the fight is won is to give up the fight. The next generation of women and men has to understand each other better (particularly the terrible traps set by tabloid stereotyping) and progress together towards an equality from which both will benefit.

Post Feminism is a fiction intended to subvert and corrupt this ambition. May we see the back of Post Feminist Woman in 1989.

news report

THE MORE ATTRACTIVE, GUTSY, SUCCESSFUL AND INDEPENDENT WE ARE, THE MORE, IT SEEMS, MEN ARE TERRIFIED OF GETTING TO KNOW US.

BY MARCELLE D'ARGY SMITH

Here's how it is. Opposites attract. Females attract males. The feminine attracts the masculine. Whoops, I hear you cry—and this article started out on such an optimistic note. Could it be that you don't feel feminine enough? Could that be why you don't seem to be attracting enough men? Okay then—any men? What do you have to do in order to be feminine? What's a woman supposed to be in today's world?

Listen, you're asking the wrong person here. I probably know more about the London drainage system than I know about being feminine. I have spent my life not being feminine. Female—yes, sexual—yes, feminist—yes.

Could this be why today I am without a man? Yes, it could well be. But don't let's lose heart. I just looked up feminine in my dictionary. Funny that I never thought of it before. To me the word conjured up frills and sweetness, a sort of baby-faced manipulation of big strong men. And, as you tend to reject what you can't be, I've rejected femininity.

But I should have looked it up sooner. I'd have felt better. My *Webster's Dictionary* defines the word as "female, of women or girls", "having qualities regarded as characteristics of women or girls such as gentleness, weakness, delicacy, modesty." Give me a break. This I can live without. Well, for sure as hell you wouldn't survive very long in a modern world if you had those qualities—if indeed it were ever possible. But it was possible and it still is *provided you have a strong man to depend upon for support and protection.*

You'd obviously have to be very nice to him, otherwise you wouldn't survive. This is the way we were. And, by the way, it is the way a lot of men would still like us to be. But, of course, by now you've probably noticed.

In a fascinating book, called *Eye to Eye—your relationships and how they work,* edited by Peter Marsh (Sidgwick & Jackson, £15.95), are published the results of a survey in the United States where young men and women were asked to select and rate potentially desirable attributes in a partner. In order ▶

PHOTOGRAPH BY MEL YATES. Hair and make-up by Sue Moxley. Clothes and accessories: see stockists, page 244.

What we
really are,
really want

What we really are

◀ of importance, most sought by men in their perfect woman were the following attributes:
Physical attractiveness
Ability in bed
Warmth and affection
Social skill
Home-making ability
Dress sense
Sensitivity to others' needs
Good taste
Moral perception
Artistic creativity.

The attributes most sought by a woman in a man were these:
A record of achievement
Leadership qualities
Skill at his job
Earnings potential
A sense of humour
Intellectual ability
Attentiveness
Common sense
Athletic ability
Good abstract reasoning.

As Amanda said, when I read her this list, "What about my leadership qualities and my intellectual abilities?" I said, "Not what they're looking for." What is true, however, is that some of the brightest and best women I know could be ticked on both check lists—although if I'm being totally honest with you, athletic ability is not their strong point. I only know one man who scores the maximum on both lists and he's gay. But at least now I can understand why I liked him so much.

It is particularly galling, therefore, that so many attractive, gutsy, successful and independent women—many of whom, as I've said, score highly on both male and female lists of desirable attributes, the people the tabloids call "career women"—find it singularly hard to attract men.

Whereas women are delighted to find men who possess some of the desirable female attributes, many men positively shy away from females who possess attractive male characteristics. They have desperate ideas about women who hold down good careers. See some typical comments below left.

In vain can you try to explain to men that women who excel at work can be warm, affectionate, tender, caring and that a bloke could positively double up on his quota of pleasure and fun. No, it's ingrained somewhere in a male brain that if a woman is an achiever she has "masculine qualities". And the last thing he wants when he comes home from work is masculine qualities. He remembers his mother as feminine. He remembers his favourite early girlfriends as feminine as well as sexual. He wants feminine.

To illustrate the point, about three months ago my friend Jo met a man called Martin on a country weekend. They got on well and laughed a lot together. He rang her when she got home and said he was coming to London for the weekend in a couple of weeks and it would be nice to spend some time with her. So why didn't they meet for lunch in the meantime? They lunched on Thursday in a brasserie near her office. Jo said the lunch was lovely and sort of intimate and such a welcome break from her working day. She said she was really looking forward to the weekend. Martin cancelled the weekend with no explanation. Jo said that's life. And I said it can't be. He called again a few weeks later to explain why he'd cancelled: "It was that lunch, Jo. I hated it. I hated the place and all those people you knew. It was like a business meeting. You were different from when we met."

So here's how it is. Jo thought the lunch was lovely even though the brasserie was crowded with her workmates and she only had an hour. But she saw Martin as a man she liked, who was warm and amusing and she was excited to be spending some time with him. Martin saw Jo as a hurried, powerful businesswoman in a tailored suit who could barely afford him an hour of her precious time. Jo said should she perhaps have worn a pink angora sweater and taken the afternoon off work? We both said probably.

THE "PERFECT" WOMAN

Another truth is that unless you are actively trying to please men you are seen as unfeminine. Men dream, fantasise about the ideal feminine woman. Curiously enough, she looks like the heroine in a Mills & Boon novel. All too often she has long blonde hair and she definitely needs a man to depend upon for support and protection. Well, maybe deep down she doesn't, but in male eyes she looks as though she does. She's the woman, according to the media, many powerful and rich men (who certainly don't need working wives) seem to marry. She's the fairy princess. When, in social history, women en masse have cut their hair, it was seen as a gesture of defiance, a rebelliousness—as in the 'Twenties. It meant that women were demanding certain freedoms, they were no longer prepared to go along with the accepted order of things and be submissive. And I know of a stunning, bursting-with-vitality beauty editor who in the long hot days of

CAREER WOMEN—WHAT MEN SAY

"Who wants to come home tired out at the end of the day and have to start some intellectual discussion with a career woman about her day?"

"You have to be tough to get where she's got. Who wants to live with a tough woman?"

"She's so into her career, it's obvious she couldn't possibly have time to spare for a man."

"You can't have two stars in a family and my job's very important to me."

"Her career is so obviously a substitute for having a man and a child in her life."

"She has everything; she doesn't need a man."

"Can you imagine two of us with demanding jobs and schedules? I need someone restful."

GENTLEMEN PREFER "LITTLE" WOMEN

Most men, although not all, still have a vested interest in women being traditional and feminine. Who will run their homes? Bring up the children? Do the shopping? Find their socks? Be there when they're needed?

Fathers are still terrified their daughters might not marry. Men friends are terrified their wives-to-be might not be wives in the true senses. "Gina loves her job in television but she's not ambitious, thank God."

Husbands are scared that they might be left holding the baby. "Of course Lucy is giving up work once she has the child. Would you work in PR if you didn't have to?" Live-in lovers are much the same. "I don't mind Susie taking on more work but I do object to the housework going to pot." And men hate being left to fend for themselves. "Jane's got a great job and she's doing marvellously. But I am sick of all her travelling. What am I supposed to do at home on my own when she's away for weeks at a time?"

her summer holidays suddenly tired of her long hair and had it chopped off to just below her ears. It was practical and she looked great. Her younger brother was completely stunned. "Why did you do that?" he asked. "Why do women have their hair cut so they look ugly?"

And in these subtle and not so subtle ways women are discouraged from being too "masculine" and urged to be more "feminine". Do most women want to be alone in their brilliant careers? No they don't. And so women of all ages drop out at all levels in their careers, even when they've masses of potential, because no-one is urging them upwards and onwards; also, subconsciously or consciously, they've seen that they risk alienating men if they continue to regard their work as so vitally important.

Even as we're winging our way into the 1990s with women flying ever higher, there are still too many men who regard job success as a masculine prerogative. Although it's a common and worldwide problem for working women, it does seem to be a special "disease" among British men. We live in a class system and few of the wives of royalty or the "aristocracy" seem to take work very seriously, although there are notable exceptions. Successful men here often think it's a mark of success to have a non-working wife; I have only to look at the wives of the directors and senior executives in the company where I work. Not one of these men has a wife who goes to work outside the home. I'm sure these women are very busy. It's not easy running a home, caring for children and a demanding husband. But the message from the men is perfectly clear: "Look at me, I've made it. My wife doesn't need to work: she looks after me, the home and the kids."

And a further message is reinforced: if you want a successful man, be prepared for your work to take a back seat. He's driving, he's in control. He's masculine, all male. He wants feminine, all female to complement him. It's fine if this arrangement works for him and for you. It's hell on earth if it doesn't.

There are still masses of men who are convinced the majority of women wouldn't work if they didn't need the money. And it's true that some of us wouldn't. But like the men in our lives, most of us would—for the intellectual stimulation work provides.

ANDROGYNOUS—AND VERY WELL-ADJUSTED

Frankly I don't know what to do about my lack of femininity. Although I don't have a bad score on the list of desirable female attributes, I'm damned if I'll curb my masculine attributes. It's taken me years to acquire most of them and I'm rather proud of them. I'm simply not prepared to carry out a suggestion in the *Daily Mail* last spring whereby I wriggle into "boudoir lingerie" and get into "a striking risqué pose" in order to have my photograph taken to give to the man/men in my life.

This, apparently, will help me to release my repressed femininity and compensate in the eyes of my man for the status and power I seem to have in the workplace. Getouttahere—is that newspaper crazy? The answer, according to *Eye to Eye—your relationships and how they work*, is to find a well-adjusted man. (Yes, I know, I know. I'm writing to the editor of the book to tell him this is easier said than done.) But he does exist. A couple of my friends have even married him.

The well-adjusted man is, well, androgynous (he combines masculine and feminine qualities to an almost equal degree). Well-adjusted people, the book's editor assures us, do not necessarily conform to rigid sex types. Well, you have to admit that's the most enormous comfort. It means, in terms of being seen as psychologically healthy, most of us women are absolutely right to be exactly what we presently are.

So here it is. The search is on. Now I know what I'm supposed to be looking for, I will be able to throw away my dog-eared copy of *Smart Women, Foolish Choices* (Bantam, £3.50). I want an androgynous man. If you know of one you don't need who could possibly be interested in an eccentric, well-meaning writer, perhaps you'd ask him to get in touch with me. And not to be put off if I'm in a two-hour meeing. But then he wouldn't be, would he?

GOODBYE

How will the Eighties be remembered? As a decade of disasters and the prelude to a Greener, safer world or for nouvelle cuisine and Princess Diana? We take a look at what the decade meant to us. **By Mike Davis.**

If the Fifties were Never-Had-It-So-Good, the Sixties were Swinging and the Seventies were Soporific, what can we call the Eighties? Extravagant? Expensive? Execrable? Get Rich Quick And Stuff The Poor? Or is it just Too Early To Say? Before amnesia, nostalgia and TV retrospectives cloud our memories of them too much, let's look back and say a few fond farewells and heartfelt goodbyes.

In the Eighties, people said "naff" and "crucial" a lot, wore puffball skirts and patterned hosiery, and bought records by Richard Clayderman. Hob-nobs and Wispa bars emerged, along with listeria, salmonella and AIDS. Jane Fonda exposed us to the "burn", the F-plan to beans, the BBC to *Bread*, the *Sun* to bonking and the City to the Big Bang. Inflation fell and house prices rose, and vice versa. The Ecology Party turned Green, the *Herald of Free Enterprise* turned over. *Neighbours* and *EastEnders* came; *Dynasty* and *Crossroads* went. Summers got hotter and the Cold War thawed.

Some of the things listed on these pages may not have affected your life very much, if at all. Sorry if we've left out that new job you got in 1983, the man with the nice teeth you met in 1987 and the fact that your local sweet shop no longer stocks Snowballs. Whether the Eighties were happy or sad for you depends, no doubt, more on matters like these than on what people wore, watched and listened to.

WE'LL MISS YOU

The ozone layer. Clean beaches and clean seas (yes, they *have* been disappearing for ages, but now it's official). Inexpensive holidays abroad. Being sure when you fly that bits won't start to fall off the plane. Spending less than 24 hours at the airport. Eating chicken, hazelnut yogurt and home-made mayonnaise and still expecting to live. Life without faxes. Live Aid. Living in a big city and not turning your home into Fort Knox. Having only four television channels. *The Young Ones*. Pirate radio. Listening to bands that don't use computers and lasers. Red telephone boxes. High tech. People writing letters. Successful films not having a sequel. Bette Davis. Being able to park your car—occasionally. Finding a fishmonger still trading in your local high street.

PHOTOGRAPHS BY ROBERT HARDING, LFI, BARBRO, PHOTOGRAPHERS' LIBRARY, TRANSWORLD, PETER SAKAS, REX FEATURES, ARIEL, SKELLEY, NIALL McINERNEY, JOHN FORTUNATO, SCOPE, KOBAL COLLECTION.

TO ALL THAT!

GOOD RIDDANCE TO . . .
Female newsreaders being regarded as freaks. *Crossroads*. *Dynasty*. Dirty Den. Asbestos. O-level examinations. Life without videos. Novels about women from humble beginnings clawing their way to the top. Eddy Shah newspapers. Yuppies, Buppies, Guppies, Muppies, post-feminist, post-punk, post-modernist, and social commentators coming up with new terms like these every week. Four-hour "working" lunches. Nouvelle cuisine. People smoking on the Underground, in cinemas, in restaurants, etc. Aerobics. "Aciid!" Celebrity fragrances. Beauty with cruelty. Steroids winning the Olympic 100 metres. Sir Robin Day.

POLITICAL EXITS
The Liberal party. Publicly owned corporations. Docklands with real dockers in them. Honest unemployment figures. Rates. The Cold War. Married women taxed as adjuncts of their husbands. Peace camps. Property as a rock-solid investment. The Falklands. 1984. Ronald Reagan. Greens being regarded as nutters. A powerful welfare state. A left-wing party in opposition.

OUT OF THE CLOSET
(Or stashed in the attic until the Eighties revival.) Patterned hosiery. Ripped jeans. Puffball and rah-rah skirts. *Dallas* shoulder pads. ▶

Left: Loved and lost . . . A clean coastline, *The Young Ones*, billets-doux, water we're happy to drink and big red boxes. This page: We'll never forget . . . Fast Ben, *Dynasty*, life before video. Farewell to: Public smoking, *Crossroads*, Liberals, dockers, and Reagan.

THREE THINGS WE KNOW NOW:

- **Materialism got totally out of hand**
- **Bob Geldof was truly a hero for the Eighties**
- **All of us thought too much about style and not enough about each other**

◀ Smiley badges. Real fur coats. Bustiers. Stilettoes. Surfing shorts. Chanel handbags. Doc Martens. Ray·Bans. Slogan T-shirts. Patterned boxer shorts. Rolexes.

THROWN OUT OF THE BEDROOM

Expressions like "kept woman" and "good in bed". Free love. Sleeping around. One-night stands. Playboys. *Playboy*. The New Man. Younger women not knowing what a condom looks like. Older women having faith in the Pill.

NOTEWORTHY SILENCE

Haircut 100. The Specials. Frankie Goes to Hollywood. Paul Young. Wham! Echo and the Bunnymen. The Teardrop Explodes. Madness. Nik Kershaw. The Police. Culture Club. Alison Moyet. Big Country. The Human League. Bronski Beat. Adam Ant. Sex and drugs and rock'n'roll.

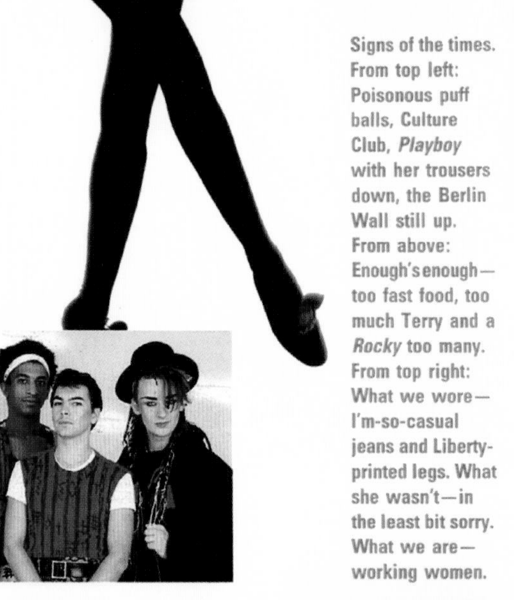

FADING FAST

Women who don't take their work seriously. Men who don't take seriously women taking their work seriously. Deep suntans. CFCs. Leaded petrol. Clothes with labels on the outside. Matt black finishes. "Yoof" programmes. Bad teeth. Men who think they're macho.

IF ONLY WE HAD SEEN . . .

Jimmy Connors win more at Wimbledon. Margaret Thatcher say, "I made a mistake." Much tougher penalties for rape. The appointment of more women judges. Tabloid excesses curbed. The Berlin Wall knocked down. Apartheid junked. Pollution and men wearing shorts with socks and sandals outlawed. Terry Wogan and TV mini-series off the air. AIDS, crack, cocaine, heroin, amphetamines, heavy drinking, smoking and pot noodles eradicated.

Signs of the times. From top left: Poisonous puff balls, Culture Club, *Playboy* with her trousers down, the Berlin Wall still up. From above: Enough's enough—too fast food, too much Terry and a *Rocky* too many. From top right: What we wore—I'm-so-casual jeans and Liberty-printed legs. What she wasn't—in the least bit sorry. What we are—working women.

WHAT WE'VE LEFT OUT

How, then, will you remember the Eighties? What did you find special about them, peculiar to them, good about them? Write and tell us. Can you think of a word or phrase which best sums up the Eighties? Tell us about that, too.

And do you have friends who still wear *Dallas* shoulder pads, say "Brill!" and smoke on the Tube? Do everyone a favour: tell them. ☺

COSMOPOLITAN

November 1980 • 50p

Maria Callas in love: an intimate portrait by Arianna Stassinopoulos

Reach for the sun in sherry country! Enter our £3,000 contest

His depression can be catching. How to pull yourself out of the depths

Hate November? Cheer yourself up by living in red, cooking Sally Vincent's hot dinners, meeting marvellous men and reading how the famous whoop it up!

Where are men now? Tom Crabtree reports from the battlefront

Adopt a handyman, plant a holly hedge, stock up on plonk-check our survival plan for the '80s

The many styles of loving-find the perfect match for you

Want to get a campaign going? Find encouragement from three women who succeeded

Stepping An uninhibited novel about the intricacies of modern marriage

COSMOPOLITA

June 198

Cover girl Nastassia K launche bare-faced for more scant esse see pag

Surrogat the does it v

Must wome bitc Must men be asks Erin P

No, the typew is not a trap, Shirley Co

Would your we

The working jum only

Fi Asking When an indeper woman dares to be diff

Dance crazy? Win a chance to dance for your living! See page 164

What to do when you're hooked on a heel

Want to improve your memory, kill pain, conquer fear and write a best seller? The future-drugs could make it happen!

COSMOPOLITAN

December 1984 • 75p

Real women expose the myth of perfect sex

Before you see Ghostbusters see page 101

Illegitimacy the new norm

Better than bingo! Win a fantasy frock glittering jewels flying lessons brilliant books

Why Boy George would kill for love

All I want for Christmas is a new nose

On the game men are better

Fiction Saga of a gangster's moll by Hilary Bailey

COSMOPOLITA

January 198

thrive!

48-PAGE ZEST EXTRA

Why men are downing tools

Win £5000 worth of high-tech treats

Glamour Irma cracks the image

Che Dozer wa live i

Have lu with

Fic The Bottom

The Sharp

Fay We